'A model of autobiography'
Humphrey Carpenter, *Sunday Times*

'Recounting her story with humour and insight – and drawing on personal correspondence not previously published ... it is a fascinating insider's account starting in 1956, when British Theatre discarded its post-war constraints' Carole Woddis, *Glasgow Herald*

'It is no surprise to find a clear, calm, measured voice emerging from her autobiography'
Rupert Christiansen, *Spectator*

'The book is suffused with the warmth and common sense that was the hallmark of Plowright's stage performances'
Michael Arditti, *Independent*

'Her twinkly, grandmaternal wisdom is the keynote of *And That's Not All*. It is the literary equivalent of tea with an aged relative, who has a tendency to digress and to pronounce platitudes, but has lived such a fascinating life and is so full of goodwill that she can only be a pleasure to listen to. Plowright's voice is remarkably lacking in luvvie-ness' Thomas Hodgkinson, *Literary Review*

'A full-on treat for stage buffs ... The gilded life of the First Lord and Lady of Theatre has a supporting cast of stars (Nivens and Redgraves, Maggie Smith and Richard Burton, Noël Coward, Ralph Richardson and dozens more), and backgrounds from Moscow to the Algonquin'
Julia Sutherland, *Financial Times*

Joan Plowright was born in Lincolnshire and educated at Scunthorpe Grammar School, the Laban Art of Movement Studio and the Old Vic Theatre School. She made her first stage appearance in *If Four Walls Told* at the Croydon Rep. Early London appearances included Orson Welles' production of *Moby Dick*. After playing at the Bristol Old Vic and Nottingham Playhouse, she joined the English Stage Company at the Royal Court in 1956 and appeared in her first starring role as Wycherly's *The Country Wife*. A variety of roles followed in plays by Nigel Dennis, Ionesco, Shaw, Brecht, Arthur Miller, and most notably, Arnold Wesker (*Roots*) and John Osborne (*The Entertainer*). She married Laurence Olivier in 1961. She acted in the opening seasons of the Chichester Festival Theatre, and joined the National Theatre Company where she played many leading roles. Her performance as Shaw's *Saint Joan* won the *Evening Standard* Best Actress Award. She also won a Tony Award for Best Actress in *A Taste of Honey* in New York. In the cinema she was nominated for an Oscar and won two Golden Globes for *Stalin* and *Enchanted April*. Her other films include *Tea With Mussolini*, *101 Dalmations*, *I Love You to Death*, *Avalon*, *Equus*, *Dennis the Menace*, *Drowning by Numbers*, *Jane Eyre* and *Surviving Picasso*.

And That's Not All

....

JOAN PLOWRIGHT

ORION

An Orion paperback

First published in Great Britain in 2001
by Orion
This paperback edition published in 2002
by Orion Books Ltd,
Orion House, 5 Upper St Martin's Lane,
London WC2H 9EA

Copyright © 2001 Joan Plowright

The right of Joan Plowright to be identified as the author of
this work has been asserted by her in accordance with the
Copyright, Designs and Patents Act 1988.

All rights reserved. No part of this publication may be
reproduced, stored in a retrieval system, or transmitted, in
any form or by any means, electronic, mechanical,
photocopying, recording or otherwise, without the prior
permission of the copyright owner.

A CIP catalogue record for this book is available
from the British Library.

ISBN 0 75284 840 2

Printed and bound in Great Britain by
Clays Ltd, St Ives plc

For my parents and my family

Contents

Illustrations

Photographs used are taken from the author's albums, except where otherwise indicated

William Ernest Plowright
Daisy Margaret Plowright
With brothers Bob and David
On holiday at Mablethorpe
With Bob and David, and cousins Geoffrey and William – just before and
    during the second world war
Obviously a novice, but still in the saddle
Learning to pose for the camera, aged fifteen
The School for Scandal at the grammar school
Drama festival winners, with my mother and David
As Sadie Thompson in *Rain*
First wedding: with Roger leaving St Hugh's Church, Old Brumby
A cartoonist's view of the Orson Welles version of *Moby Dick*
At Nottingham Rep in Ben Travers' *Rookery Nook*
With Shelagh Delaney and Angela Lansbury in *A Taste of Honey*; and how
    a Los Angeles cartoonist saw the production
As Margery Pinchwife in Wycherly's *The Country Wife*
With George Devine in *The Chairs*
As Beatie Bryant in Arnold Wesker's *Roots*, with Gwen Nelson[1]
With Laurence Olivier in the film version of *The Entertainer*
New York wedding night after our shows: walking through Shubert Alley
    with Richard Burton, Sybil Burton and Lauren Bacall
First born: Richard Kerr Olivier
Richard now joined by sisters Tamsin and Julie-Kate
The playbill for the first Chichester festival theatre season, 1962
Two scenes from *Uncle Vanya*, with Michael Redgrave, Sybil Thorndike
    and Fay Compton; and with Larry[5]
Family scenes: Tamsin on Brighton beach; in the garden at Brighton; on
    holiday in Ischia; Larry with Tamsin and Richard; Larry with Richard;
    lolling about on Franco Zeffirelli's cushions on a hot night in Positano;
    Larry with Richard; Tamsin and Julie-Kate; Larry with Julie-Kate

On the day of Larry's introduction at the House of Lords as Baron Olivier of Brighton

The last night of Larry's reign as Director of the National Theatre with Denis Quilley at the piano

As *Punch* saw the building of the new theatres on the South Bank

Letters from Larry

Filming *The Three Sisters*

Views of the Malthouse before and after extensions

Old friends: Larry with Ralph Richardson; Helen Montagu pouring champagne for John Osborne; Maggie Smith and Beverley Cross

Larry rehearsing *Othello* with Maggie Smith

Rehearsals for *Saturday, Sunday, Monday* with Frank Finlay, and Larry and Gawn Grainger; Franco Zeffirelli directing

Theatre roles: as *St Joan*; with Anthony Hopkins as Petruchio in *The Taming of the Shrew*[3]; as Hilde Wangel in *The Master Builder*; as Jennifer in *The Doctor's Dilemma* with John Neville. As Arkadina with Helen Mirren as Nina in *The Seagull*; in New York in Eduardo de Filippo's *Filumena*; La Poncia in *The House of Bernarda Alba*; and, as Edith Cavell. As Lady Pitts, having had one too many in *Daphne Laureola*; as Alma getting one of her headaches in *The Bed Before Yesterday*. In *The Merchant of Venice* as Portia, with Jeremy Brett, Derek Jacobi and Anna Carteret. In *Way of the World* with Maggie Smith[4]

Larry as *King Lear* for Granada Television: Diana Rigg and Dorothy Tutin; in Washington with Ronald and Nancy Reagan following a special screening at the White House

At the Malthouse following Larry's funeral: With Julie-Kate, Tarquin and his daughter Isis, Richard and his wife Shelley, and Tamsin; Larry's chair and crown; grandson Troy with Hamlet the cat; Richard and Donald McKechnie; with Douglas Fairbanks; Maggie Smith, David Plowright, Lady Richardson, Mary Evans, John Mills, Laurence Evans and Mary Mills; Franco Zeffirelli

Seventieth birthday party: Edna O'Brien and Helen Mirren; Vanessa Redgrave and Ned Sherrin; Frank Finlay; Alec McCowen; Tamsin and Julie-Kate with the cake; Julie-Kate with David Heyman; Twiggy, Leigh Lawson and Patrick Garland; Cleo Laine and Johnny Dankworth; Chris Larkin, Richard and Tamsin; with Simon and Tamsin, Julie-Kate, Richard and Shelley, Troy and Alessandra; Anthony Page, Norma Heyman and Maggie Smith; Geraldine McEwan and John Mortimer; John Stride and Edward Petherbridge

Film roles: *101 Dalmatians*; in *Dennis the Menace* with Walter Matthau; in *I Love You to Death* with Keanu Reeves, River Phoenix and William Hurt; with Sting in *Brimstone and Treacle*. In *Tea With Mussolini* with Lily

Tomlin, Cher, Maggie Smith, Judi Dench; with Armin Mueller Stahl in *Avalon*; comedy dance in *Dance With Me*; with Jim Broadbent and Mia Farrow in *Widows' Peak*; with Polly Walker, Josie Lawrence and Miranda Richardson in *Enchanted April*[3] All the family – in the garden at the Malthouse; and the next generation: Troy, Alessandra and Wilfred

The Author and the Publishers wish to thank the following photographers:
[1] Zoë Dominic
[2] Snowdon
[3] John Timbers
[4] Alastair Muir
[5] Angus McBean

Introduction

Some fifteen years ago I was commissioned by George Wei-
denfeld to write a book about my life. Eighteen months later I
gave him his money back as I hadn't even started and couldn't
think how to do it. When Larry died in 1989 and I was going
through private letters, I become absorbed in the memories
they evoked and realized that they could provide a springboard
for a book. Hence this memoir, which is not an autobiography
in the strict sense of that word. It is a personal selection
of events, people and places and how they affected my life
significantly in one way or another. Nor is it always in chrono-
logical order; the contents of the letters quoted sometimes send
me back and forth into the past and the future. And occasionally
it is a present day snippet of news which sparks off comparisons
with remembered times gone by.

There is a Pirandello play called *Right You Are If You Think
You Are* about the way those people who are involved, remember the same sequence of events quite differently, and from
their own particular point of view. These recollections are from
my point of view, aided and abetted by letters when possible,
and the title, of course, is the simple truth.

I have written intermittently for nearly two years, in between
film engagements and want to thank those who have provided
the support and sustenance which allowed me some freedom
from the practical business of day to day living.

Helen and Clive and the helpers at the Malthouse, plus Jean
and Gary; Sharon in London; Simon from SimonPaul, and of
course Penny.

I also wish to acknowledge here the wise counselling and
friendship of our advisors, Laurence Harbottle and Peter Hiley.

Special thanks are due to Janet Macklam who put up with my shilly-shallying and constant rewriting, overcame my doubts, corrected my grammar, and put it all into her computer. And to the editor, Ion Trewin, for his guidance, encouragement and patience.

I am grateful for permission to use letters from the following: Lindsay Anderson, Robert Bolt, Alexandra Boyd, Richard Burton, Lord Chandos, John Dexter, Jill Esmond, Douglas Fairbanks Jnr., Mia Farrow, Trader Faulkner, William Gaskill, Sir John Gielgud, Sir Alec Guinness, Sir Peter Hall, Vivien Leigh, Donald MacKechnie, Jack Merivale, David Niven, Peter O'Toole, Ronald Pickup, Barbara Priestley, Vanessa Redgrave, Sir Ralph Richardson, Toby Rowlands, Paul Scofield, Peter Shaffer and Kenneth Tynan.

My brothers, Robert and David Plowright and their families have supported me through thick and thin and deserve my gratitude for always being there when I most needed them.

And finally I would like to say that I cannot envisage life without the help of my own loving family. And so, in the order in which they came into it, I bless Richard, Tasmin, Julie-Kate, and their partners, Shelley, Simon and Paul; and grandchildren Troy, Ali and Wilfred; together with those as yet unborn who may perhaps arrive after I am gone. Not that I envisage leaving the planet in the near future – my mother lived to be ninety-three years of age – but because I always remember the motto from my Girl Guide days 'Be Prepared'.

JP

The Malthouse, 21 June 2001

One

·······················

Hibaldstow

If I had been born twenty-two years earlier we might, just might, have met in Hibaldstow, a Lincolnshire village, where Larry's father was temporarily the priest at the local church. And where, as a boy, he drove through the streets in a pony and trap, which he fell out of and suffered a wound to the head. It left a dent in his scalp, which many years later he traced with my finger and said, 'This hole was made in Hibaldstow.'

Twenty-two years later I would ride through those same cobbled streets on my pony, on my way to the show ring of the local gymkhana. And unaware that he had ever been there until our May–December love affair began and we told each other everything about our childhood.

Two

....

Dark Green Velvet

I have no photograph of myself in the dress which has imprinted itself so indelibly in my memory. And there is no black and white record of the confrontation with my mother when I refused to wear it. But the recollections come with such vivid intensity that I'm sure they are as near to the truth as it's possible to get, though only the conventional bourgeois side of my dual-natured mother emerges here.

'Either you wear that dress or you don't go,' said my mother as she carefully pressed the jacket of the Marlborough suit she had instructed her youngest son to wear for the important Goodwin family's 'party of the year'.

'But it smells,' I shouted, thrusting the dress under her nose. 'Go on, you smell it! It smells of mothballs and cleaner's stuff ... It's sickly and velvety and ... all those buttons.' My voice broke and tears started to trickle down my cheeks. 'And ... oh, it's horrible.'

I flung the offending dress across a kitchen chair and myself into the other chair on the opposite side of the fireplace.

'It's the only decent dress you've got,' said my mother implacably. 'It's beautifully cut and made and you look very well dressed in it. The Goodwin girls are always beautifully turned out; I won't let you go round there in anything cheap, it's not fair to your father or to me. Those sort of people always recognize good taste when they see it. You'll learn about that sort of thing when you're a bit older.'

It was, indeed, a tasteful dress. Made of dark green velvet, it had two rows of dark green velvet buttons running from the dark green velvet belt up to the round, Peter Pan collar, of the selfsame material. It had been purchased second-hand, but in very good condition, through the columns of *The Lady*, a magazine which enabled the impecunious, professional classes to wear with pride and confidence the cast-off but unimpeachable garments of the Upper Middle and occasionally, the Very Top, Classes.

But in my fourteen-year-old adolescent world, good-taste dresses usually sentenced their wearers to a whole evening as a wallflower.

It was no good complaining that the boys much preferred Linda's way of dressing. Linda had a low-cut, mauve taffeta frock for parties, and wore tight skirts and sweaters and provocative off-the-shoulder blouses to our Saturday night church hall dances.

'She's very lucky to have a mother who's up-to-date and not so stuffy about clothes as you are,' I said.

My mother merely remarked that she could hardly be expected to model herself on Mrs Harris, and added that she was surprised Linda had been asked to the Goodwins' party.

'Because the Goodwin boys said they wouldn't turn up at their own party if they couldn't have Linda,' I shouted triumphantly. 'Anyway, we had her to our party.'

'That's quite different,' said my mother. 'We've known her since she was a child. She's a very sweet girl, but things have changed a bit now you're older and going to different schools.'

I was bursting to knock the wind out of my mother's sails by telling her about my brother's secret assignations with Linda. How he pedalled furiously across town to meet her and braved the jeers ('Green cabbage, green cabbage!') of her secondary modern school classmates on account of his dark green, grammar school blazer. It was considered a risky business for a 'green cabbage' to walk alone among the swarm of muddy brown blazers emerging from Linda's school.

Many a friendship cemented at the junior school had suffered irreparable damage on the day the eleven-plus exam results came through. Children wept openly in the classroom if their name was not mentioned when the list of successful grammar school candidates was read out; and the segregation into different ways of life and uniforms took time to get used to.

Linda was fortunate enough to be among those who had never harboured Dark Green ambitions. She had other assets, which she very well knew, and I wanted my brother to go on seeing her as there were things I urgently needed to talk to her about.

Besides, I suspected that my mother would 'have a few words' with Mrs Harris if I told her, and that would have made things very uncomfortable for all of us. Mrs Harris came into the house for three hours every morning, and had done so for the past five years; and though they were on very friendly terms, my mother still referred to her as 'my daily woman'.

Despite my objections to the clothes she chose for me, I thought the ones she acquired for herself from the same source looked wonderful. Her model suits, and the little hats perched stylishly on her auburn curls, were the envy of many of the more wealthy, Aquascutum-addicted ladies in the town. And I always felt proud to be with her when we went on our cultural jaunts together. Whenever the Royal Ballet or a top theatre company visited Leeds or Nottingham, she would arrange my leave of absence from school. Off we would go on the train in search of a more poetic world and the enchantment of the Forest of Arden, or Swan Lake. We went on a pilgrimage together to Haworth Parsonage in Yorkshire, where the Brontë sisters had lived, written their books and died. It seemed that every window in their house looked out onto gravestones; and we thought it was no wonder Emily took to striding on the moors all day to get away. My mother liked Charlotte best, and though I identified closely with Jane Eyre, I was fascinated by Emily's more dangerous nature, and we were both quite fond of Anne. I think we had read almost everything they had ever written. Both of my parents were great readers and had generated the same passion in their children.

My mother came from Kent originally, and my father was born in Worksop. They were from similar family backgrounds, comprising headmasters, music teachers, English teachers, Methodist ministers and a farmer or two, with the occasional orchestral musician and journalist thrown in. Both came from large families and each had lost their father when they were small children. He had also lost two sisters to the same disease which had carried off the Brontë girls, and my mother had lost her only brother in the First World War.

As a child she had wanted to be a prima ballerina and at sixteen had engaged herself to a touring ballet company, but had been fetched back home as the life was considered too precarious.

I know how she and my father first met, but I don't remember where. She had taken a temporary job teaching ballroom dancing; and he, feeling the need to acquire some social graces, had come in for a lesson. She, Daisy Margaret Burton, married my father, William Ernest Plowright, in 1926 in Gainsborough, Lincolnshire, where Sybil Thorndike was born, and where he began his career as a journalist on the local newspaper.

In 1929 when he became Editor of the *Lincolnshire Star*, they moved with their first child, Robert, to a small country market town called Brigg. It was there that I was born in October the same year and my brother David one year later. In two years' time he would be promoted to the editorship of a larger paper in a bigger town where my mother hoped to lead a more fulfilling existence.

When they first moved to Scunthorpe in 1931 my parents found a four-bedroomed house in a lane comprising twenty-four semi-detacheds, twelve on each side, and boasting a 'No Through Road' sign. Surrounded on three sides by pastureland, it was considered a desirable place to live, marking the spot where town finished and countryside began. We could wander down the hill and spend whole afternoons in Fairy Dell, an ancient quarry now magically overgrown with bushes, trees, tall grass and wild flowers, with hiding places, and odd little hills and valleys and sheltered spots for picnics. It wasn't spectacular compared with some English countryside, but to small children who had known no other, it was paradise.

Within the next ten years, Scunthorpe was to become a 'boom' town, producing more steel than Sheffield; most of the neighbouring farmers were bought out by the borough council, and a rash of new and hurriedly erected houses began to obliterate the pastoral land around us.

My brothers and I mourned the loss of the fields as a playground as much as my parents lamented the unaesthetic look of the buildings closing in on them. My mother, who had loved the quiet and the space and the freedom to walk alone, was filled with a deep unrest and a yearning to escape; and she began the first of her exhortations to us three children to get out and away in search of a more promising world.

She had the same longing for a cultural paradise as Chekhov's three sisters had for Moscow, though she worked a great deal harder for it than they did. But, like them, she had to compromise and make the best of what she had; and she did it with huge flair and style.

She became a leading light with the Amateur Players (in which she was much talked about as an unforgettable Elizabeth Barrett Browning), sang with the Operatic Society and choreographed her own ballets on the lawn. During the war she founded her own drama group, directing as well as acting in it, involving her whole family in all its operations and even painting the scenery when no one else was available.

It may sound paradoxical to describe her as nervous, shy, reticent and reclusive, but she was all these things and said to me once, 'There were times when I couldn't have crossed the road without your father to guide me.' An imaginative and resourceful housekeeper, she worked day and night with my father to improve their standard of living and in the late 1930s, life began to look good.

With Nurse Penistone to look after her children she could sally forth at night in a glamorous evening gown to dazzle the town; and she was thrilled to bits the night my father looked up from his accounts and said with a huge smile, 'By Jove, Pop, if we go on like this, we shall be in Easy Street.' (Pop was his own affectionate nickname for her, shortened from 'Snap, Crackle, Pop' on account of her red hair and temperament to match.)

A week later, sitting in shocked silence in front of the radio, the family listened to Mr Chamberlain's solemn announcement: 'We are at war with Germany.' Overnight my father's income was cut by half; Nurse Penistone had to go, the daily maid went; the car was sold, and my father went to his office on a bicycle. The Old Empire Theatre, where my mother had acted, became a Forces canteen; the professional Savoy Theatre went dark; and a blackout descended on the town and on all my mother's life-enhancing activities. Though she wept for what might have been, and the unfairness of two wars in one lifetime, she set about making the best of yet another compromise.

All her ingenuity went into making new clothes out of old ones, coping with the housework alone, inventing recipes to relieve the monotony caused by rationing, and turning the dining room into a four-bunk bedroom where we eventually slept, ignoring the air-raid siren and its implied injunction to rush out to the Anderson Shelter in the garden.

The first bomb to be dropped on England fell on Scunthorpe, according to my father. (The actual first was dropped in Scotland.)

Ten days before war was declared, forty German technicians had been at work on the erection of a new steel plant at Appleby. Their sudden recall left everyone deeply suspicious, and no one was surprised when the first of several attempts to bomb the steelworks occurred on the second night of the war. The Germans missed their target by about a mile and never did us any great harm; but we were constantly being fetched out

7

of our beds for what often turned out to be a false alarm.

As children we found it all rather exciting, and watching the shells of the anti-aircraft guns exploding in the sky seemed merely a more impressive kind of fireworks display.

We adapted very quickly to a different way of life, unaware of the struggle and deprivation of our parents; the sacrifice of my mother's portions of butter, eggs and meat, which we unknowingly consumed, and of my father's clothing coupons, which caused an eminent solicitor to accost him in the street: 'Good God, Plowright, you're not wearing any socks!'

My mother was deeply grateful to Lord Woolton for instigating the British Restaurants, where we could get a good, square meal once a day; and she revived her good spirits with enterprising projects for her drama group and concerts to raise money for the Spitfire funds.

But unable to travel far in search of good theatre, ballet or concerts, she became more and more aware of the limitations of her existence, and more determined that her children should not suffer them.

My father, quite naturally, did not share her restlessness. He led a very full life: as editor of the *Scunthorpe and Fordingham Star*; chairman of both the Cricket League and the Allotment Holders' Association; a director of Scunthorpe United Football Club; Entertainments Officer for the troops; vice-chairman of the Music Festival; co-founder of the Amateur Operatic Society; and head of the Hospital Carnival Committee.

He was not in the house long enough to notice its shortcomings. There was, after all, a decent sitting room where he could teach us to play bridge, or push us out of when he was phoning local news to the national dailies. There was a dining room where he could conduct political discussions across the table whilst my mother went back and forth with the food. There was a largish kitchen where all things necessary to life could be done without impinging too much on his consciousness, and we three all had our own bedrooms, though they shared theirs.

He dealt with a good-sized garden, putting a lawn and flower beds nearer the house, and vegetable plots, rabbit hutches and a chicken run at the further end. He built us a large, wooden playhouse at the side of the house, with a painted sign on the door, proclaiming its name as Bohemia. Inside Bohemia we played Fathers and Mothers, Doctors and Patients, and other exploratory childhood games with small and timorous friends.

Those were reticent days of family life, and none of us had seen our parents naked, except, shockingly, by accident. It was not deemed right to expose us too early to the brutal facts of life, and as young children we were desperately short of information about sex. The very word itself caused eyelids to be lowered, cheeks to redden and parents to exchange glances. Carnal knowledge was supposed to be acquired indirectly, and gradually, through a humorous and wholesome contact with animal life at the bottom of the garden; until such time as gentle talks, and nature lessons at school, could be given without embarrassment. But we were intensely curious, and watching rabbits and dogs copulating was not much of an introduction to the fascinating intricacies of human relationships. We felt shut out from the adult world but discussed endlessly with each other instances of their sometimes baffling behaviour. Grown-ups were forever shutting the bathroom door hurriedly, whisking newspapers out of sight, hiding books they were reading, talking in hushed tones of mysterious illnesses and shushing each other reproachfully when caught swearing.

My own parents' turbulent quarrelling, which involved competitive plate-smashing and, on occasion, the loss of an entire dinner service, provided an endless source of material. There were the silent days, when they addressed each other only through their children.

'Tell your father I shall be out on Wednesday night.'

'Ask your mother if I'm to get tickets for the Barbirolli concert next week.'

The days of shouting were more embarrassing because of the neighbours and the flimsiness of the walls. We adopted the subterfuge of playing the piano, violin or saxophone very loudly to disguise the exact nature of the discord behind our curtains.

If my mother's voice rose to screaming pitch, I would start to sing music-hall or popular songs, which could be given a raucous, Gracie Fields rendering: 'Gimme, gimme, gimme what I cry for,' I shrieked. 'You know you've got the kind of kisses that I'd die for.'

We also spread vague rumours, acceptable because of my mother's renown as a gifted amateur actress, that the house was never free from people rehearsing violently quarrelsome plays.

Fortunately their sense of humour always reasserted itself before too long, and they celebrated their reconciliations with considerable élan on a Friday, going amicably together to choose a new dinner service, and then repairing to the Majestic Cinema Café, where we joined them after school to eat a high tea of poached eggs, sausages or sardines on toast. Then, a united family once again, we walked light-heartedly up the red-carpeted stairs to catch the 5.30 showing of the current film; then home to unpack the new crockery and round off the evening singing Ivor Novello songs at the piano. My mother and father knew many duets which they liked to sing, but they tended to get rather snappish with each other halfway through, bandying mutual accusations about not coming in on the right beat. Neither of them could read music and it was left to my elder brother, Robert, the musician of the family, to mediate between them.

He would be much missed when he went off to join the Royal Marine Band to fulfil his National Service obligations; and the Trinity College of Music in London would take him away after that, first as a student and later as a Professor of Music on the staff. He was the only one of us who went to Uncle Lambert's Ashley House Boarding School, and David and I were overjoyed when he returned after three years and brought music back into our family life.

As we moved into adolescence, our wooden Bohemia acquired bookshelves and easy chairs around the stove, and reverberated to the sounds of jazz band practice, parties, rehearsals for plays or Spitfire concerts during the war. Twelve evacuees from London were once bedded down there for two nights before being moved to safer territory in the country.

My mother was the driving force behind all this, throwing herself passionately into our development and accomplishments in preparation for our necessary escape into that larger, more promising world, and deviating from the normal pattern of mothers around her, whose dearest wish was to see their children married and settled down as near to them as possible.

We were rather an odd family by other people's standards. We were not on visiting terms with our immediate neighbours, most of whom held positions of authority at the steelworks. My parents met them on large celebratory occasions, but never entertained them to dinner, though we played with their children. The same evasion was apparent in their dealings with the church.

We were made to attend at least one service every Sunday and take communion after we had been confirmed; we joined the choir and benefited from all the facilities of the church hall. But, though they encouraged and pressured from afar, they never set foot in the church, apart from occasional weddings and carol services, or when my mother was producing the nativity play. They enjoyed the company of a few chosen friends, often separately, and my mother entertained Gentlemen Callers, whose probably quite innocent visits my father seemed to condone.

The headmaster and the bank manager were the two most steadfast of her admirers. They would call at different times on a Thursday evening when they knew my father would be away all night, putting the paper to bed at the printing works. The *Star* was a weekly newspaper and it came out on the streets early on Friday mornings.

The same charade would be played out each week with my brother and me and the Gentlemen Callers.

'Hello, Joan/David. Is your father in?'

'I'm afraid he's not at the moment.'

'Oh well . . . perhaps I can have a word with your mother if she's not too busy?'

'Come in Alex/Bill,' my mother would call and we would retire from the scene, rolling our eyes at each other.

My father behaved with great generosity towards my mother, it seems to me, aware as he was of her longings and frustrations and despite the fact that she did not much welcome his attentions in the bedroom. She told me later that as neither of them knew very much about the art of lovemaking, she had bought a copy of Marie Stopes' *Married Love*, and left it lying around in the hope that he would read it too. For us children he was a vital, energetic and protective force in our lives. Though outwardly an undemonstrative sort of man, he couldn't hide his deeply emotional nature from his children. We had seen him weeping at the Hallé Orchestra's concerts, though of course we never said anything about it.

He was as closely involved as my mother in the Operatic Society and the Amateur Players, acting as a kind of business manager and promoting and publicizing their activities in his newspaper. He campaigned for the restoration and reopening of the Savoy Theatre after the war, and was delighted when our family's entry in the Drama Festival held there won first prize.

A shortened version of *Pride and Prejudice* called *I Have Five Daughters*, it had me as Elizabeth and brother David as Mr Darcy; Mrs Bennet was played by my mother, who also produced and directed. In addition it boasted a small orchestra, formed and led by brother Robert, which played before the curtain rose and during the interval. If I seem to be going on a bit about the family achievements, it is not out of vanity, merely an attempt to evoke the kind of childhood that parents like ours provided before television and computers and video games.

When I acted with my mother, whose gifts I admired so much, I found that I was not intimidated in any way for we had surrendered our identities as mother and daughter. I enjoyed acting and felt somehow freer and more confident when I was appearing as someone other than myself. On stage I could experiment with all those different 'Is' milling about inside me without having to settle for just one to present to the world.

The vexing problem of matching clothes to a shifting identity did not apply in other areas where achievement mattered more than appearance. Competing in gymkhanas, I wore more or less the same outfit as everyone else and, as it too had been acquired by courtesy of *The Lady*, it had an air of impeccable suitability.

My father had engaged an ex-cavalry officer to teach us to ride, a conscientious but stern man who forced us back in the saddle when we had been thrown, ignoring, it seemed to my dazed mind, all signs of incipient concussion.

He would be stationed with my father at the entrance to the show ring to monitor our performances in competitions, and to stop me retiring from the jumping class when my nerve began to fail.

David and I both rode our best jumper, Springbok, though in different classes, and he knew very well which rider he had on his back. With me in the saddle he would come to a sudden and deliberate halt at the wall jump, leaving me to sail over it unexpectedly, and ungracefully, by myself. Yet with David he would clear everything including the five-bar gate, with six inches to spare, and carry off the silver championship cup.

I much preferred the dressage class, where I rode our better-bred Princess, and we performed various well-rehearsed man-oeuvres together with no such risk of humiliation.

Gymkhanas were the main source of entertainment at week-ends in the summer months during the war. Another kind of theatre, they involved us in hours of dedicated practising, the mounting excitement of dressing up our ponies and ourselves, and the last-minute notes and advice before we appeared in front of the public.

In a neighbouring farmer's horsebox, we travelled miles

across the flat Lincolnshire landscape to Keadby, Hibaldstow, Epworth, Winterton, Brigg and Gainsborough, with an occasional foray into the big time at Doncaster. Away from show business, we rode through woods and countryside for fun and in search of adventure, daring each other to gallop under the lowest branches, thundering past sedate groups from posh riding schools, and giggling over the havoc we left behind us.

At Scunthorpe Grammar School, I was back in dark green again, but this time it was uniform and nobody was allowed to deviate from it. A scholarship girl, I was in the A form but still feeling slightly out of place with my classmates, most of whom were from very dissimilar backgrounds. Girls from my sort of family were mostly sent to convents or Brigg High School for Girls, which was considered more ladylike.

I had two inspirational teachers, an English master and a French mistress, who took me through to gain distinctions in their subjects in the Higher School Certificate; both were inordinately fond of the theatre and, with Miss McKay, I acquired the ability to appreciate *Le Cid* and *Phèdre* in their original language, a skill I have unfortunately lost since. But I was hopeless at maths and science, though I fell in love with the maths master's son.

My next-closest friendship was platonic, with a kindred spirit who bought *Theatre World* each month and talked with awe-inspiring familiarity of 'Noël and Graham'. He was surprisingly knowledgeable, at fifteen, about their recent difficulties in rehearsals for *Sigh No More* and was even able to tell me where they had spent the last weekend together. It was a mystery to me where he got it all from, for, as far as I know, he never left Scunthorpe; but as I was more interested in 'Edith and Sybil', Peggy Ashcroft, Wendy Hiller and Celia Johnson, I never pursued the matter.

Because of my experience in my mother's drama group, I was a seasoned performer compared with other girls at school, and the English master cast me as Lady Teazle in his production of *School for Scandal*. There was a very good review in the local paper, written by the director of the Harry Hanson Repertory Company, playing at the reopened Savoy Theatre. My father had invited him to be Critic of the Week, with the direct intention, I believe, of assessing my chances in the profession that he knew I was longing to enter.

A year later I made my first appearance on the professional stage after winning the Harry Hanson Trophy in the Drama Festival, plus one week's engagement with his company at the Savoy, for which I was given leave of absence from school.

When Harry Hanson suddenly advertised for actors in the *Stage*, I was not the only young hopeful to apply. A struggling actor and would-be playwright, called John Osborne, also wrote for a job. He would later describe in his autobiography, *A Better Class of Person*, the true standing of Harry Hanson as viewed by other members of the profession: 'Harry Hanson ... was a by-word for tatty, ill-paid, tyrannical, joyless work. He ran about half a dozen companies with queenly ruthlessness and he had a legendary wardrobe of various coloured wigs which he was said to change according to any bout of ill-humour he was indulging.' To me, however, in my innocence, he was the gateway to that glorious world of theatre I was about to enter.

I travelled up to Soho in London in my green school raincoat and matching beret, brimming with youthful confidence until I joined the queue of platinum-blonde, fur-coated and seasoned actresses in a shabby waiting room outside his office. I took my place beside them, overcome with uneasiness at the sight of their skilfully painted faces, silk stockings and high-heeled shoes, and the initialled silver cases from which they drew, and smoked, endless cigarettes. Unaccountably, I was called in first.

Harry Hanson had opted for a flame-orange wig that day, and he sat, looking like a ravaged carrot, behind a desk littered with photographs and letters and overflowing ashtrays. Raising his dyed eyebrows in disbelief when he saw me, he managed to assume a benign, avuncular characterization for a few minutes before gently dismissing me. (He had no doubt been reminded of the trophy I had won and, more persuasively, of my father's position on the local newspaper.) Pointing to several waste-paper baskets, filled to the brim with discarded letters, he said, with a sweet and melancholy smile, 'Go home, my dear, go home.'

One day, years later, filming Merchant–Ivory's *Surviving Picasso* in the South of France, I was huddled under an umbrella with Anthony Hopkins as torrential rain put an end to the entire day's work. 'It is a blessing in disguise,' stated Ismail Merchant firmly.

'Why?' we asked.

'That I do not know,' he answered, 'but it will become apparent.'

I must say I envied that serene belief and carefree attitude towards the black clouds in one's life; but looking back I recognize that there was an instance of it right under my nose.

Three
....

Drama Student Days

Two years after the black cloud of my rejection in Soho I auditioned for Glen Byam Shaw, Michel Saint-Denis and George Devine, and gained a place at the Old Vic Theatre School in London.

The blessing in disguise became apparent when I went back home as advised by the tatty Mr Hanson, and met a remarkable man of the theatre called Wilhelm Marckwald.

He had worked with Max Reinhardt before fleeing from Nazi Germany; and his first job when he came to England was as Head of Drama for the Adult Education Department of Hull University, where my mother and I attended his first summer drama course. He recognized my longing to be an actress, shaped my theatrical tastes, and developed my talent with intensive coaching, before sending me off to the Old Vic School audition. George Devine told me later that they had been genuinely surprised to see me performing the girl's mad scene from *Danton's Death* by Büchner (instead of the usual Saint Joan or Juliet), not to mention a detailed and accomplished mime (a required audition piece).

The mime was the result of a year's wonderful training at the Rudolf von Laban Art of Movement Studio in Manchester, which had also been arranged by Marckwald.

A centre of contemporary dance drama, the Studio was extending its curriculum to include a few students who were pursuing a future as actors rather than as dancers. Now called the Laban Centre, and based in London, it trained Matthew Bourne, the brilliant choreographer whose stunning, and now legendary, production of *Swan Lake* with all-male swans created such a furore in 1995 and won some twenty-five international awards. And there are plans a-foot, I am told, for the Centre to occupy a new building in 2002 to be designed by the architects of the Tate Modern.

The work at the Laban Studio led to my introduction to a newly formed communal theatre group who were incorporating Laban's theories into their theatrical presentations. They lived en masse in a huge old house, worked at other jobs in the day and rehearsed at night. They were led by Joan Littlewood and Ewan MacColl and were called Theatre Workshop. I was invited to go along and work with them, but was nearly frightened off the first evening by the sardonic MacColl's greeting: 'So this is Marckwald's little protégée, is it?' Miss Littlewood was more cheerful and welcoming, though not yet the dynamic and celebrated figure she was to become in the London theatre ten years later.

I loved their enthusiasm and commitment, whilst being somewhat alarmed but intrigued by all the free-love and wife-swapping which was going on, which I tried to persuade myself was properly bohemian.

All those experiences I owed to Marck (as I now called him), and I was inordinately grateful. My only quarrel with him was when he found fault with Laurence Olivier's *Hamlet* (on film) and spent an entire afternoon going through it with me, explaining why. I had loved the film and was not best pleased to have him sowing doubts about it in my mind.

The next and the greatest architect of my fortunes in the theatre was George Devine, who along with Saint-Denis and Byam Shaw provided a wonderfully comprehensive training, best described by his biographer Irving Wardle, as follows:

The Centre saw itself as a classical school, but naturalism was not excluded from the training. For acting and technical students alike, theatre history was divided into three main phases. First was the 'big style' which hopefully embraced everything from the Greeks to Shakespeare, and implied a drama dealing with cosmic events; this also had to do with the return from the proscenium to open staging. Second, there was a style they were forced to label 'Restoration', as Saint-Denis felt there must be some English equivalent to Molière: this inclined to improvisation and the commedia, acknowledging the presence of the public and treating theatre as a game. Third came the 'modern' or 'realist' style, which meant everything from Chekhov onwards: the determining convention here was the invisibility of the audience. (Devine's term for this style was 'aquarium theatre'.)

The uniqueness of the triumvirate who ran the Old Vic Theatre School lay in the fact that they were not primarily teachers but practising professionals. All three were directing plays at the Old Vic Theatre and thus, as well as handing out criticism to their students, they were on the receiving end of it themselves from critics in the national press. This did not take away from their godlike status in our eyes but it made them seem more vulnerable and human. They were idealistic men with a vision of an ideal theatre company; and they had devised a training which could hopefully produce the kind of accomplished actors they knew they were going to need.

They laid great emphasis on originality and the development of the actor's imaginative powers, but not at the expense of his technical prowess.

Technique is a word that has fallen into disrepute in recent years. English actors were accused of having too much and consequently lacking the spontaneity and naturalness of their American brothers. But the Americans are mostly in training for films where the ability to heighten and project a performance is not required; in the theatre it is essential. The film actor is allowed the freedom to stop and start again; he only has to act in short bursts and can keep going back over the same few lines until he gets them right. Once the curtain goes up in the theatre, nobody can say, 'Cut.' Technique is simply a necessary skill, a knowledge of your craft, and an actor without it is like a car with its engine out of order, or a violin with a broken string. The actor's only instrument is himself, his body and his voice, and both must be properly tuned before inspiration can successfully take over.

We had movement classes to exercise every part of the body, to correct individual faults such as round shoulders, knock-knees, cramped arm movements and general bad posture. There were voice and singing lessons and speech delivery classes, for an actor's voice must be supple, capable of great range, and always audible. Knowing how to breathe properly is as essential to the actor as to the opera singer; otherwise he won't be able to get to the end of a sentence by Bernard Shaw, or Congreve, or Shakespeare, without gasping for breath in the middle.

No audience wants to be made aware of the effort that goes into a performance; it makes them feel worried and uneasy. They want to be able to sit back and relax, confident that they are in safe hands, and marvel at the brilliance and apparent ease of the performers. The best acting comes from a point of balance between technique and inspiration. Michel Saint-Denis said it was like holding a bird in your hand: 'If you clench your fist, you will kill it. If you loosen your hand too much, it will fly away.'

Apart from these more traditional classes there was the Stanislavsky-influenced animal improvisation. We had to choose an animal, go to the zoo and study it, and then work to perfect the physical characteristics of that animal; slinking around on all fours as a tiger, slithering about the floor as a snake, or hopping around as a chicken. After about four weeks we had to perform it on stage for the staff and other students. If we were successful, they would be able to identify the animal by its eating habits, the way it moved, whether it was timid and frightened, or an aggressive hunting animal. All that is not as silly as it may sound, for an actor needs to apply the same intense study of movements, habits and peculiarities to the creation of a human character. That doesn't mean to say that a man who can be an extremely good chicken will necessarily be a good actor. In fact a potentially good actor can be a very bad chicken . . . but it will have taught him that though he may have believed fervently and passionately that he was a chicken, he was not able to express it physically to his audience. His body was not yet trained or capable of carrying out the tasks imposed upon it by his imaginative powers.

We did have one rebellious young actor who simply went up and crouched on the stage, where he sat perfectly still with an intense expression on his face but did nothing at all for the whole five minutes. As we had no idea what he was doing, Michel Saint-Denis asked him to explain. He said that he had been a chameleon and that while he was sitting there he had changed colour several times, and that he had felt it very deeply and sincerely, and if we hadn't been able to see it, he was sorry.

Alongside were classes in mime, masks and acrobatics, and, most enjoyably for me, classes in George Devine's special field of comic improvisation. We could dip into a great pile of clothes, funny noses, half-masks, wigs and hats and become whatever we wished. After we had found a character we would begin to move it around and start relating to others. Wearing a mask, or half-mask, tended to bring out more primitive move-ment or energy; you became larger than life-size with more ferocious appetites and fears. George himself would enter into the spirit of the game with huge abandon, demonstrating with great relish an armoury of the tricks of the trade. How to speak with a cleft palate, or whistle through your teeth; how to perform comic trips, pratfalls and double takes; and how to move the diaphragm to produce hysterical laughter. He would wander around, attaching one or the other of these physical aids to students who were still too tentative and self-conscious.

There was one girl, a beautiful ex-ballet dancer, for whom these classes were a torture. While the rest of us were working on a dentist's waiting-room scenario, she sat miserably on the sidelines, immobilized by fear and a sense of failure. Finally, George put her into a shapeless old raincoat and loaded her with parcels. She didn't have to act at all; she simply walked in among us, trying to cope with too many bundles. All her own misery was focused on that impossible task, where to put the parcels down, where to move them when other people came in and glared at her. That became the central motif in the scene and it was hysterically funny. It taught us something important about playing comedy and farce; the actual emotion must be completely genuine and the character's predicament taken very seriously, not played as though the actor thinks that what he is doing is funny.

There would come a time in the future when undue stress and strain would cause me to forget that golden rule. In 1975 I was playing Alma in Ben Travers' *The Bed Before Yesterday*, which had become the comedy hit of the year (and won me a Best Actress award). It had been running for some time. It was summertime and we were playing to packed houses that by now were made up mostly of foreign tourists, few of whom understood English. It was very hot, I was very tired, my husband had been ill and I was worrying about my children. But my director, Lindsay Anderson, renowned for his Scots puritanism, quite rightly had no time for my excuses. He came, and saw, and was dismayed. He made notes and came again, and wrote his stern letter:

The Bed Before Yesterday: Performance of Thursday　　　*Lyric Theatre*

Dear Joan,

I thought the performance distinctly improved – less external decoration and 'signalling', more reality. The audience may have been better – but the performance helped.

When characteristic movements (originating, that's to say, in genuine psychological observation and invention) exaggerate into mannerism *– it isn't only that reality is lost. More seriously, what is destroyed is* EMPATHY *– the ability of the audience to laugh* with *– to enter into the character's feelings. Instead they laugh* at. *The character becomes an object. But this is to sacrifice the most precious and unique qualities of* *your performance (and also to diminish the play). Negatively this is due to lack of concentration, proper emotional and imaginative effort. And positively it is due to playing for the easiest kind of laughter.*

You mustn't let yourself get deflected, or your performance distorted, by feeling that the house is full of Japanese. In the end truthfulness of feeling and reality of character will always win – if you don't let yourself get panicked by losing laughs. (You know very well anyway that size and frequency of laughs is infinitely variable, and never the sole factor by which one can judge the success of a performance.) . . .

Love, L

I adored Lindsay with his insistence on the refinement of acting, on simplicity, truth and strength, though I frequently told him he could be too unbending. He directed me as Arkadina in *The Seagull*, and as Madame Ranevski in *The Cherry Orchard*, two of Chekhov's greatest plays; Tennessee Williams wrote in the *New York Times* that the production of *The Seagull* was the only one he had ever seen that had got it right. During rehearsals I remember asking Lindsay if we could be having a picnic in Act II, so that we could all have a glass of wine or something whilst Trofimov is philosophizing. 'Why?' asked Lindsay. 'Chekhov didn't say they were having a picnic. Why don't you just listen to what Trofimov is saying? Russians would find it perfectly natural to sit still and listen to a serious speech – only the English would need to giggle or find bits of business to do whilst he is talking. Why don't you just EXIST?'

With Chekhov still in mind, let me return to the Old Vic School training. We were required to investigate the historical background of each author; to study the manner of dress and movement of each different period; and to appreciate the particular style of each written text. We attended art galleries to study painting, and parks, pubs and the big railway stations to study people. There were lectures on political movements and their development, and how they affected the dramatists of their time. If I take Chekhov as an example it is not just because he's my favourite author but because it is impossible to play his

23

characters properly without an understanding of the enormous social upheaval in Russia at the time of their creation.

The training was rigorous and demanded total commitment. 'Acting is a serious business' was the message we were being given.

I was sent home early at the end of the first year. My parents were warned that I was in a state of nervous exhaustion and must have rest and quiet. It was discovered that I had been staying behind night after night, when everyone else had gone home, trying to come to grips with Medea. And Litz Pisk, our wonderful movement teacher, warned me that I must not allow such an obsession to take hold again.

When I first arrived in 1949, the school was still inhabiting the Old Vic Theatre, which had been damaged in the war and closed as a playhouse for some time. The actual Old Vic Company were installed at the New Theatre and we had the place to ourselves. As the auditorium was full of rubble and leftover scenic debris from past productions, classes took place in the foyer, the bars and the big rehearsal room at the top of the stairs. The place was so full of atmosphere and tradition that we didn't care about the discomfort. We just felt privileged and happy to be there. When plans were made for the Acting Company to move back in 1950, the school had to find new premises in West Dulwich, and we students helped to load all our equipment into removal vans.

Extract from a letter home:

It was terribly exciting as the Old Vic Company, playing at the New Theatre, came in today to rehearse. They are using it now we've moved out. They were rehearsing in Room 42 which is right at the top, up eight flights of stairs. We had formed a chain (thirty-six of us) from the top down to the stage and were slinging things down and across to each other and singing 'She'll Be Coming Round the Mountain' at the tops of our voices. I was in full swing and had just go to 'She'll be wearing Woolworth's corsets when she comes' when I swung my chair round to Christopher, next to me, and nearly hit Michael Redgrave in the chest instead. He stood there, looking rather amused, but I was mortified, and my voice trailed away and so did everyone else's; and he had to walk on up the stairs, past rows of breathless, gaping students who were only roused from their stupor by indignant shouts from the top of the chain.

When we assembled on stage for further instructions the rumour began to spread that L. Olivier had come in too. The boys made a concerted dash for the doormat and came back holding it aloft and crying, 'He wiped his feet on this.'

Extract from second letter home:

I've been to see Hamlet and it was wonderful to see it performed by marvellous actors after studying it for two years for Higher School Certificate. My pleasure was greatly enhanced by the fact that I knew most of the speeches by heart; those lovely passages of poetry really are poetry when spoken by Michael Redgrave. He took the famous 'To be or not to be' well down near the front of the stage, and so quietly and simply that it made Olivier's beautiful diction, dramatic pauses, loud music and despairing cries sound like pure unadulterated ham. Now I know what Marck meant when he said it was Olivier's Hamlet, but not Shakespeare's. I don't say that Redgrave was perfect, but he was more moving because of his stillness and intensity. He was dressed in the traditional black and he had his hands behind him and just brought his right hand forward at the end to make one significant gesture which was the more beautiful for being the only one.

I was quite startled to read that passage when my father, who had kept all my letters home, sent them back to me a few years ago. I don't remember feeling like that about the film; I think I was just trying to impress my parents. And somehow the speaking of Shakespeare's poetry seems more appropriate on the stage than on film. In the way that some films work better in black and white than in colour.

I was just as bumptious and judgemental about my first opening night experience:

On Tuesday I went to the first night of Ralph Richardson's new play,
Home at Seven. It is by the same author as Journey's End, but not as
good, though the acting was very good indeed. But I think I enjoyed the
experience of being at a first night almost as much. We sat and gazed
down in wonder on 'London Society' plus a sprinkling of famous theatrical
names in the stalls and dress circle. They all looked resplendent in full
evening dress, and sparkling jewels, though some of them seemed more
interested in looking at each other than in looking at the stage. However,
the play received a rapturous reception, especially from the gallerites (we
were in the upper circle) who let themselves go shouting 'Bravo' and
stamping their feet and crying, 'Author, Author.' As various people in the
stalls looked up at them with amused smiles and said, 'Shh, Shh,' we
could only assume that the poor chap was dead. Richardson's performance
was, of course, marvellous and I was glad to have seen him but there is
one thing about London theatre that makes me quite cross. The houselights
go down and there is a sudden hush, and the audience becomes very still
and waits with mounting excitement for the curtain to rise on whatever
world has been created up there on the stage; then, as a door opens and
the first character in the drama appears, there is a sudden intrusive outbreak
of clap-clap-clapping because it's Ralph Richardson or whoever, and the
spell is broken completely. Entrance rounds, they call them, and they are
as disturbing to a play's performance as their brethren exit rounds, and I
wish to goodness someone would put a stop to them.

Of course, like every other struggling actor I learnt to be
grateful for such a show of audience approval. It meant that the
management would place a higher value on your contribution
and offer to extend your contract. But that doesn't mean to say
that I would miss such displays if they never happened at all to
anyone. They are like prizes for acting; few people believe in
them but if prizes are going to be given, it's nicer to get one
than not.

At the end of the two-year training came the annual show,
which involved everyone in the school. Scenery and costumes
and props were provided by the design students; lighting and
stage management by those on the technical course, and we all

had our first taste of professional theatre. Because of the renown of the school's three directors, and the results they achieved, there was an eager and professional audience for these events.

My letter home after the school show, 1951:

... *The show is over! It finished in a blaze of glory with several distinguished visitors coming up to the dressing rooms to offer congratulations. We all gave it our utmost as it might be our last opportunity to give a performance for quite some time unless we are lucky enough to get a job. I was better on the second night because I wasn't so nervous, and I could barely get through my big solo speech because the audience were laughing so much.*

Roger Livesey came to the dressing room and said in a beery voice, 'Where's the little girl who played Mae West?' The part was actually the Courtesan in Shakespeare's The Comedy of Errors, *which George Devine had directed with such invention and such relish. The Old Vic actress, Pauline Jameson, also came up to me and said, 'You've converted an anti-Shakespeare gentleman friend of mine to a Shakespeare lover.'*

So you see, now I know I can do it because other people think so too! I'm determined to stay and find myself a job, and I'm sure I will if I don't give in too easily at the start.

I had an offer that night from the John Gliddon Agency, which I have since found out is a very good one – John Gliddon launched Vivien Leigh! I was warned, however, that he had a reputation with the ladies, and that I must 'watch him' when I went to the agency offices.

He was extremely brusque and said such things as, 'I'm told you were very good. Are you very good?' Well, what does one say to a question like that? He then took me into his personal office and there on the wall was a large photograph of his discovery, the beautiful Vivien Leigh.

I did two audition pieces for him, one an extremely emotional speech from a modern play, Granite *by Clemence Dane. He told me that he usually gave that speech to older, more experienced actresses and that I'd done it very well. 'You've certainly got something,' he said, and then came over and took my hand and said, 'In fact you've got far more than I'd imagined.' Which means, according to those in the know, that I've got to watch my step.*

I asked Norman Ayrton, an Old Vic actor and tutor at the school, whether I should go to the next appointment. 'Certainly you must go,' he said. 'He's a damn good agent – only take your roller-skates and keep your wits about you.' But, oh Lord, it's so maddening to have to cope with all that when all you want is a job.

I obviously turned my back on Mr Gliddon and the roller-skating it involved, for in my next letter, shortly afterwards, there is no more mention of him and I am about to acquire a new, and safer, agent.

Another letter home:

Now for some very special news. I don't know why I've put it last as it's terrifically exciting but I somehow didn't want to say anything in case it all falls through. Anyway . . .

Last week Jimmy Fraser of Fraser & Dunlop, who are very good agents I'm told, rang and asked if I could get some photographs round to his office by 11 a.m. next morning. He had seen me in the school show and had recommended me to Lovat Fraser, manager of Laurence Olivier Productions, who was arranging auditions for the part of Bianca in Orson Welles' Othello. They rang back after the audition and asked me to come for a personal meeting with Mr Welles. So . . .

Last Saturday I went to the St James's Theatre to audition for the great man himself. I stood on the stage in the midst of the Antony and Cleopatra set, all huge pillars and rostrums (on which the Oliviers are playing at night), and a young man came on with the book to read Cassio for me. Orson Welles stood in the centre aisle about halfway back and when he saw I had no book, he grunted, 'Do you know it?' I just nodded my head (I had played it at the Vic School), being too dazed to speak, and he said, 'OK, go ahead.' So I went ahead.

When I'd finished he walked slowly towards the stage and stopped and looked at me and said in a deep voice which shook the theatre, 'Who are you, you're very good, who are you, what have you done?' Honestly, he did! . . .

Yesterday they called and said Orson wanted to see me again next Wednesday when he comes back from Paris. Jimmy Fraser says he believes that it's now between me and one other actress. Now don't get too excited, will you? I am trying not to.

Another letter, two weeks later:

Ah well. The other girl got the part. Jimmy Fraser says she's a Rank starlet who can get them more publicity, but they had told him that Mr Welles had said he'd keep me in mind for the future.

Four

....

Orson Welles' *Moby Dick*

Orson was as good as his word. In June 1955 he cast me as the only girl in his extraordinary version of Melville's *Moby Dick* at the Duke of York's Theatre. He had explained to me that he needed versatile actors willing to take risks and able to mime convincingly as there would be no scenery, and could I play the piano? (The 'piano' turned out to be a small harmonium on which I played mood music occasionally to enhance the dramatic action.) He also warned me that it would be like nothing I had ever done, or seen, before. Or since, I should add, in retrospect, for it was the most brilliantly imaginative, exciting and unpredictable theatrical experience of my life.

Rehearsals were long, arduous and chaotic. Some days Orson would be in a thundering bad temper, changing scenes and dialogue all the time and working the actors into the night. Other days he would be chuckling and wreathed in cherubic smiles as some kind of order began to emerge. On yet other days he would suddenly abandon us altogether, being forced to dodge the attempts of exasperated creditors to have their writs served upon him. He would return the next day with huge hampers of food from Fortnum & Mason, chomp his way through two chickens, pâté de foie gras, quails' eggs and succulent pastries, and down a bottle or two of Chablis without a care in the world. We marvelled at him, and sometimes cursed him, but despite what he put us through, we loved him and wanted his quixotic adventure of a production to succeed. And though critics would pick holes in it, it was variously described as 'Dazzling' and 'Astonishing' and 'An evening of sheer theatrical virtuosity'.

It started off as a play about an 1890s travelling theatre company. Appropriately dressed for the period, the cast are gathered on an empty stage with their Actor-Manager (Orson) preparing to run through a scene from *King Lear*. They have barely begun when a messenger hurtles on with a pile of new scripts, which the Actor-Manager has been expecting; it is his adaptation of the story of *Moby Dick*. The scene from *King Lear* is abandoned and rehearsals begin for the new play.

I was Cordelia to Orson's Lear for about seven minutes only and was then required to take on the part of Pip, the mad Negro cabin-boy, on my knees (because he's a small boy) and in a bustle (because I am an 1890s young actress). The other actors, who included Patrick McGoohan, Kenneth Williams and Gordon Jackson, were assigned various parts and Orson himself became Captain Ahab. We perused our scripts for about two seconds, then there was a change of lighting denoting a time lapse, the scripts were abandoned, and the evening moved into the realm of the surreal.

Aided only by astonishing lighting effects, choreographed mime and movement, with the actors playing several parts each, the story of Melville's classic unfolded on a bare stage, stripped of everything except the lumber of an old-fashioned theatre.

Ropes descended from the flies and were swung violently from side to side, as, simultaneously, the actors staggered from side to side, to suggest a storm at sea. Multi-coloured spotlights created stained-glass windows for a scene in a chapel, and an old wooden rostrum became a rowing boat. The theatre electrician's bridge became the ship's bridge, and that was where Orson and I as Ahab and Pip played many of our scenes. Below us on the stage, which became the deck of the ship, the crew played out their scenes separately from us, and the lighting sequences alternated between the two arenas. Orson and I would be lit for our scenes on the bridge, whilst the crew below stood immobile and in darkness; conversely, we would freeze into immobility when the lights switched off from us and focused on them.

But things went a bit awry on opening night.

The first scene involved the crew on the deck, but as they began to speak, the lights went out on them, and instead shone brightly on Orson and me, who had nothing to say. Consequently, of course, the minute we began our scene we were plunged into darkness and the lights came up on the actors below, who had finished their scene, and who sat mute and petrified (and brilliantly lit) wondering what the hell was going on.

Orson cut our scene in half, and hissed at me to go down to the prompt corner and tell them to get it right. I managed to scramble down the ladder and up again in time for our next scene, but was sent down again ten minutes later to deal with his wife. The lovely and devoted Paola was worried to death about her husband's seemingly precarious grasp of his lines, and was crouched on the opposite-prompt side of the stage with a flashlight, poring over the script. She didn't know, as we all knew, that he delivered his lines, and held his pauses, quite differently at every performance. Consequently, whenever there appeared to be an unaccountable silence she leapt frantically into the breach with a loud prompting, which was as audible to the audience as it was exasperating to him.

He was also having trouble with his false nose. In the film world there are skilled make-up artists to do the work, but in the theatre the actors do it for themselves. Orson hadn't had a lot of practice with the nose putty, and so it had begun to crack and drift downwards quite early on in the evening. He kept pressing it back into place with his fingers whenever he could turn his back on the audience. But in the end he lost his temper with it, snatched the whole thing off his face and threw it on the floor.

Orson believed that actors should go on trying out new ways

of playing a scene every night in order to retain true spontaneity. He would sometimes reel off a great speech that we had never heard before. Having worked on his adaptation for several years, there were obviously chunks of it that had not been included in the present version, and which he would revert to without any warning when the fancy took him.

He would also come up behind actors on stage, during a performance, and hiss at them to 'Hurry up' if he was getting bored; Kenneth Williams was once told to 'Get off' just as he was launching into a big scene as the Carpenter. Kenneth had the presence of mind to say, 'God bless you, Captain,' so as not to lose face with the audience before slinking off to the wings to stand, as he wrote in *Just Williams*,

next to Joan Plowright . . . 'What happened,' she whispered, and out of the side of my mouth I replied, 'He told me to get off.' She looked heavenward: 'What about your speech?'

'It's cut,' I whispered. At this point she realised it was her scene which followed the now absent Carpenter episode. She rushed on saying her line, 'Oh Captain, put thy hand in mine, the black and white together . . .' with such incoherent haste that Orson was quite taken aback, but Joan rattled on with the speed of a Gatling gun about white being black, and black becoming white until it sounded like a high-speed detergent commercial.

The concept of the production was such that none of this perturbed the audience in the slightest. Captain Ahab was also the Actor–Manager directing what was, after all, a rehearsal; so, for all they knew, anything that happened could have been in the script.

Apart from the mishap on the first night, Orson never did anything like that to me, even when Kenneth Tynan, the critic he most admired, wrote unkind things about my performance, and complained that the scenes between Ahab and Pip had been too much expanded.

It was the sort of notice that makes an actor reluctant to go out in the street, in case anyone else has read it, and I spent that entire Sunday alone in my flat until my mother rang at six o'clock in the evening.

'You're not to take any notice of that man in the *Observer*,' she told me. 'The Mayor of Scunthorpe was in front last night, and he says you were very good.'

If that brought the ghost of a smile to my lips, it did nothing to dispel my nervousness about going on stage again on Monday night. There had, of course, been good notices too, but it is always the bad that stay uppermost in the mind, particularly when they emanate from the pen of an influential critic. I went early to the theatre to stoke up my courage before the performance. Orson was already in his dressing room, and his door was open.

'Congratulations on your notices,' he called as I approached.

'*Which* notices?' I asked gloomily, looking and feeling rather forlorn. He was prepared for that and dealt with the matter quite brusquely.

'You've had just the same mixture of good and bad as I've had,' he said. 'And I've been in the business forty years, and you're just starting. Why should you presume you will please everybody?' He continued, 'If you're going to spend your life in this profession, there's something you should understand, something everybody has to learn. There'll be the hits when everybody is excited about you, in parts you were born to play, and everyone loves you. The other times there will always be a percentage of the audience, perhaps very small, sometimes a bit bigger, who don't go for your chemistry. There's nothing to be done about that. But if they don't go for your chemistry, make sure they admire your skill.'

He gave a magnificent performance that night, full of such passion and power and depth of sorrow that we actors were all mesmerized and felt we were in the presence of a wayward genius. He couldn't always do it like that; if he wasn't in the mood his wicked sense of mischief would reassert itself.

'I ad libbed a great deal,' he told a biographer, 'and tried to

My father William Ernest Plowright.

My mother Daisy Margaret Plowright (née Burton).

On holiday at Mablethorpe, Lincs.

Mablethorpe again – 'I don't wish to be photographed in this outfit'.

Brother Bob, me and brother David in our Sunday best.

Me, brother Bob, cousins Geoffrey and William, and brother David. And, below, all of us again some years after war had begun.

Obviously a
novice, but still in
the saddle.

Learning to pose for the
camera, aged fifteen.

'Lady Teazle! By all that wonderful.' *School for Scandal* at the grammar school.

Top left: drama festival winners. My mother holding the cup, me in my dress decorated with milk bottle tops; brother David behind us.

Left: vamping it up as Sadie Thompson in *Rain* – West of England Theatre Company.

First wedding: with Roger leaving St Hugh's Church, Old Brumby.

FRIDAY, JUNE 17, 1955

1955

JOAN PLOWRIGHT and ORSON WELLES
—eerie madness, virtue and "ham."

A contemporary cartoonist's view of me with Orson Welles in his version of *Moby Dick*.

At Nottingham Rep in my first Ben Travers play, *Rookery Nook*.

'Look this way ladies! Smile please!' With the author Shelagh Delaney (left) and Angela Lansbury promoting *A Taste of Honey* in New York.

As a local cartoonist saw it after our Los Angeles opening.

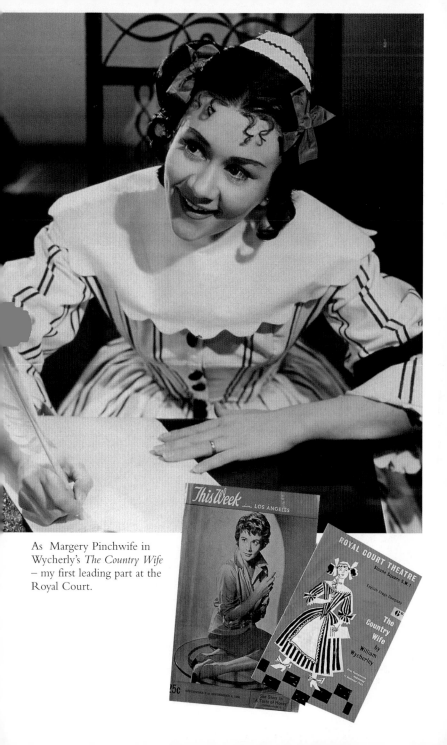

As Margery Pinchwife in
Wycherly's *The Country Wife*
– my first leading part at the
Royal Court.

George Devine was a major influence, at the Old Vic Drama School and the Royal Court, where we played together in *The Chairs*.

Arnold Wesker's *Roots*. Gwen Nelson as my mother; me as Beatie Bryant.

take the mickey out of all the actors. They were all young and solemn.'

But he told the same writer, '*Moby Dick*, I think, is the best thing I ever did in *any* form.'

And Tynan, despite disliking me, described it as 'Dazzling' and 'A sustained assault on the senses which dwarfs anything London has seen since perhaps the Great Fire ... With it the theatre becomes once more a house of magic.' How sad then, that such an evening should be lost for ever, recorded only in the memory of those who saw it; for it proved impossible to capture that magic on film.

I have a vivid image still in my mind of Orson in his dressing room one night, after a performance. The beautiful Paola (the Countess di Girfalco) was kneeling on the floor with a basin of water, bathing his feet. He was gazing down at her with the grateful eyes of a small boy, when I stopped by to say goodnight. 'Where are you going, Snooks?' he asked me. (He had christened me 'Snooks' on the second day of rehearsal.)

It was perhaps the two bottles of wine under my arm that had prompted the question. I told him we were having a cheese-and-wine party in Kenneth's flat. 'Why wasn't I invited?' he asked plaintively. I tried to explain the obvious unsuitability of such a party and place for someone like him.

'That's the trouble, once you get into the star dressing room,' he said. 'People think you're going out every night to much grander places than they can offer, so nobody asks you anywhere.'

Though I suspected him of exaggeration, he looked so vulnerable and deflated that I felt I could willingly have joined Paola on the floor and helped to bathe his swollen feet.

Five
....

South Africa and First Marriage

In between the two encounters with Orson Welles, I became a married woman. I was engaged by the Old Vic Theatre Company to play small parts and to understudy; so was a handsome, ace student from the Bristol Old Vic Theatre School called Roger Gage. Together we sailed with the company in 1952 to southern Africa, taking Shakespeare to, amongst others, Cape Town, Johannesburg and Durban.

We fell in love during the voyage over on the SS *Pretoria Castle*, revelling in the romanticism of moonlit nights on deck, singing duets together in the ship's concert, dancing to soft music and gazing at the stars.

We rose at dawn on the day of our arrival at Cape Town to watch as the famous Table Mountain loomed into view, and marvelled at the beauty of the desert skies at night when we travelled on the train to Johannesburg.

The actress Irene Worth was our leading lady. As dinner was being served she asked the waiter the name of the town we had just passed through.

'Mafeking,' he said with a deadpan delivery and then dumped her soup down in front of her with quite unnecessary force.

Irene was not to be put off so easily, and after we had passed the next village, she repeated her request.

'Mafeking,' he said again with the same expressionless face. There was now no mistaking his hostility towards the English, and we were to meet it again from some other members of the Afrikaner community. We were of course welcomed and lavishly entertained by the pro-British contingent, but we found our first experience of racial segregation difficult to accept.

The theatres were for white people only. And so were the pavements of the streets, I thought, as I watched a burly white farmer elbow a black South African contemptuously into the gutter.

After some indignant reactions from members of the company, arrangements were made by sympathizers for us to go out to a settlement and play to a community of black people only. They provided us with the most stimulating audiences of the tour and the performances became an interactive experience. Not knowing the plays, the audience were taken by surprise at every twist and turn of the plot, murmuring anxiously when Hamlet was about to make the dreadful mistake of killing old Polonius. By the end of the evening, they had grown more excitedly vociferous, feeling the need to warn the actors about poisoned chalices and the tips of swords. We all thought that Elizabethan audiences must have reacted in the same fashion when they watched the plays for the first time. And it is a reaction which is encouraged (when it is genuine) at Shakespeare's Globe Theatre on the South Bank in London. Pioneered by the American actor Sam Wanamaker, it opened in 1996. An exact replica of the original seventeenth century Globe Theatre, it has become an essential part of London theatregoing.

The South African trip had provided a wonderfully adventurous start to our romance, but Roger and I came down off our cloud with a bump when we returned, unemployed, to England. We rushed off to get married in my home town at St Hugh's Church, Old Brumby, and then dashed back to London in search of work.

On the strength of my singing debut in the ship's concert, I was offered the soubrette part in Julian Slade's musical, *The Merry Gentleman*, at the Bristol Old Vic. Behind me, as I sang

37

'I am a first cousin twice removed' was a chorus of girl students co-opted from the Bristol Drama School. One of them was already the possessor of a fine contralto voice and her name was Patricia Routledge. I delighted in the warmth and gaiety of the company, in Julian himself, his collaborator, Dorothy Reynolds, and his leading lady, Jane Wenham.

During the run Roger came to Bristol after finishing an engagement in London and he introduced me to an actor friend from his drama student days there. His name was Peter Nichols and he was already gifted with the mordant sense of humour that would serve him so well as a notable playwright in the future.

When *The Merry Gentleman* finished at Bristol I was happy to move with the company to London for Julian's next musical, an adaptation of Sheridan's play *The Duenna*. His greatest hit was of course *Salad Days*, which ran and ran, but we had quite a respectable success with *The Duenna*, which opened at the Westminster Theatre in July 1954. Though not exactly the West End, it marked my first appearance in a London theatre before Orson's *Moby Dick*.

After the mad Negro cabin boy, I was still frantically in search of my identity as an actress and obviously leading a very precarious life.

Nottingham Playhouse

Dear Ma and Pa,

Chaotic change of plan! I have an offer from Nottingham to play Lady Basingstoke in the Peter Ustinov play No Sign of the Dove *so accepted as it is only for four weeks. It is to be broadcast from the theatre in three weeks' time so you'll be able to listen if you want to. Let me just say that the part is something I have never played before in my life and I can't think for a moment why they cast me in it! She is a sophisticated 'femme fatale' – married three times – and has innumerable lovers, and is described variously in the play as 'a goddess of love in this arid Olympus'; as 'having used her proud body as a sterile altar for sensual delights'; and 'as stupid and as animal as a woman should be, with a gallery of disarming pretensions'. Now, do you honestly think all that adds up to me? However, they all seem to think I can do it, so on their heads be it. I shall certainly have earned my £12 a week by the time I get through this one.*

It was whilst I was giving my version of Lady Basingstoke that the summons came from George Devine in London. He told me about the new company he was forming with Tony Richardson, and asked me to come and audition so that Tony could see my work.

Ironically enough, Roger was engaged as the leading man at Nottingham shortly before I was due to leave, so, like many other couples in the theatre, separations had often to be endured.

Six

Royal Court Theatre
and Consequences

On 9 March 2000, forty-four years after I first stepped onto its
stage, I attended a celebratory gala evening at the Royal Court
Theatre. After being closed for three years because it finally
became uninhabitable, the newly restored theatre opened to a
clamour of congratulations and much rejoicing in the profession
and from the press. For though its work had been going on
elsewhere, the newly exposed walls of this unique small theatre
hold memories of such great moments in theatrical history that
it claims a special place in all our hearts. As Richard Findlater
says in *At the Royal Court*: 'When people talk about the Royal
Court, in the world of the arts, they don't just mean a playhouse
in London, on the eastern side of Sloane Square. The Royal
Court is more than a building. It is an attitude, a discipline, an
inheritance, a global constituency whose members are scattered
through the performing arts.'

After everyone had left the auditorium, I stood on the stage
and gazed around those familiar walls, feeling suddenly as
though I had been transported back in time. Prompted by
Stephen Daldry and Ian Rickson, the current Artistic Directors,
standing in the wings, I took up the position on stage from
where I had poured out Beatie's last triumphant words in *Roots*,
the play that put me on the map in 1959. And into that
expectant silence, as the empty seats gazed back at me, came
echoes of the voices of beloved past colleagues, with whom I
had shared the excitement and camaraderie of those early days.

When George Devine asked me to join the newly formed English Stage Company in 1956 I felt for the first time totally at home in a theatre. I was in touch with people who cared, as I cared, about creating a theatre which was to do with the twentieth century. I found my own voice as an actress, and an exhilarating sense of purpose, which had been sadly lacking elsewhere.

Though primarily a writers' theatre, the Court became a special place for actors too. Until then I had been mostly concerned with the work of dead authors, so it was enormously stimulating to be working alongside live ones, talking to them in rehearsals, arguing with them in the pub afterwards, and even acting with one or two occasionally. There was literally no other place in existence where I could have become involved with such diverse talents as John Osborne, Arthur Miller, Arnold Wesker, Nigel Dennis, Eugène Ionesco and Samuel Beckett, not to mention brilliant young directors like John Dexter and William Gaskill, with exciting futures ahead of them.

It was an unpredictable theatre for the actors, who were just as diverse in their talents as the writers. We were not a permanent company, though there was a nucleus of promising young people, chosen by Devine and Tony Richardson, who could hopefully encompass a large variety of styles. The style, after all, was going to be determined by the authors, not the actors.

When Osborne's *Look Back in Anger* with its anti-hero Jimmy Porter first exploded on the stage, it provided the Royal Court with an identity not previously envisaged by George Devine. And its author joined the ranks of a new and rising young intelligentsia who had come of age under a socialist government. Many of them were the product of a free and better educational system, and state scholarships to Oxbridge; they shared a ferociously irreverent attitude towards the current ruling classes. Often of semi-proletarian origin and from the provinces, they were surprisingly sophisticated, articulate and self-confident (Ken Tynan, for example, Peter Hall and Tony Richardson), and seemed intent on changing the face of British culture. Some of England's young film directors and critics had also started to rail against 'the genteel vacuity of British cinema', and were promoting commitment to reality and social truth. Writers like Kingsley Amis, John Wain and Iris Murdoch had already achieved some celebrity with the iconoclastic anti-heroes in their novels, but Osborne was the first to put one on the stage.

Look Back in Anger was not well received (except by Tynan) when it first opened but it grew into a cult and was ultimately acknowledged to have changed the face of English theatre at that time. All of us at the Court were excited about the play, but uncertain of audience reaction.

On the night of its first dress rehearsal, nerves were stretched almost to breaking point. We were all encouraged to watch each other's rehearsals. I was sitting in the stalls with an anxious George Devine, as Kenneth Haigh (playing Jimmy Porter) and director Tony Richardson started on another of their fierce arguments. We watched John Osborne leave the auditorium, unwilling to take sides; but things finally calmed down and the dress rehearsal ran its course. After the final scene of whimsical reconciliation, George asked me, 'What do you think of that squirrels and bears business?' I admitted that it made me feel a bit queasy. 'Thank God,' he replied, 'I thought it was just me getting old.' He was aware of the play's faults but recognized its brilliance and would not dream of forcing his opinions on its author at this stage. He was often chided for his attitude to writers, which some people thought was too indulgent. But he believed the artist should be guided, not pushed; that he must learn from his own mistakes and develop in his own time.

After the five-year gap since drama student days, I had to get to know him all over again. He had changed. He had greater authority, his humour was more abrasive, now that he was his own boss and had the weight of a whole organization on his shoulders. The zest and passionate enthusiasm were still there, but directed to a new cause – the search for new writers, new material and new forms of theatre. His great tolerance and patience were now extended more to young authors than to actors – and rightly so. The new authors were his students. Actors who came along were expected to be already properly equipped to interpret his authors' works. He cared about our development, of course, but it was not now his first consideration.

George and the people he gathered round him were interested in every aspect of modern life. He wanted us to be aware of new developments in art, music, education, politics, even industry; and he wanted that reflected in the work at the Court. He cared passionately about creating a contemporary theatre, (a) because there was a great lack of it and (b) because he would say, 'Theatre is an immediate art.' He was not interested in 'political theatre' as such, and his search for new forms of theatre would include occasional forays into the classics.

It was short-sighted of people to label us 'kitchen sink' or 'angry young men' (and women), but we were all irretrievably identified with that image after Look Back in Anger, whether we had appeared in it or not. I only played in it once when John (the author), George Devine and I presented a potted version of the English Stage Company's work at a gala evening in Rome. But the label 'angry young woman' stuck firmly to me throughout my first visit to New York in January 1958 with the Ionesco double bill of The Chairs and The Lesson. It had nothing to do either with the ninety-year-old lady I played in The Chairs, or the seventeen-year-old pupil in The Lesson, but it was indicative of the impact made by the Royal Court in a very short time, even in America.

In 1959 I was justifiably slotted into the 'kitchen sink' category after the first night of Roots. I say 'justifiably' only because there was a real sink on stage, not to mention a real stove on which real liver and onions were cooked. The play itself, however, was concerned with a great many other, and more weighty, matters. I am eternally indebted to Arnold Wesker who provided for the contemporary actress what Osborne had provided for the actor – a character who spoke to and for our own generation and who had never before been seen on an English stage. The play would be remembered, according to Tynan, as a portent; and he wrote of its impact in *Curtains*, his summing-up of British theatre in 1959:

. . . the daughter of a family of agricultural labourers comes home, after a long stay in London, full of progressive ideas she has learned from her lover, . . . with a vocabulary that succeeds only in alienating her from her background. In the last scene a family gathering is reluctantly convened to welcome her urban boyfriend, who fails to turn up. A smug reaction of I-told-you-so prevents anyone from comforting the shattered Beatie. If this were an English play of the traditional kind, the jilted girl would at this point recognise the futility of her intellectual aspirations and snuggle back to the bosom of the family. Not so Beatie. She rounds on her relatives, blaming their conservatism and their suspicion of independent thought for her own inability to communicate with intelligent people . . . At the end of this tirade she realises that for once she has not been parroting the opinions of her love, but has been thinking for herself. With the wonder that is cognate with one's first sense of identity, she cries, 'I'm beginning. I'm beginning!' And the play is over. I stumbled out in a haze of emotion, on a sticky, baking July evening. The theatre, I noticed, was full of young men and women who had been distracted from the movies, from television, and even from love-making by the powerful lure of a show that concerned them and that could help as well as amuse. Joan Plowright played the awakened rustic, and the director was John Dexter, and in neither case can I think of an alternative half as good.

Four months before *Roots* I had been lured away to the West End by Robert Morley. He had worn down my initial resistance to his comedy *Hook, Line and Sinker* by remarking how dreadfully pale and overworked everybody looked at the Royal Court. Not to mention underpaid. He said it would do me the world of good to get away, and offered to conduct rehearsals on the beach at Cannes. I was currently playing in Ionesco's *The Chairs* and *The Lesson* at night and rehearsing Shaw's *Major Barbara* during the day; by the end of the run of the Shaw play, Mr Morley's offer had begun to look extremely inviting. Though the sojourn in the South of France put the colour back in my cheeks, the play itself gave little satisfaction to anybody. One matinée, Robert wandered into my dressing room and said, 'I understood you were the darling of the intellectuals. Kindly explain the half-empty house this afternoon.' Another night he came in and asked plaintively, 'Should we do something worthwhile together at the Royal Court in the spring?' On hearing this, the director Bill Gaskill (Devine's eventual appointed successor) promptly offered him *The Man of Mode*, which sadly he turned down, and John Dexter turned up with the script of *Roots* for me. After the notices came out, it was clear that it was one of those 'hits' which Orson had talked about.

The *Daily Telegraph*'s critic W.A. Darlington reported ... *'Joan Plowright, who is to my mind one of the most accomplished, quite the most interesting and easily the most versatile of our young leading actresses, scored a personal triumph on Tuesday at the Royal Court, London, in* Roots *by Arnold Wesker.'*

THIS PLAY CAUTERISED ME – IT WAS WHITE HOT was the headline of Bernard Levin's notice which ended ... *'It is helped by a faultless production by Mr John Dexter ... it is also helped by fine acting which, in Miss Joan Plowright's mammoth performance as the bud which has begun to open, reaches true greatness.'* (Daily Express, *31 July 1959)*

I wished that Orson had been able to come and see it. But Margot Fonteyn came; and Katharine Hepburn, who said I should take it to America (which I didn't); and Sybil Thorndike, who said I should play Saint Joan (which I did). And there was a second-night telegram from Robert Morley and his producer Robin Fox:

JOAN PLOWRIGHT ROYAL COURT THEATRE SW1
  HAD NO IDEA YOU WERE GOING TO MAKE SUCH A SUCCESS
OR WE WOULD OF COURSE HAVE SENT A TELEGRAM EARLIER
STOP = YOUR LATE BUT LOVING MANAGEMENT.

King of the Establishment

I have leapfrogged over a momentous time in my life, which preceded *Roots*. I must go back to its beginning, to the time in 1956 when Osborne's *Look Back in Anger* with its anti-hero, Jimmy Porter was mainly responsible for the Court becoming identified, in Richard Findlater's words, as 'a symbolic centre of rebellion and dissent among young artists, intellectuals, and theatre workers. It was the time of Suez, Hungary, and the Campaign for Nuclear Disarmament, and a surge of feeling against the political and cultural establishment, the social system, the traditional theatre and all authority and institutions...'. It was into the maelstrom of this left-wing and radical rebellion that Sir Laurence Olivier, king of the Establishment, suddenly and unexpectedly propelled himself in 1957. The magnet was John Osborne's new play, *The Entertainer*, together with a growing dissatisfaction with his life in general and his image in particular.

Our first meeting took place in a dressing room at the Royal Court. George had given me my first starring part in Wycherley's *The Country Wife* and it had turned out to be a lovely success. 'A gorgeous little "goof"', wrote Tynan, making up for his nastiness the first time round. I was playing opposite Laurence Harvey, a popular film star brought in for box office appeal, and we were about to transfer to the West End. Larry and Vivien had come round to offer congratulations; and he wrote afterwards, in *Confessions of an Actor*, of his feeling that in our eyes he represented everything my generation were trying to change in the theatre: 'I was titled, necessarily self-satisfied, pompous, patronizing, having obviously come to visit in a spirit of condescension – I could see it all.'

As I remember it we were rather shy, very curious and perhaps a bit wary; but there had been a genuine buzz of excitement at the news that he was coming to act at the Court. And we were very pleased that he was coming to see us at work. There may have been a few mutterings about the Establishment 'joining because they couldn't beat 'em' but they certainly didn't come from the actors. It was perhaps true that to a younger generation he and Vivien seemed somehow outside the profession, existing on a different plane and in the constant glare of publicity as a famous couple. We secretly felt that he was wasting his talent in vehicles like *The Sleeping Prince*, despite their success with a huge audience. So Olivier's decision to risk appearing in a controversial new play and possibly offending his usual audience came as a welcome surprise. It was at a time when connoisseurs of great acting were beginning to voice their discontent over his apparent acceptance of the role of consort to Miss Leigh on the stage. It was Tynan, of course, who came out with it in a vitriolic article after the 'Cleopatras', which earned him the enmity of both for a while, though Larry told me later of a conversation with Lynn Fontanne after Alfred Lunt had died. She had said, rather sadly, that Alfred could have risen to the heights as a great actor, but becoming famous as 'The Lunts' and feeling obliged to choose plays with parts for both of them had prevented him from achieving that stature.

Devine's production of *The Country Wife* packed the theatre for the first time that year. It came after a string of new plays which, though arousing interest and some acclaim, had lost money. The Court was in the red. 'The contemporary theatre,' George commented afterwards, 'was saved by a classic revival.'

For me it was a joyous experience; but for Alan Bates and Robert Stephens (who had not benefited from an Old Vic School training) it was sheer torture. Trying to walk naturally in high-heeled buckled shoes on a polished and steeply raked stage, and wearing unfamiliar eighteenth-century costumes, long wigs and large-plumed hats, they approached every per-formance with fear and dread. As Alan Bates said: 'It's the only time I can ever remember having drunk before a first night to get myself on. I fell into every sort of trap, and I came on wishing I wasn't there. I remember George coming up to me in the wings and saying, "For Christ's sake, boy, enjoy yourself." It kept me out of classical plays for five years.' Laurence Harvey was under contract to the Boulting Brothers and they were hatching a scheme to make a film version of *The Country Wife*, updated and set in contemporary London. They had made it sound very attractive to my agent, except for the stipulation that I would have to sign a seven-year contract. Even so, I was tempted. But George Devine advised against it, saying that if the film succeeded, I would be typecast for life, and 'You've got more important things to do.'

He had become the most influential person in my life at that time. We had enjoyed acting together in four plays during that first year; particularly as the decrepit old couple, welcoming imaginary guests into their home in Ionesco's *The Chairs*. We got used to the sound of the odd seat being slammed up as people walked out, saying, 'Surrealist rubbish.' We would ad lib to each other, 'What was that?' or 'What did he say, dear?' pretending they were part of the invisible throng around us on the stage. We had great fun.

The Making of Moo, a satirical attack on organized religion by Nigel Dennis, caused even more offence. On the first night, George broke his own golden rule and attempted to make a curtain speech, explaining his reasons for doing the play. It is never easy to distinguish between boo-ing and bravo-ing when you are bobbing up and down, taking very fast curtain calls. But when George stepped forward, indicating that he wished to speak, it was only the cheering lot who fell silent; and the field was left wide open to the dissenters shouting 'Boo', 'Rubbish' and 'Disgraceful'. He never made that mistake again.

My erstwhile relationship with George of pupil and mentor

had changed completely as soon as we started acting together. On stage we were just two old pros together and at the beginning of a deep and abiding friendship. He was entirely responsible for transforming me from an actress contracted to 'play as cast' into a leading player with a choice of scripts, and I owe him an enormous debt of gratitude.

When people went out, shouting and grumbling, into Sloane Square, George would watch through his window, smoke his pipe and think, That's what I'm here for. He would never look out of his window when they were all gliding out into their Daimlers after a Restoration revival.

This takes us back to *The Country Wife*, which by now was playing at the Adelphi Theatre, in the West End. Along with George's advice to turn down the film came his request: 'Would you think about taking over the part of Jean Rice in *The Entertainer* when it transfers to the Palace?' Olivier had played just the usual six weeks at the Court with Osborne's play, but its huge success meant that it could pack a theatre for much longer. The part of Archie's daughter had originally been played by Dorothy Tutin, who was not going with it into the West End.

Neither George nor I had any inkling of what rested on my decision during that final week at the Adelphi.

Palace Theatre *September 1957*

Dear Mummy and Daddy,

Thank you so much for your first night telegram. It was very sweet of you to remember. I've really stepped into quite another world of theatre at the Palace. It's on a much bigger scale; and just the fact that I'm acting with Olivier (with my name up in lights) seems to have afforded me more recognition than when I was doing The Country Wife *in a much better part! I had lots of bouquets of flowers; some anonymous and some from 'Royal Court theatregoers' which was really very touching. But in spite of the fuss and excitement, I think I still prefer my Royal Court world. Of course there's more money in this one, but it isn't half as genuine.*

Olivier is fabulous in the part of Archie Rice and wonderful to act with, but the rest of the play's characters don't really mean very much, and that includes mine. I feel there's nothing to get my teeth into. But it certainly is an experience.

The street at the stage door is packed every night with autograph hunters. No other actor in the country is such a draw at the box office; and though they're really waiting for him, it takes me nearly half an hour to get through them as they want the rest of us to sign their programmes too.

In his autobiography, Larry wrote: 'I went to see *The Country Wife* and was entranced by the Margery Pinchwife of Miss Joan Plowright, whose very name was enough to make me think thoughts of love.' On my first day of rehearsal with him, he pretended to have forgotten that name, and rechristened me 'Miss Wheelshare'. He said it was equally agricultural.

He was bristling with energy and his smile was full of mischief; it was as though he had been let off a leash. He obviously adored playing Archie Rice whom he liked to claim was nearer to him than any part he had ever played. Rehearsing in an open-necked shirt with braces holding up his trousers, he had banished all traces of that titled gentleman of the Establishment. He was simply an actor among actors, but one of such extraordinary accomplishment, and with such electricity crackling around him, that I was both exhilarated and exhausted by the end of the day. Larry was very kind and patient with me, though he kept up the game of 'Miss Wheelshare', establishing a sort of jaunty intimacy between us. The name made me laugh. I was very flattered and began to feel more at ease on stage with him.

Taking over a part is always difficult; everyone else is ahead of you, having already reached performance level. Tony Richardson was directing and, as he and I were by now close friends, it was a little unnerving to find that he and Larry were giving me totally conflicting advice. There wasn't a lot you could do with Jean Rice, as Tutin had discovered before me, but I spent a lot of time trying to invest her with a more substantial character; until Larry told me to relax and do it all more quickly, just letting it flow. 'You are trying too hard to establish yourself the minute you come on. You don't need to,' he said. 'You have a presence on stage which you don't seem to trust – you've been very successful in a wide range of characters but you have not yet been required to come on as yourself. So it's as though you have a top register and a bass register, and no middle; and it is that centre you still need to find.' He told me that he had been given that advice by someone (I think Sybil and Lewis Casson) years ago when he was too fond of disguising himself with make-up and false noses, and exaggerated physical characteristics.

We became companions in the lunch breaks, joined sometimes by George Devine with whom he enjoyed a friendship reaching back some twenty years to early days at the Old Vic. It was there, too, that Michel Saint-Denis had directed him in the legendary *Oedipus*.

And when Michel, George and Byam Shaw founded the Old Vic Theatre School, it was Larry who gave the opening address to the students:

An actor, above all, must be a great understander, either by intuition, observation or both, and that puts him on the level with a doctor, a priest, or a philosopher. If I can get more fun from him than just belief, then I feel both fortunate and overjoyed ... There are many dimensions in the art of acting, but none of them ... [is] good or interesting ... unless they are invested with the appearance, or complete illusions of truth.

The difference between the actual truth and the illusion of the truth is what you are about to learn. You will not finish learning it until you are dead.

He had moved on out of their world, with the fame of his films and the obligations of his successful partnership with Vivien Leigh. Now he seemed to be reaching a hand back to them. He had recently played the lead role in *Titus Andronicus* for

Byam Shaw, who was now Artistic Director of the Royal Shakespeare Company; and he told me that he envied George the passion and the purpose of his life at the Royal Court.

In an article for Findlater's book, *At the Royal Court*, he explained his feelings at the time of *The Entertainer*:

My rhythm of work had become a bit deadly; a classical or semi-classical film; a play or two at Stratford, or a nine-month run in the West End, etc., etc. . . . What I felt to be my image was boring me to death. I really felt that death might be quite exciting, compared with the amorphous purgatorial Nothing that was my existence. And now, suddenly this miracle was happening . . . I could feel in this opportunity a great sea change, transforming me into something strange. I felt in fact that I was starting a new life.

And in his autobiography, he says: '. . . more and more my impulses were to create a condition of detachment from my marriage, and a sharp change in the direction in my career might help to form such a wedge.'

He appeared to be living apart from his wife most of the time; he was staying at a cottage in Chelsea owned by his old friend, the designer Roger Furse, and we had all been round there for drinks during rehearsals. As there had been so much gossip and speculation about their marital problems in recent years, it came as no surprise. But he and Vivien still appeared together at first nights and official functions. I was still living with my husband, though our marriage had run into difficulties after the work at the Royal Court began to take over my life. Rehearsing all day and performing every night, I was hardly ever at home except for Sundays, and they were often taken up with lunch parties at George Devine and Tony Richardson's house in Hammersmith where Roger knew few of the people present. Years later, when Larry and I stayed with Sir William and Susana Walton in Ischia, William said to me, 'You're as fanatical about work as he is.' And it was true at that time, and before I gave birth to my first child. My girlhood dreams had never been about living my life through a man. I had wanted to be like Florence Nightingale or Saint Joan or Odette of the French Resistance whose lives seemed so exciting and purposeful and fulfilled; or of course to be an actress, and able to play all of them on the stage.

I never dreamt that what was happening to me now could happen, that I could be so spellbound by the flirtatious charm being directed like a laser beam towards me, even though I knew that my predecessor had been the target before me.

But what was infinitely more dangerous was the way my heart was touched by the bleakness in his face when he wasn't acting or flirting; by the way Archie's cynicism and gallows humour came so easily to him; and by his admission that his only anchor in life now was the theatre, where he could 'knock their eyes out' with his performances and forget about finding happiness in any other form. Talking one day of Archie's reaction to the news of his son's death, Larry recalled his own desolation when his much-loved mother died. Unashamedly devoted to him, she had been the main source of his happiness in a childhood dominated by the father who he felt disliked him. Only twelve years old when it happened, he was assailed by the belief that he would never be happy again and might as well put an end to his own life. ('An early fatalist' was how a friend of the family once described him.)

But those feelings were soon to be replaced by a smouldering anger, which found an outlet in productions of Shakespeare at school, where he could display the talent so encouraged by his mother and savour his first taste of popularity among his schoolmates. His celebrated performance as a thirteen-year-old Katharina in *The Taming of the Shrew* was based, he told me, on minute observation of his mother; but his anger, he said, was his own. Ralph Richardson once admitted: 'I don't have Laurence's splendid fury.'

Tynan wrote that he had 'a pipeline to childhood pain', and I would write to him later, after we had acknowledged our love: 'I want my love to bring you happiness and peace – more than it is doing at the moment. I do not know how I can ever bring you complete relief from pain – I met you too late for that and you will always have a certain grief that I can do nothing about. But I'll do all I can, I love you with such an aching love . . .'

But at the beginning when I was in such danger of being swept off my feet, I took a few steps backwards, suspecting that for him, it could be simply a routine flirtation. I was not a promiscuous girl, and though it was naturally enjoyable, my pride was hurt by the thought that I might be just one of a long line of ladies singled out for such attention. I grew more wary, and made a point of disappearing during breaks in rehearsal; or sitting and talking with Richard Pasco who played my brother or, more pointedly, with Brenda de Banzie, who played his wife and whom he thoroughly disliked. She was apparently guilty of making herself cry as she came on for her curtain call, so that the tears streaming down her face would be a reminder of her emotional scene earlier in the evening, and elicit loud shouts of 'Bravo' from a sympathetic audience. It took a bit of the gilt off the gingerbread when he came on after her for his own call.

None of my evasive tactics was of the slightest use. And finally I knew that I didn't need them; there was a bond between us, a strange feeling of kinship which had nothing to do with casual flirtation. We had fallen very much in love.

The Solace of Work

We played together in *The Entertainer* for six weeks at the Palace but then I had to leave the cast. I had a previous commitment to go to New York with Tony Richardson and the Ionesco double bill of *The Chairs* and *The Lesson*, and so Geraldine McEwan took over Jean Rice for the rest of the run in London. We were to be together again some weeks later when *The Entertainer* came to New York. After my stint in the Ionesco plays at the Phoenix Theatre, I rejoined Larry to play Jean Rice for the Broadway opening at the Royale Theatre in February 1958.

And there in New York our relationship grew deeper and more binding. Away as we were from the people in our lives from whom we were keeping secrets and about whom we were feeling guilty (or certainly I was), we could enjoy a precious time of happiness together. We told each other everything about our past history and the present state of our marriages. He confided that he had suggested divorce to Vivien two years ago but that she had vehemently opposed it and even threatened to take her own life if he went ahead. She wanted the legend and the marriage to continue, though she conceded that each of them could be free to enjoy liaisons elsewhere. I knew, as indeed half of London knew, of the Peter Finch affair among others, and he told me about his own romance with Dorothy Tutin.

He cared deeply about Vivien's well-being but he was adamant that their life together was over and there was no going back. It was hoped that after a time of separation she would recognize the futility of keeping up the pretence and possibly find a new love of her own. He could not bear the thought that any precipitate action of his might be the cause of some irrational act on her part. And he feared even more, and so did I, the effect such a happening would have on our own relationship; we would carry the burden of it for the rest of our lives. He knew that I had no experience either of being hounded by the press or in such a situation, of probably being reviled by the public; but he of course had been through something similar before. When he and Vivien had left their partners, and their babies, some years previously it was she who had received the most vitriolic of the letters of condemnation. Somehow it seems that it is always the woman who has to shoulder most of the blame. As though the world is resigned to the fact that men cannot help behaving badly in affairs of the heart but women are expected to weigh the consequences and put aside their passion and behave better.

After four months our New York idyll came to an end and we were back to England and the solace of new work. Letters and telephone calls kept us in touch, and there were occasional suppers with George Devine and Jocelyn Herbert, the great theatre designer, at her studio in Flood Street. They had been through a similar time of heart-wrenching difficulties themselves, and gave us, constantly, their wise, generous and loving support.

The Royal Court decided to present me in the Ionesco double bill for a short season, as only one of the plays had been seen previously in London. 'That it is the same young actress of twenty-six we are seeing in both plays, is hard to believe,' wrote Alan Dent. When George and I had first played in *The Chairs*, Tynan had called it 'an enthralling experience', despite the fact that on paper it seems merely 'virtuoso nonsense'. He went on: 'The audacity of the idea is breathtaking; here is pure theatre, the stage doing what only the stage can do', and he finished by stating that 'as a comic inventor he [Ionesco] is superb and classical'. On the second time around he lost patience with the 'anarchic wag' and worried about the impact of the Royal Court's promotion of his work. 'The point of the programme,' he wrote, 'is to demonstrate the versatility of Joan Plowright, who shed seventy years during the interval, and to celebrate this nimble girl's return from Broadway, where she appeared in both plays under Tony Richardson's direction. Yet there was more in the applause than a mere welcome home. It had about it a blind, deafening intensity; one felt present at the consecration of a cult ... an Ionesco cult, and in it I smell danger.' He expressed his dislike of Ionesco's nihilistic view that communication between human beings is impossible; and went on to chastise those who championed the playwright's evocative escape from realism. He warned that it must not be held up for emulation as the gateway to the theatre of the future. This sparked off a vigorous controversy on the merits of the Romanian-born author, and escalated into a debate on the role of the artist in society. Ionesco wrote to the *Observer* in his own defence, claiming 'a work of art has nothing to do with doctrine' and saying that a critic's job was to look at it and decide 'whether it was true to its own nature'. Devine wrote defending his author's conception of theatre as an art and Orson Welles joined in on Tynan's side, saying 'an artist must confirm the values of his society; as he must challenge them'. The correspondence grew larger as half of London's artistic and literary community battled it out. Ionesco was not impressed by the contemporary playwrights who, Tynan claimed, had created the lasting body of twentieth-century drama (O'Casey, Sartre, Arthur Miller, John Osborne, Tennessee Williams and even Brecht), and called them the 'new *auteurs du boulevard*'. And as far as society was concerned, he wrote: 'the authentic human community is revealed by our common anxieties, our desires, our secret nostalgias ... no political system can deliver us from the pain of living, from our fear of death.'

'Nor can any work of art,' Tynan answered, 'but both are in the business of trying.'

I found it exciting to be involved in such a hullabaloo, and of course it meant that the theatre was packed every night. In a way I belonged equally strongly to both sides. As an artist I delighted in Ionesco's surrealist imagination, and the scope it gave to the actor; as a human being I would rather look, along with Tynan, for the artist 'who concerns himself, from time to time, with such things as healing'.

It is interesting to note that *The Chairs* was revived by the Royal Court in 1997 with great success, and transferred a second time to New York with Geraldine McEwan now playing my part of the Old Lady.

George then decided it was time that I had a change of direction after the eccentricities of Ionesco, and offered me the leading part in Shaw's *Major Barbara*. He had high hopes that Orson Welles could be tempted to play Undershaft, the rich armaments manufacturer who comes into conflict with his Christian daughter and tramples on her belief that poverty is of less importance than salvation. Orson entertained the idea for a short time but was too busy with other commitments. I had some qualms about accepting the part; the English class system still had some power over people's minds back then, and Barbara was supposed to have come from South Kensington, not Scunthorpe. But George prevailed over my doubts and nervousness, saying that it would be an excellent preparation for Helena in Shakespeare's *All's Well that Ends Well*, which he was planning to do the following year. Larry came to see the Shaw play and wrote that night from Notley where he was living alone and studying *John Gabriel Borkman* for a television production.

First of all I was really very impressed by how far you had managed to go to collar this not at all rewarding part along most difficult new lines for you.

By the way, please tell Georgie, who came to talk about All's Well that Ends Well, *that I am absolutely happy, having seen you in this, that it will hold no terrors for you. You could knock off Helena on your dainty black head, darling. You have an absolute natural poetic quality and without any sign of strain, which is the whole bloody thing.*

Now then, I think when you essay to alter your personality as radically as you are required to do for Barbara you must be prepared to throw out some of those qualities which have stood you in good stead in your earlier triumphs at this theatre.

You have an absolutely marvellous uncalculated, impish sense of humour which is strongly laced with an aptitude for self-mockery. This last can be an invaluable but also a dangerous quality which should be used judiciously . . . the first is priceless, but must not always be relied upon because it will not always get you out of a hole.

In any untoward circumstance which might make one unusually self-conscious, or when overtired, the basic elements of our personality will predominate naturally, as they are the first things within us we unconsciously grab hold of to make us think we can do it at all, as any mannerism is developed subconsciously to cover up some weakness . . .

disjointed pauses by one who is frightened of drying up . . . exaggerated gait in one who thinks he is ungainly, e.g. JG etc.

But in this role, or any in which the background is different from our own, we must be strong and prepared to face the fact that these elements may not be suitable and bloody well create something else that is . . .

Acting is basically a humourless craft, and that's what makes people like us suffer so.

I think you are a little frightened of the part and it's hard to love anything you're frightened of. But you must love Barbara. Love her as she's never been loved before. Love is (among other things) the exaltation of understanding. Now understanding is the absolute must in our work, and the means whereby we can inform. Love is the means whereby we can bring that information home.

Please don't think I am saying it is a bad thing to be frightened of a part at the beginning.

A humble approach to our work is essential and there is a dreadfully stern law which ordains that 'No True Artist May Expect Satisfaction From His Work'. But how do we equate the essential humility towards the work with the full possession of the confidence required to carry it off?

Not that last night's audience were given any other impression than that you were sailing along confident in your prowess and presenting a perfectly plausible Barbara for their enjoyment and approval. But you and I know that you have brought her towards yourself . . . and into you . . . instead of going out to her. And that is what leaves you with that niggling sense of dissatisfaction.

I think my dissatisfaction was compounded by the knowledge that with me on stage (playing the small part of my sister) was an actress unknown as yet, apart from her surname, who would have been absolutely perfect for the part. She was Vanessa Redgrave.

Some weeks later when I was on the pre-West End tour of *Hook, Line and Sinker* with Robert Morley, Larry wrote again from Notley, on 28 October 1958, to share with me his grave concerns about his brother, who was suffering from leukaemia.

Notley Abbey
Your Birthday
Still   11.55 *p.m.*

... *The day has been a poor one, my love, one third of it devoted to writing another of 'those letters' to V ... Then Dickie has taken a turn for the worse. Hester came over to dinner with me and we discussed if, and how, we should tell him. I don't know – I simply don't know. I think I should want to be told but I suspect my judgement in human matters is coloured by my sense of the dramatic and so, as so often happens, I am deeply perplexed in my dealings with a really human matter. I think I would want to be told and I think I would rather be told by my brother. But, oh Lord, I can't really trust myself for true judgement. Hester, I think, wants me to tell him within the next few days. I wish I could talk to you. I know that you would help me and that in your judgement I would always have faith, my darling, in human matters, indeed probably in all.*

... Please, my love, be sure to send me the phone number of the hotel in Glasgow and the one in Edinburgh. I envy you having two and a half hours in the day when you have to concentrate. All through my trying to learn my words, my thoughts fly through them to you. Your letters are such heaven to me ... God bless you my dear, wonderful girl.

In an earlier letter to Vivien, Larry had suggested that it was time to make their separation legal. The repercussions were not of the kind expected. She wrote back from the Apollo Theatre on 25 October: 'Thank you for writing to me so fully and gently – I agree with almost everything you say – in any case on the main decision of it – completely. I would very much like to keep the announcement quiet until I finish in this play.' It was around this same time that she complained quite reasonably to Rachel Kempson: 'If he was going to do it, why didn't he do it when I had Finchy in tow?' The long-term love affair with Peter Finch had continued intermittently until quite recently when they had apparently agreed to go their separate ways. But in answer to Larry's second plea, she wrote to him again, in a letter dated 2 November 1958:

... Because I have had a day entirely on my own and able to think clearly, I have come to the conclusion (a fearfully painful one) that a clean and absolute break is the only path to follow – so I intend to divorce you on the grounds of desertion, mental and physical – as soon as our present chores in the theatre and television are over. We are, in any case, separated ... I think our lives will lie in quite different directions. I feel confident I shall make my own life – and you have always made yours.

This was so much more than Larry had hoped for that it seemed too good to be true. We were not to know that the divorce was contingent on her getting back together again with Peter Finch. She had, apparently, decided to try and reclaim her former lover and start a new life with him. But Finch was now involved with Yolande Turnbull whom he would later marry. He evaded Vivien's attempts to meet him alone and left her letters unanswered. She enlisted the help of his mother whose dearest wish was to see them reunited and who succeeded in arranging a meeting between them at her mews house in Chelsea. Peter insisted on taking his reluctant bride-to-be with him; and that final confrontation with Vivien is described in detail in *Finchy*, the book Yolande Finch wrote after her husband died.

For some reason in his book, *Olivier*, Anthony Holden has seen fit to recast this scene with Larry and me as the Finches, and to move the setting to Sardi's in New York. This is pure invention, like much else that has been written. For the record, there was never any confrontation between us three in Sardi's or anywhere else, and in fact Larry never wanted Vivien and me to meet.

When Peter Finch disappeared from a possible future, there were more violent scenes and she abandoned her plans for divorce. I was beginning to realize the implications of that kind of illness, and to understand more clearly what Larry had suffered in recent years. And I feared it might be too much for me to cope with. The stolen happiness, the secrecy and the uncertainty as to when, or indeed whether, we would be able to start a proper life together was becoming unbearable. I suggested to Larry that we should have a year's break; we must not meet or phone or write until the year was over and the future clearer. And meantime I needed to get on with my own life, and to know that I could exist without him if necessary. But he was so miserable at the thought of it that I didn't have the heart to insist.

As it happened there was an enforced separation when Larry accepted work in America, first in New York and then a film in Los Angeles. It brought a relief from all the tension and provided time for more thought and decisions. We wrote to each other constantly of our hopes and fears.

From LO to JP:
New York

. . . Some of my most burdensome considerations have been to do with the knowledge or the contemplation of what this has all been doing to you . . . and the recurring thought I have had since I first fell in love with you, that it would be more charitable to do what you so often almost begged me to do — for your sake to cut the thing off — 'sign off' — and that if I really loved you that is what I should do. Oh my darling, I love you all right, I can't believe I could love you more, but there is too much love of myself in my love for you for it to be a really selfless love. It is just something about our love, something about you, about us, that I want so much that I could never put it from me — a communion of heart, spirit and body that is so beautiful that I am absorbed by it and obsessed by it and live by it. You can only turn your back upon something which is outside you. Already by the end of NY Entertainer it was beyond that.

By now I too was separated from Roger and living in Ovington Square. He had sensed my withdrawal and asked if there was someone else; as I trusted him completely I had told him the truth. As it happened, because of my frequent absence he too had become involved with someone else, and we had agreed, amicably, to part with no immediate plans for divorce. At the end of that year, I went home to spend Christmas with my parents and my brother and his wife. On Christmas Eve I attended Midnight Mass in St Hugh's Church, Old Brumby, and it was on that day Larry wrote his next letter.

Beverly Hills Hotel   *Christmas Eve*

Darling my love,

I have made out a little message and I will get it sent from Tucson which may fox the Old Brumby Post Office. But a phone call which I have been itching like a crazy lunatic to make is I know too dangerous and would anger and worry you. O my darling love, I have been thinking of you without ceasing. I wonder if Scunthorpe has ever had such a barrage of thought and longing. I hope Georgie remembers to phone you today or perhaps yesterday. 2346 is right I hope. Nothing from my love in New York and nothing here. Oh baby, I do hope I hear some little word from you soon. But I know what it is if you are feeling sort of paralysed.

He hadn't heard from me because I worried about my letters being intercepted and because I wanted him to feel free for a while, not pursued by letters and obliged to write back. I had wept during that midnight service in church, not for any reason in particular, but perhaps because it reminded me of childhood and lost innocence and a time when I didn't have to take such responsibility for my actions. I wrote to him the minute I arrived back in London.

From JP to LO:
London

. . . A love that is compounded of so much joy, pain, gratitude, beauty, tears and laughter, such gentleness and such sacrifice is like God's love, and is infinitely precious. Oh my darling, if I could only pray and really pray in the way I did as a child when I fully believed and had no doubts. My faith had been tinged with doubt for some time, my life was progressing satisfactorily and complacently and it seems I had no need of God, no

need of a faith other than faith in myself. Then you came into my life and through you I feel the need of God again ... it's as though I've been uprooted, lost my bearings and am a prey to something that the mind cannot explain or understand ... Those moments when you are standing stockstill – perhaps in the garden at night – and emptied of everything to do with this world and suddenly invaded with an overwhelming feeling of awe and reverence which permeates your whole being but is gone before you have time to comprehend. If you try to hold onto that moment – you can't. If you try to recapture the feeling – you can't. But I believe it is only vouchsafed to those who are suddenly illuminated with a deep and all-embracing love. Either love of a human being or I suppose a true love of God. And the love has a way of spilling over onto other people.

Tolerance and sympathy, patience, integrity and compassion are all awakened in a powerful way – and the ability to admire and praise without envy or malice. It is a kind of serene acceptance of life – the good with the bad but it does not exclude vivacity, joy, laughter and the will to fight rousing battles for what one believes is true. Your love has given me a new strength and courage – I want my love to give that to you whether we are together or not. Be strong and have faith, my darling wondrous and good man – you are a very special human being with great gifts. My spirit is with you now and for ever more – I love you, I love you, I love you – nothing can take that away from you, it is yours throughout eternity. Let it help you my dearest and not hinder you. You seem to inspire great love in many people and thus must be capable of such love yourself – use your love well, my darling, and be worthy of other people's ...

Larry had gone to Los Angeles to film *Spartacus* early in 1959, and I was ensconced in the West End with Robert Morley. We talked on the phone whenever we could, and he told me that he had begun to feel that our situation was more hopeful. Vivien had a new man in her life, Jack Merivale, with whom she thought she was in love, though she was still reluctant to talk of divorce. Larry was committed to Stratford-upon-Avon in June to start rehearsing *Coriolanus*, and in preparation for his return to England, wrote to Vivien of his intentions.

... I am quite sure in my mind and heart that both are firmly made up not to return to our life together when I come back in June. In fact, I think it best that we do not see each other. And so I shall be going straight to Stratford when I do get back. We have ten weeks before this happens in which to decide what is best to do in the way of announcement or statement if any; and that is why I think it best to reaffirm at this point my decision of last September–October which I have reiterated each time we have communicated since then. I think it's time now that we dropped the legend which is being kept up for press and public, and before I return have some statement ready on the true state of affairs.

The repercussions this time were more extreme and more upsetting, as my next letter from Larry revealed. It began: '... Darling Joanie, I had one of those disastrous letters from V. Stiebel.' Victor Stiebel, a close friend of Vivien, had written on her behalf in answer to Larry's request and warned that if Larry refused to see her on his return, 'her reaction will be to give up any treatment she may have started'. He added that the proposed announcement would 'make the illness worse'. He begged for another postponement and asked if Larry 'would consider a normal homecoming', on condition that she started the treatment, in which case he was sure 'she would really bust herself to get well'. He then added: 'This all sounds like blackhearted blackmail, which of course it is ...'

Larry's letter to me continued:

... Now, darling, I want to say this – when I read that my heart did not sink, my brain did not reel. I simply felt without causing it or forcing it a complete and solid cold determination even while reading it, and then felt lighter and lighter than for ages – isn't that curious? Through the hell, something has happened to me – Something through the ordeal that I didn't know was happening – Funny from Victor actually, I did confess to him (and only him) some months ago that I was in love with someone else. 'You know I understand the 1001 ramifications,' he says. What sort of a lie does he think I can live ... I could never act off the stage anyway. Well, there it is, my love – I don't know what's going to happen except

that that is not. And since it all (yesterday) still still lighter, much lighter. I think some harp-string must have broken somewhere and not only in me. Some astral telepathy. What do you think, love? I tried phoning last night but you had left, I suppose, for your weekend already. No room left to tell you sweetly of my love which is as constant as the pole star and eternal as life anywhere. Yes, DO Lady Teazle on TV, very good idea, Roots too if you can. I feel so calm, so calm, my love.

His feeling of lightness gave him the courage to go on the wagon after a few years of what he admitted to be heavy drinking to drown his sorrows. And he wrote to me again on 18 April 1959:

Beverly Hills, California

. . . Enjoyed myself surprisingly much last night in spite of being on the wagon. Never thought I'd be able to endure it — the worst is when you first get there and need something to get you going, to conquer the shyness and tide you over that dreadful stretch before dinner. Spent most of the evening with the French faction. Louis Jourdain and Claude Dauphin. Louis said I was quite another person, not myself at all, when I drank and this was the first time he'd ever met me . . . made me think a bit. Maybe I'll keep it up for good? ('Oh shit, no, Christ, what have I said?!!) But I'm certainly beginning to feel much better and healthier — but I will not drink Ovaltine, do you hear me? . . .

Larry's calm was not to last long. Cecil Tennant, his personal manager, came to see me, having also received Larry's ultimatum about not seeing Vivien on his return. He and his wife, Irina, had extended their warm friendship to me too, and poor Cecil had the unenviable task of keeping all of us out of trouble. He told me that Vivien was in a worryingly destructive state and that whatever it entailed, she must start the treatment as soon as possible. I wrote to Larry after Cecil's visit, explaining the gravity of the situation, and suggested that he and I should

not meet either when he came back until we had to be together
for filming *The Entertainer* in October.

*The cost to us both of secret meetings while she is in this sort of state
would, I think, be too much. Can you understand my fear that it might
in some way destroy our faith in each other? That it would sap our
strength and integrity and that finally we would make some silly mistake,
or take a risk which would land us in an awful, undignified mess. It is
suggested that she meet you at the airport in the company of Cecil and a
few others, so that it will not be a terribly personal demonstration, but a
more formal one. You can all go for a meal somewhere together and then
you go on to Stratford when you need to. This will quieten speculation
among any press waiting around and satisfy the conditions necessary for
the commencement of her treatment. I don't see how you can do anything
but go along with it, my love, until she is better.*

Though Larry knew he must bow to the inevitable, he
felt in some way unmanned by the necessity to give in again,
and go back on that firm decision he had made. He began
to sound more depressed on the phone, saying it was wicked
of him to ask me to put my life on hold until he was free.
I was back in the fold at the Royal Court with all my old
friends – John Dexter, Robert Stephens and his wife, Tarn
Bassett, Albert Finney and Frank Finlay. The excitement of
Roots was upon me and Larry had rung one night when I
had a few people round for supper. Among them was the
actor Robert Shaw, who was playing alongside Peter O'Toole
in *The Long and the Short and the Tall*, which had just
transferred from the Court to the West End. Robert, bent
on mischief as usual, picked up the phone before I could get
to it and I knew by the look on his face as he handed it to
me that he had recognized the caller. 'Who's the young
blade?' Larry had asked with some apprehension, as soon as
I answered. We talked with more privacy the next night and
I laid his fears to rest; and then wrote to reassure him of my
love and understanding.

From JP to LO:
London

. . . It is so much easier to be born without a conscience; but both you and I belong to the group who are possessed of an overworked one, and so we must just face the fact that life is always going to be difficult in that direction. What happens to me, in my heart, mind and body when you walk into a room I am in is so indescribably wonderful that it is probably just as well that it can't happen too frequently. Otherwise I think I should suffocate beneath the intensity. Though we have tried so often to express to each other everything we feel, there is something between us that is absolutely indefinable and inexpressible by the ordinary means of communication. When you say to me simply on the phone, 'You must have learnt by now that I am a weak man,' or something like that, my heart just contracts with love and desire. I suppose it is your goodness and honesty which fill me with such ardent passion and love.

I only know that the way you said it on the phone has stayed in my memory for days and each time I think of it, I experience the same intense emotion. My darling love, I love you so much and know that always, always you have tried, and are trying, to do your best for all of us.

In the autumn of 1959 we made the film of *The Entertainer* together and then went for a brief holiday in France with Michel Saint-Denis, talking long into the night about a possible future.

Although Vivien was still with Merivale, she remained firmly opposed to divorce. She knew by now of our relationship but was not prepared to make it easy for our love affair to prosper. Perhaps she believed that if she held out long enough, I would be unable to endure the kind of life that I was forced to lead and would put an end to the relationship. Her illness was intermittent and no one seemed to know when it was coming on. She could seem to be out of control and behaving badly off-stage, and yet still be able to function properly when performing in the theatre at night. Larry admitted that he could never be quite sure whether the tantrums and rages were the result of illness, or simply the prima donna behaviour of a very beautiful woman who was used to getting her own way. She had been born on 5 November (Bonfire Night in England) and he said once, with grim humour, that she had been so spoilt as a child that she believed the fireworks exploding all over the place that night were in celebration of her birthday. I, of course, knew only his side of the story, though it was backed up by his close friends who urged me to stand by him whatever Vivien might do, because they said the hell had gone on long enough. Nobody underestimated the depth of her genuine distress at the break-up of the marriage and the legend, or the effects of the illness; everyone remained deeply sympathetic and gave her all the support and help they possibly could. Nor did they underestimate the strength of her desire to turn the clock back and have things the way they were; and I was warned of the possibility of visitations at home or at the theatre.

Larry himself grew fearful at the thought of it, knowing the violent extremes of her manic behaviour and where they could lead her.

Peter Finch's biographer, and long-term friend, Trader Faulkner, was an actor in Larry's company in Stratford in 1955. He became a friend to both Vivien and Larry and remembers dinner parties where Finch, who came for weekends, was also present. He witnessed 'a great deal of the agony' caused by Vivien's indiscretion and described how the rest of the company 'dreaded to be drawn into the crossfire'. The affair had caused most concern in 1953 when Finch and Vivien were filming *Elephant Walk* in California. Finch's wife, Tamara, went out to try and reclaim her husband but, Faulkner reported, 'Vivien was quite determined to take Peter from Tamara.' And when he tried to end it, Peter confessed, 'I didn't realize the tenacity and determination of the woman I'd fallen for.' As the manic phase of her illness took hold, Vivien became out of control; at a party that she arranged for Peter to meet other celebrities in Hollywood, he told Faulkner: 'Vivien went for Tamara with a pair of scissors and had to be forcibly restrained.'

It was this knowledge which made Larry determined never to admit that he was in love with me until a legal separation or divorce had been obtained. (It made me feel sometimes that I was living in a Charlotte Brontë novel.) But too many people in the profession now knew of our relationship for it to be kept secret from her any longer. He would write in a panic from New York in early December:

Algonquin Hotel   *Wednesday night, 12.30*

... My heart leapt a great height tonight when I saw your letter in my pigeon-hole, 808. You see your last up to tonight was written last Wednesday, and yesterday I had one from the previous Sunday, and I thought oh God – the visitation *has occurred, and she's upset. I know, I know, my love, it's most unreasonable because after all we did talk on Sunday night but the spec[ial] deliv[ery] never seemed to arrive ... I couldn't get you on the phone today and my imaginings have ballooned up sky high, I suppose, thinking that you weren't answering the phone and that you were in bad trouble of some sort ... You see I thought I had cheered you up on Sunday and that you were comforted by my conjurations that you were not to weaken if the visitation took place ...*

I knew enough by now, even without those words of comfort, to feel certain that we would eventually be together. That he and Vivien were temperamentally unsuited, each had acknowledged some time ago when their preference for quite different lifestyles had become so apparent.

Maggie Smith has told me of the time she was taken by her agent to Notley Abbey one afternoon, to a kind of garden party. She didn't know the Oliviers and neither, she said, did a lot of the other guests. People were there to enjoy the garden, to say that they had seen the Abbey and perhaps to meet Vivien herself – though Larry was nowhere to be seen. When one of the guests was suddenly taken ill, Maggie's help was enlisted to find a spare room in the house where she could lie down. As they milled about at one end of a corridor, uncertain which door to open, a man came out of a room at the other end, politely showed them where to go, and then went back in again without any further communication. 'It was Larry, of course,' said Maggie. 'He didn't want any part of it.'

Larry told me later of his sadness when the Notley he had so loved and visualized as a home, had come to seem more like a stage set, where an audience was always necessary in order to dispel the feeling of emptiness between himself and Vivien. But his patience, born of the guilt he still felt at leaving his first wife and child, and an almost religious sense of duty towards preserving this second marriage whatever the cost, had come to an end.

And life had changed since those privileged days when Vivien could sit in the drawing room with Larry and Peter Finch and ask, with no fear of retribution, 'Which one of you is coming to bed with me tonight?' It was a story told with great relish and amusement around Stratford, where it had happened, and in London. But underlying the laughter was the sympathetic realization that such humiliation is not easily borne and, though it may have been condoned, may not be entirely forgiven. And finally in everyone's mind was the certainty that she would have gone off more than happily with Peter Finch had it proved possible, which would have solved all our problems. The knowledge of that at least released us from feelings of guilt and allowed our enjoyment of life to resurface, though it could not do away with Larry's feeling of responsibility.

Letters from New York

In order to maintain his separation, he had agreed to direct Benn Levy's play, *The Tumbler*, with Charlton Heston, in New York. He had gone over in December 1959 to solve the problem of where he could safely spend Christmas. It was, he admitted, a desperate measure; he was not passionate about the play but none of his other projects had come to fruition. And it was not possible for us to be together without the risk of precipitating a scandal, and neither of us was ready and willing to do that. But we wrote to each other with a deepening knowledge of what our love meant to us, putting down on paper some of those things we had thought but never yet said.

From LO to JP:

Algonquin Hotel

. . . Dear love, do you know how important you are to me? — how vital? — how essential, more part of me than my guts, more living in me than my heart itself? I worship you so my darling, darling, Joanie. Oh forgive me the pain and the anxiety I have caused you. I believe you know I couldn't help it, please say you will never hold it in your heart against me. It is night-time for you and you will be baby-snorting away — how I long to be gazing raptly down at you from a few inches away — Occasionally giving your nose a little pinch and you will swallow and make a little grunt or two and start shifting your legs about. I have watched you so often when you are asleep. The dim light from the long narrow window at Cheyne falling across your face, pale in the serene beauty of after love, and other times rolled up and gypsy dark, witch-baby with the dolly's black hair. There are so many of you, my darling girl. Every shade and change of you enraptures me so with such tender sharp ecstasy, my own true wonderful girl. With what wealth of gratitude do all my memories of you fill my heart. My love. My Darling. My girl. Child of God. Wumpy Scrumpy . . .

From JP to LO:

London
Saturday, 3 p.m.

My darling love,

 I had such a beautiful letter from you this morning, full of Scrumpys and Wumpys, very sexy sort of letter and it made me so happy I've had a song in my heart all day long. Oh God, I do love you, love you so. I feel so close to you, so much an integral part of you when you write those sort of intimate things about when I'm asleep and you are watching me. It fills me with such an indefinable ecstasy, a wondering love and a so strange longing, oh I can't explain it. It is always with me really, but at certain times it is absolutely overwhelming. And it was this morning when I read that letter. It seemed to hit me right at the bottom of my solar plexus or wherever the seat of the emotions is supposed to be, and my whole inside rolled over with the impact of it. Everything that is truly me without any affectation you seem to know and love. Sometimes you seem to know me better than I know myself. You say things to me occasionally which quite stun me for a moment with their perception, and very often I will deny them out of shyness or unease or simply rage that you know so much. And the knowledge that I will never be able really to hide anything from you, that you will probably always know exactly what I am feeling or thinking in any situation. It's rather wonderful in one way, and slightly irritating in another, but it is all part of this wondrous, mysterious experience of being wholly, devastatingly, shatteringly, deeply in love. You cannot surely be afraid that it could die?

From LO to JP:

*Algonquin Hotel
January 1960*

. . . Don't think, dearest, that I know you more than you'd want me to – I really don't think I do – and I'm sure no better than you know me – and that only worries me when I think it makes you laugh at me in a way which makes me think that it will not be long before you despise me. And that is the only element which could possibly make me think your love could die. I respect so utterly, my darling, your complete honesty, your goodness, sense, gravity and judgement – things I find myself leaning on more and more throughout every day – and your heavenly humour which restores me and wipes all cares away instantly. The sort of pride that I admire and your glorious ample generosity and your lovely loving love. Oh your lovely loving love . . .

Oh I wish you would take my advice about Mrs Harding as well as the massage. Yes to be honest I did feel all that you explain about your resistance to the idea – but I did entertain the possibility of something else which I thought was perhaps a sort of pride. 'He ought to love me as I am – things can't be quite right if he wants me to alter something' – No? I've had so much to alter in my life – more concentratedly in my body – and it's taken all my life to do even what I have. You can't really imagine what physical disadvantages I had at seventeen! And even at thirty, and I'm inclined to be intolerant if people won't take the more obvious step. I think one owes it to the public, and much more important, to oneself – and more important still to one's gifts – to meet the Giver halfway.

From JP to LO:

. . . your words have inspired me to make super-human efforts. And yes, all right, I'll go to Mrs Harding, even if it kills me . . . You always bring me back to the knowledge that we are all capable of more than we think. Because life has a way of dampening down one's idealism again and again so that resignation takes the place of courage and striving. We feel it is perhaps wiser and braver to admit our limitations but it can become an excuse for taking the easy way out. I don't mean that we should always pine for the moon and never never accept second best. I know by now that compromise (which we despise when we are very young) is sometimes inevitable and essential – but it is important that it should still be looked upon as compromise and not as the best thing to do. Then next time maybe we won't have to compromise because we will still be aware that the best thing has not been found and we will go on looking and fighting for it . . . Take care of yourself, my darling. I sometimes feel such a peacefulness come over me when I think of you, or write to you – a gentle tenderness and serenity. A feeling devoid of all violence, passion or shattering longing.

It makes me go out into the street with a smile on my face and in my heart for everybody.

I was by now engaged in a re-shoot of one small scene from *The Entertainer* at Shepperton Studios where the film was being edited. And Larry had just begun rehearsals with Charlton Heston, Rosemary Harris and Hermione Baddeley.

From LO to JP:

Algonquin Hotel
1960

Darling beloved Joanie,

It's 9.30 a.m., and Monday, 11 January and your sweet letter has come and set my heart high for the day and the week. And I am wearing my tie for luck as we are up on our feet and blocking today – no more mumbling in my sitting room. I have been thinking of you, my darling, since I awoke and all through the bathroom time – mostly I have thought of you in the bar at Shepperton with Tony or else you might have skipped lunch and be lying down in your dressing room – One of four places anyway – bar, dressing room, restaurant, set – possibly projection room (no, I don't think so). Anyway my heart has managed to take in and spread itself entirely over the whole of Shepperton so as to be all round you in any situation, and ready for you any time your thoughts should turn my way . . . Saw Ben Hur *after we'd phoned on Monday. Golly – it's long, and that is almost the entire impression – except for the very spectacular bits, the sea battle and the chariot race; though no better done I swear than in the old silent version with Ramon Navarro. Oh, and that overall sense of* piety *which I find rather sticky in a picture. I must say my heart sank rather at the relentless good-kid ingenuousness of Chuck Heston. How I'm going to get him attractive-cruel, stricken-deer, and Lucifer-humorous and wiseguy-Heathcliff I don't quite know . . .*

He would later be full of admiration for the way Heston set to work and delivered an excellent performance. On the phone Larry told me that Stanley Kubrick had been to see him about making a film of *Lolita*, and I had obviously sent him my thoughts on it (not many of my letters to New York survived).

From LO to JP:

. . . You must know, darling, that I seek and long for and adore to get your advice, and I don't think that could ever be unacceptable to me . . . as one of the virtues in you that entrances me beyond all measure is your

75

sweet loving wisdom. And I agreed with every word you said about Lolita, *and even if I hadn't agreed with them, I would have been grateful and happy that you had proffered them.*

Oh my love, my longing for you has been all-else-obliterating today and hard to attend at rehearsal. I need, I absolutely require my Joanie – you are essential to me like water and air. Oh God how I thirst for your loved and loving company – my companion, my consciousness and light . . .

Perhaps this is the time to explain why so few of my letters to New York have survived. But to do so I must move two months into the future when Larry was returning on the boat to England after *The Tumbler* had opened.

From LO to JP (on the boat back from New York after *Tumbler*):

. . . I've just come in from throwing your letters over the side and my heart is still stabbed with the pain of it. I woke up at 8.30 a.m. and read through them all and by the time I was through I felt completely limp, as if I had relived with you all the first six months of the year. (No, I did not part with quite all, I couldn't quite do that, and I stuck the two photos into my wallet as I said I would.)

It felt more than anything just vandalous to throw away such beauty, such precious heartbeats, such a history of love, gallantry, patience and heaven-sent understanding – but there, we said we would, and I have.

Clearly I didn't throw any of his letters away, but then I was living at home and had a safer place to keep them.

But to go back to the time when he was still in New York and writing his letters and making his phone calls. There came another evening when he rang; Robert Shaw answered the phone again, and told him in jocular fashion that there was nothing to worry about – that he knew all about Larry and me and that he and I were simply old friends and supper companions. Robert's wife had gone back to Jamaica with their children for a time so he was often at a loose end. A few years back, he and I had been involved in an on–off relationship, which neither of us took very seriously. I knew of his ambition to be a writer, which was far more important to him than acting. And we would spend Sundays, sometimes, working out plots for the play we might write one day. Knowing that I was now separated from Roger (and his wife being away), he had asked me to supper one night. I told him immediately about my commitment to Larry. He admitted that he had heard the rumours but had no idea that it was serious. With that he asked my help in finding him a mistress who was 'on his intellectual level, but of course nice and dishy into the bargain'. He began to turn up on Sunday mornings after playing squash with the critic Alan Brien and I would take him to Hammersmith where Tony Richardson held open house each week. It was there that he came into contact with Mary Ure (then Mrs John Osborne) who would later become his wife. In case Larry hadn't been convinced by Robert on the phone, I added my own explanation by letter. He wrote: 'Darling, I feel so grateful to you for explaining about the "Young Blade" who I know has only ingrate feelings, nay, delight-in-tripping-up feelings towards beneficent and blessedly *absent* ex-employer. Oh I do love you . . .'

The phone can be a treacherous instrument as his next letters reveal (I had obviously been making some complaints about his lack of sensitivity).

LO to JP:

. . . There are some things one never seems to grow out of, and in the days when one first made transatlantic calls I think there was a three-minute limit and so on long-distance calls one always has the instinct to conduct them like a telegram. And sometimes when the conversation becomes dilatory or very pause-full my wretched sense of parsimony comes up and I think, 'Come on now – more than £1 a minute – was that pause ten-shillings-worth?' Ghastly isn't it. But sweet darling, you know it isn't

the dough. It is deep dyed in me that extravagance is wrong – unless one enjoys it – then I suppose it is all right. But there is dreadful workaday economy bred in me that if a thing isn't going well – then cut it out – you have seen in me I know from time to time to your annoyance – 'no profit in continuing further' sort of thing. Sweet darling, this is not recrimination, it is not even excuse, it is quite honestly a pardon-begging for my shortcomings, my lack of imagination which allows the thought to cross my mind, 'She is not enjoying this, I am not either, let's be practical and save it for next time.'

Algonquin Hotel

. . . Oh God, I can't get over the muddle about the phone conversation! I was so moved and emotional after it and I think I had to write and say so, and what do I see was your impression? 'Unfeeling bastard,' I read. I have only the vaguest recollection of anything that was not sweetness and tenderness itself, I have a vague memory of a little gentle raillery but only of the most flattering kind. Properly concerned that you should not work unless you want to, properly solicitous about thermal baths and health measures and properly jealous of male company, and all I get is furious blame for your appalling driving the next day. Well, all right, I'll consider myself ticked off.

He was due to leave New York at the end of February but had no idea what he was going to do next; and his indecisiveness was naturally aggravated by the continued uncertainty of our personal situation.

LO to JP:

Algonquin Hotel
Jan/Feb 1960

. . . Really my quandary exists in the fact I feel half-committed, and half-heartedly at that, to so many things I really think you'll have to come over, if only to advise me. Cecil [Tennant], of course, only wants me to direct and play in one or the other of his 'William The Conqueror' epics –

only take me about a year – I don't seem to fancy anything. No point in a holiday unless we could do it together. Merrick has asked me to do Becket *here. Again I've half-promised [Peter] Hall for London, but again I'm not quite entirely willing to fall in with his Aldwych set-up – I feel I really ought to be doing something on my own but what??? And then, I feel sort of too fatigued and scared of the immediate future from a public relations angle to make a decisive step, even if I knew what. I'd like to be let off all half-promises, and start again.*

Walked to the Guggenheim with Roger [Furse] – didn't go in – couldn't face the queue. Rog said F. Lloyd Wright obviously hated painting from the way he'd arranged the inside, and I said he also hated architecture from the way he arranged the outside. Actually it's strangely old-fashioned – like too many imaginary pictures of buildings on other planets in science fiction cartoons.

. . . Went with the Furses to see Rex [Harrison] in The Fighting Cock. *God, it's a sad, sad play. Rex very good – play good in the second half, uneven in the first – rest of the cast quite bad and the production puzzlingly bad (Brook). It's the same old thing, they will get the biggest house to get the most dough in, and a thoughtful play cannot live in it. Stayed up late at Rex's flat and fell off the wagon but I'm on again from now on. Certain things are beyond human capability and keeping on water with Rex was one of them – at least the first time. Worry not it will not happen again – no, honest.*

During his time in New York Larry had been helping to finalize arrangements for the London production of *Duel of Angels* to open in America later in the year. It had been presented under his management, Laurence Olivier Productions, with Vivien as the star, and he knew she could have a success with it in New York. A week before he came home, he wrote:

Darling Love

Vivien rang me last night very late. Duel of Angels *was the excuse but of course the other things developed. Difficult as it was, knowing it was 2.15 a.m. her time and those pills were within reach, I remained firm and definite. No more letters, no more phone calls except on business. Somehow or other I got her laughing and managed to get her to ring off before the mood changed.*

As it happened, early in 1960, shortly after Larry came home, and before *Duel of Angels*, Vivien would go to New York to star in a musical, *Tovarich*, on Broadway. She and Jack Merivale took an apartment together in East 71st Street and from there she wrote to Larry in gentler mood: '... I hope you are happy, darling. I am – very – for I think I am in love. I did not think it possible as you know, but I have found someone kind and dear who takes good care of me. I shall try to take care of him and have his children and start a different life – I hope a more sensible and quiet one ...'

Upheaval

On 27 July 2000, I received a letter which leads conveniently into the next upheaval in my life.

Hollywood, California   *18 July 2000*

Dear Ms Plowright,

I am writing to you from Los Angeles, California. I felt compelled to drop you a line as I'm about to play you in Orson's Shadow *at the Old Globe Theatre in San Diego!*

I'm sure you have heard of Austin Pendelton's play as it has been a huge hit for the Steppenwolf company in Chicago ...

If you haven't seen or read the play, Orson's Shadow *is set at the Gaiety Theatre in Dublin and at the Royal Court at about the time Sir Laurence Olivier and Kenneth Tynan and you were starting the National Theatre. It includes Orson Welles directing you in* Rhinoceros. *What exciting times those must have been? ...*

Yours sincerely,

Alexandra Boyd

Well, yes ... the thought of working with Orson again and acting with Larry in a play was exciting. The rest of the letter (and presumably the play it describes) contains such surprising misinformation that it is tempting to think that what we accept as history was ever thus.

The National Theatre was started at the Old Vic in 1963, not at the Royal Court. Ken Tynan was still a critic on the *Observer* in 1960, and was never at the Royal Court; but Orson certainly did direct us in *Rhinoceros* at that theatre and in that year. (Though 'exciting' is not exactly the word to describe the catastrophic nature of events that surrounded that production.)

I had adored working with Orson before but I was no longer the 'Snooks' of our *Moby Dick* time together; I was Larry's paramour and he and Orson didn't get on after the first week of rehearsal. Everything was fine to begin with; they admired each other's talents and expected the combination to prove electrifying. But Ionesco's play was not of the kind that either of them was used to dealing with. Orson admitted later that the more he worked in it, the more he disliked the play; and that he had only done it to work with Olivier. Larry wanted to do something new and hoped that Orson would bring some of his magician's expertise to bear on it, and equal, if not surpass, Jean-Louis Barrault's successful production in France.

But their ways of working were diametrically opposed. Larry always prepared a production some weeks before rehearsals began, moving cardboard characters around on a model of the set and choreographing the entire play, before coming with a completed framework to present to the cast on the first day. From then on as the actors began their creative input, he would become more flexible and allow the structure to change.

Orson liked to experiment in 101 ways before making his choices and allowing some order to emerge from chaos. But actors who have been given no specific place to occupy will in most cases head straight for centre stage, causing alarming traffic jams.

Larry began in a subtle way to take over the direction of the acting; finally he asked Orson to stay away for a few days whilst he pulled it together. Orson was bitterly hurt. I felt distressed for him but was in no position to come to his defence. As he had also designed the sets, he of course came back to light his production and supervise the dress rehearsal weekend. Everyone was very good-mannered, but the heart had gone out of him and he didn't stay around after we had opened in April 1960. Critical reaction was mixed and Harold Pinter's *The Caretaker*, which opened in the same week, stole a bit of our thunder. 'Nothing could have been more fatal,' wrote Orson later of the comparison between the two productions, though he omitted to say that the acting had been praised, and that it was his direction which bore the brunt of the attacks.

Audiences packed the Royal Court, a transfer to the West End was arranged, but then came the bombshell on Larry's birthday, 22 May 1960.

I was woken in my flat in Ovington Square at 8.10 a.m. that Sunday morning by a friendly newspaper man. 'Have you heard the eight o'clock news?' I was still half asleep. 'Vivien Leigh has told the press that Olivier has asked for a divorce in order to marry you,' he said. 'Get out of your flat now.'

'But ... but ... I must ring my parents,' I heard myself say.

'There's no time,' he urged. 'Take my advice and get out now.'

Twenty minutes later the front doorbell and the phone rang simultaneously. I thought it safer to pick up the phone – I could always put it down again without speaking – but it was George Devine. 'Is there a garden?' he asked. 'And a way out at the back?' – there was – and he told me that he and Tony Richardson would be there in half an hour to take me to their house in Hammersmith. There were already several reporters outside my front door but nothing like the throng outside Larry's in Eaton Square.

Vivien had dropped her bomb, without warning, from New York; Larry felt that it was intended as a black-hearted birthday present. She had ended her statement by saying, 'I will do whatever he wishes,' which in those days was looked upon

Larry as Archie Rice and me as Jean Rice in the film version of *The Entertainer*.

Our wedding night after our shows: walking through Shubert Alley, New York, with Richard Burton, and, right, Sybil Burton and Lauren Bacall trying to stay out of the picture.

First born: Richard
Kerr Olivier.

Richard now joined
by sisters Tamsin and
Julie-Kate.

The playbill for the first
Chichester festival theatre
season, 1962. Following
the success of Larry's pro-
duction of *Uncle Vanya* it
was repeated in 1963.
Below (left) Michael
Redgrave in the title role,
Sybil Thorndike as the
Nurse, Fay Compton as
Vanya's mother; I played
Sonya; and (right) with
Larry as Astrov,
the doctor.

CHICHESTER
festival THEATRE
Box Office Chichester 4183

FIRST SEASON - JULY 3rd until SEPTEMBER 8th

directed by LAURENCE OLIVIER

| LEWIS CASSON | FAY COMPTON | JOAN GREENWOOD |

ROSEMARY HARRIS   KATHLEEN HARRISON

KEITH MICHELL   ANDRE MORELL   JOHN NEVILLE

LAURENCE OLIVIER   JOAN PLOWRIGHT   MICHAEL REDGRAVE

ATHENE SEYLER   SYBIL THORNDIKE   PETER WOODTHORPE

GENE ANDERSON   TIMOTHY BATESON   ARTHUR BROUGH
ALAN HOWARD   ROBERT LANG

POLLY ADAMS   BETH BOYD   ELIZABETH BURGER   PATRICIA CONOLLY   ROWENA COOPER
LAWRENCE DAVIDSON   KENNETH EDWARDS   DAVID PUTCHER   DAPHNE GODDARD   RICHARD HAMPTON
JANET HENFREY   VALERIE HERMANNI   WILLIAM HOBBS   TERENCE KNAPP
ROBIN PHILLIPS   ADAM ROWNTREE   JOSEPHINE STUART   DANVERS WALKER

THE CHANCES
a comedy by JOHN FLETCHER, adapted by the Duke of Buckingham
decor by Malcolm Pride, music by Herbert Menges, dances arranged by Eleanor Fazan

Evenings 7-15   July 4, 6, 6, 7, 13, 23, 25, 27.   August 9, 11, 12, 15, 17, 21, 30.   September 1, 3, 5, 7.
Matinees 2-15   July 14, 21.   August 2, 4, 8, 23, 25, 29.

THE BROKEN HEART
a tragedy by JOHN FORD   decor by ROGER FURSE, music by John Addison, dances arranged by Eleanor Fazan

Evenings 7-15   July 10, 11, 12, 14, 20, 24.   August 2, 4, 6, 8, 10, 14, 22, 25, 27, 29, 31.   September 4.
Matinees 2-15   July 12, 26, 28.   August 1, 16, 18, 22.   September 6, 8.

UNCLE VANYA
scenes from country life by ANTON CHEKHOV, translated by Constance Garnett
designed by Sean Kenny, costumes by Beatrice Dawson

Evenings 7-15   July 17, 18, 19, 21, 26, 28, 30.   August 1, 3, 7, 16, 18, 20, 22, 24, 28.   September 6.
Matinees 2-15   July 19, 25.   August 9, 11, 15, 30.   September 1, 5.

PRICES: 25/-, 20/-, 15/-, 10/- (unreserved available on day of performance at 5/-)

THEATRE RESTAURANT AND CAR PARK AVAILABLE

During the Festival Season British Railways are running a special train leaving Chichester at 10-30 each weeknight and arriving at Victoria at 12-15.
All evening performances are timed to enable patrons ample time to catch this train. The Management regrets that owing to the action of the plays,
entry to the auditorium must be restricted once the performance has begun, and latecomers cannot be guaranteed admittance.
KING PRESS LTD, LONDONBRIDGE

THE FAMILY GROWING UP

Left: on Brighton beach. A helping hand for Tamsin.

Right: in the garden at Brighton.

Left: on holiday in Ischia. Larry with Tamsin and Richard, and below (left) Richard with earache in his sister's bathing cap.

Below: Lolling about on Franco Zeffirelli's cushions on a hot night in Positano – and not keen on being photographed.

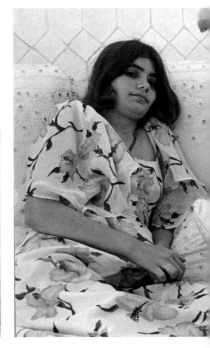

Top: Larry with Richard; above, Tamsin and Julie-Kate; and below, Larry with Julie-Kate.

We are now Lord and Lady Olivier. Photographed on the day of Larry's introduction at the House of Lords as Baron Olivier of Brighton.

Sing-song in the rehearsal room at the Old Vic on the last night of Larry's reign as Director of the National Theatre with Denis Quilley at the piano. Despite the *Punch* cover the new theatres on the South Bank would open without him.

LETTERS FROM LARRY

27th Jan. Wed night 1250

HOTEL Algonquin
59 WEST 44TH ST., NEW YORK 36, N. Y.

Darling Baby — My heart leapt a great heepn longnt when I came back & saw your letter in my pigeon hole 808. You see your last up to tonight was written last ...

AIRMAIL

United States Lines

Noon. 21st. 12.30 noon

Dearest my Darling first. I've just come Spec. in from throwing your letters over the side I've ... and my ... is still ... with the ... write at 8.30 about ...

Beverly Hills Hotel and Bungalows
in Beverly Hills, California

Christmas Eve

Darling my Love. I have made out of a little message & I will send it from Tucson which may be the Old Boundary P.O. But a phone call wh. I have been itching like a crazy lunatic trels is I know too dangerous & would anger & worry you. Oh my darling Love, my darling Girl I have been thinking of you without ceasing — I wonder if Scunthorpe has ever had such a barrage of thought and longing. I hope Georgie remembers to phone you today or perhaps yesterday. 2346 is your I hope. Now from my baby to N.Y. & now here she is Eileen V. cagey or too miserable to write. I called George yesterday morning & he told me about 'Root' been ah off. Lock my baby one — there's nothing to be said about that is there?,

FILMING *THE THREE SISTERS*

Far left: Masha waiting for the next shot.
Left: Larry directing on the set.
Below: Masha's farewell, with Alan Bates as Vershinin.

The cast includes, clockwise from centre: Sheila Reid, Alan Bates, Jeanne Watts, Judy Wilson, Kenneth Macintosh, Larry, Louise Purnell, Derek Jacobi, me and Ronald Pickup.

as collusion and which could prevent a divorce from being granted.

It also of course made it well nigh impossible for us to be on stage together on Monday night. From George's house we all wished Larry a sardonic 'Happy Birthday'. He was holed up in Eaton Square for the entire day, having sent a note down to the army of reporters advising them not to waste their time as he would not be leaving the flat. I was by now nearly at the end of my tether, and it was decided that it would be wiser for me to leave the production.

The understudy played the last two weeks at the Royal Court whilst Maggie Smith was brought in to rehearse my part for the new opening at the Strand Theatre.

Maggie, at the time, was hoping to buy a small house from a lady who became very uncooperative on learning that she was acting with Laurence Olivier. 'You're not a friend of that Joan Plowright, I hope,' she had snapped. And Maggie, desperate to find somewhere to live, though feeling as she said like the disciple Peter, thrice denied having ever met me. She still didn't get the house.

My father drove to fetch me from George's house after a phone call and took me to stay with my brother Robert and his wife, Phyllis, in Amersham, Bucks. There I remained undetected for two weeks until the hullabaloo had died down but I was contracted to return to the Royal Court for a revival of *Roots* in June. It was a fortunate play and role in which to return to the London stage after such an eruption of scandal and gossip and shaking of heads. Beatie Bryant was hardly the epitome of a 'femme fatale', and the audience at the Royal Court was a sympathetic one, as a letter from a stranger, left for me at the stage door, revealed.

26 June 1960

Dear Joan Plowright,

I had to say how grateful I am that we shall have the chance to see Beatie again – and to wish you good luck for tonight.

Please *don't feel it impertinent when I say there are so many of us who wish you very great personal happiness and peace and tranquillity to enjoy the many years ahead.*

Very sincerely,
Marion Wilson

Even so I made my first entrance in fear and trembling, not knowing what to expect; but nobody threw anything or heckled me from the gallery. In an article in the *Sunday Dispatch* of July 1960, headed, 'AFTER THE FLOPS – A WEEK OF TRI-UMPH,' their critic wrote:

*I have seen, within six days, a magnificent film partnership by two veterans over sixty, Spencer Tracy and Fredric March (*Inherit the Wind*) – and a young English actress, Joan Plowright, putting up the finest stage performance for years.*

*In the theatre, too, Paul Scofield gave – two nights ago – an acting display which raises him to the heights (*A Man for All Seasons*). All this following Olivier's superb feat in* Rhinoceros.

Not since the war has London been offered so rich a feast of artistry, or one so varied – and I must not forget Stratford, with its wonderful match between Peggy Ashcroft and Peter O'Toole. (The Taming of the Shrew)

But though we were surviving in our professional lives, our personal troubles were far from over. Suddenly abandoning her apparent consent to the divorce, Vivien flew to London in a high state of irrationality and called a press conference. She told journalists that she had also invited me to attend. I received a note during a matinée of *Roots*, informing me that she and the press were expecting me after the performance. I didn't go. She then told the press that she would be going to see *Rhinoceros*, and meeting Larry to talk things over. When he refused to see her, knowing she would be attended by journalists, she was distraught and angry but was finally persuaded that it would be wiser to stay away. Somehow we managed to ride out the storm; the press soon lost interest in us all and Vivien flew back to America to rejoin Jack Merivale.

We took our first holiday together at the end of that summer in France; then I left for Los Angeles with George Devine to begin rehearsals for *A Taste of Honey*. Larry sent me a copy of the letter which came after I had gone, from his first wife, Jill Esmond, wishing us well.

Queen's Grove, London NW8   *23 August 1960*

Darling Larry,

. . . I have been meaning to write to you for a long time to tell you how happy I am that you have found someone you love and with whom you can be happy. I was hoping that I should be able to meet you and Joan before she went to America, that's why I put off writing. I had news of your horrid time when Viv was over here and wanted terribly to tell you how much I felt for you.

. . . I do so hope that things will work out all right for you both and that when you come back from America I shall see something of you. I wish this had happened years ago . . .

With love,
Jill

Larry followed me to America in September 1960 to begin his own rehearsals for *Becket*. With him he brought the letter from the loyal and kindly Jack Merivale, which rounded off our time of waiting.

The Huntington Hotel, San Francisco

Dear Larry,

Vivien showed me parts of your letter to her. When I came to what you described as the 'bombshell on my birthday' I asked her whether she thought she had done the right thing in giving that release to the press. She said that she was in agonies of doubt about it and then confessed that she couldn't remember doing it or how it came about. I can quite believe this as I recall the day it happened. It was a very 'bad day' – a Saturday.

After the matinée I wanted to take her straight back to her apartment so that she could eat and rest quietly; but she wanted to stop and shop, and go and have a drink, and kept giving the driver orders to go to Dunhill's or the St Regis or wherever, which, after argument with her, I would have to countermand. So we didn't get to the apartment until about half past six and by this time I was pretty unpopular.

We arrived to find David Lewin there which caused me some concern as I didn't know that she had made the appointment and didn't think this was any time for her to be talking to the press. I hardly knew David then and tried by broad hints to get him out and let her alone, but while I was in the kitchen fixing some dinner he came in and said that 'something very important' had come up and would I please let him have some time alone with Vivien. So I said that she wasn't very well and had another show to do and really must rest. But this last she overheard and said, 'Well, I've got to eat, haven't I? So David can talk to me while I do.'

So I gave up and let them alone and that's when she was persuaded that it was better to have an official release rather than let the news leak out in gossip items.

When I said to her the other day as we were talking about it all, 'Why don't you write and explain it to him?' she said she couldn't; she simply did not remember the circumstances. So she asked me to do it.

I am glad to because I want you to know how it happened and don't want you to think that it was done vindictively or with calculation. I am completely sure that she would not have done it in that unilateral fashion in any other circumstances than the ones I have tried to describe . . .

As to ourselves, I have to report that we are wonderfully happy together and the situation is totally different from when I wrote to you last. I am certain that there is a wealth of happiness for us in a life together and these are riches we intend to enjoy. I'm sure you will be glad to know that she is wonderfully well too and gives every evidence of content and well-being.

I do hope so much that the same can be said of you, Larry, and that you are enjoying your holiday.

With every good wish always,

Yours ever,

Jack

Seven

....

Across the Atlantic

It was Devine and Tony Richardson's idea to present me as Josephine in a Royal Court production of *A Taste of Honey* on Broadway, in partnership with the New York producer, David Merrick. The play, by Shelagh Delaney, had been premièred in England by Joan Littlewood's Theatre Workshop at Stratford East in London, and had earned excellent reviews for its author and for Frances Cuka, the actress who had created the part of Josephine. When George told me, I expressed some qualms of conscience about taking the part of Jo away from Frances, saying that it seemed so unfair. 'It's not a fair profession,' said George brusquely, and explained that Merrick wouldn't take Frances anyway if I turned it down. She was not known to American audiences; he was a commercial manager and needed someone who was. 'He didn't want you in 1957 for *The Country Wife* for the same reason,' George reminded me. 'Now he does. All you need to think about is whether you want to play the part or not.' Of course I wanted to play it – it was a wonderful part. But I remembered my great disappointment and George's dismay when he had to break the news to me that the American actress, Julie Harris, would be playing my part when *The Country Wife* went to New York. Five members of the original Royal Court cast, including of course Laurence Harvey, were going and would be joined by American actors for the Broadway production. But the resulting mixture of styles didn't work and the play only lasted a few weeks.

By way of compensation, Tony Richardson had arranged for his productions of Ionesco's *The Chairs* and *The Lesson* to open in New York at the same time at the Phoenix Theatre, off-Broadway. I was to play the ninety-year-old Old Woman in the first play, and the seventeen-year-old pupil in the second. The American actor Eli Wallach played opposite me in *The Chairs*, and Max Adrian in *The Lesson*. As it was New York's first exposure to Ionesco, the evening aroused a bit more interest than *The Country Wife*. (There was never much of an audience for Restoration comedy anyway in America.) I was nominated for a Tony Award for the double bill and for *The Entertainer* (also a David Merrick presentation), which followed it.

Tony had since directed the film version of *The Entertainer* and was now an influential name across the Atlantic. And *A Taste of Honey* was planned to open in Los Angeles, mainly because he was already there completing a film of Faulkner's *Sanctuary*, starring Yves Montand. Jocelyn Herbert and George came over with me; he was to take rehearsals when Tony was absent, and we were all to live together in a lovely house rented from Eva Gabor in Westwood. Angela Lansbury (who became a much valued friend) had accepted the part of Jo's mother. The English contingent of Andrew Ray (as the gay art student) and Nigel Davenport (the mother's lover) were joined by Billy Dee Williams, the black American actor who would play Jo's sailor-boy lover.

Rehearsals were a bit sticky to begin with as Tony could devote only half of his energy and attention to us, and was inclined to be a bit impatient when he did appear. And we were suddenly made aware of our art student's very occasional tendency to stammer when under great pressure. He was a talented young actor, very well cast as Geoffrey, and the problem had never manifested itself at readings and early rehearsals. But he was not conditioned to the jungle-like atmosphere of a pre-Broadway production, where time and money are of the utmost importance, first impressions are the vital ones, and where no allowance can be made for weakness. Angela and I managed to cover for him the first time it happened when David Merrick came to watch rehearsals with his henchmen. But the stammer occurred again on Merrick's second visit and this time we were unable to disguise the problem. Merrick told Tony to replace him. Tony refused, saying everything would be all right on the night and so it was; Andrew received glowing reviews for his performance.

I wrote to Larry, who was still in London, packing up the flat in Eaton Square, to let him know what was going on:

22 August 1960

... Another sweet letter when I woke up this morning. Couldn't get to sleep last night for thinking of you ... We've had good weekend rehearsals – all Saturday and Sunday afternoon and feel something beginning to happen at last. Simone Signoret and Yves Montand came for brunch on Sunday. I do adore her – think she's a wonderful woman. She told me about a film she's going to do in Paris which they were all dying for you to do but you couldn't. Christopher Isherwood came to pick us up from rehearsal at night, and came back for supper with his boyfriend, sweet boy called Don Bachardy who is a painter. Strange creature – Isherwood – gentle, kind and very intelligent – but a bit hysterical if you know what I mean. Seems to be living in voluntary exile out here. Says he can work better ...

Tony's film is going through censor trouble. Skouras saw rushes the other day and cabled Zanuck to close down the picture immediately as it would never get a 'seal' and no right-minded person would want to see it anyway. He doesn't care for William Faulkner at all. The film is still going, however, for the moment.

The Merrick entourage keep wandering in and out of rehearsal, looking like Al Capone and his gang – I've never seen such a crooked-looking bunch in my life. I expect them to pull a gun out every time they are contradicted in an argument. Merrick came in during a scene with Billy Dee Williams, the black actor, and me – in fact when we were on the bed together – and George asked him if he thought some people would be shocked. Merrick's laconic reply was, 'I certainly hope so ... otherwise I've lost an awful lot of money.'

Rehearsals improved and Merrick stayed away for a while. Friends who came to a run-through were favourably impressed, and we began to enjoy ourselves a bit more. Tony was usually happiest when juggling at least three projects simultaneously, but his temper got the better of him this time when Larry disapproved of the first cut of *The Entertainer*, which he had just seen. They had a blazing row on the phone, some of which I overheard. George advised me to stay out of it, not even to think about it, and to leave them to sort it out themselves. But I felt I had to say something about it in my next letter, which began:

. . . If only you were here with me everything would seem much better. David Merrick is doing his usual day-to-day economy drives – suddenly scrapping the ramp on stage because it would cost too much to build – thus making much of the set invisible from certain parts of the house. We don't have the designer here because the designer is now working on Becket *(your play!) and as far as he's concerned* Taste of Honey *is behind him!*

Apart from that, naturally I've been worrying about you and the row with Tony. As I don't know sufficient about it, I'm not in a position to say anything until I hear from you but I realize that it is a clash between two people who have grown more and more apart in ideas and ways of working . . . And it is so very difficult for me because I am quite obviously with you, behind you and for you – and I finally have more faith in your judgement than anyone's. Yet I believe in a certain talent that Tony has though perhaps he's lucky to have got this far on it. But I have to work with him at the moment and we've shared some exciting times together and I'm also very fond of him as a friend . . .

However, my darling, enough of that. Johnny Mills rang me yesterday. He and Mary asked me round for the weekend though I shan't see much of them as we work from 3 p.m. to 6 and then again from 8 to 10.30 but it will be lovely to be with them for however short a time . . .

Though I didn't mention it to Larry, it would also be lovely to get away for a while from the turbulence which had invaded our rented house. John Osborne had joined us, bringing with him his current mistress, a model called Francine, whom none of us had ever met before. His wife, Mary Ure, was in New York and about to start rehearsals for *Duel of Angels* in which she would be acting opposite Vivien Leigh. Mary, naturally, wanted to come to Los Angeles for weekends, to join her husband whenever she could; and the model had to be bundled out, often at very short notice, and not allowed back until the coast was clear. We never quite knew whom we would meet at breakfast or supper from Friday night until Sunday, and it was beginning to get on our nerves. That John had a mistress was nothing to do with us; it was his affair, and if he had chosen to live somewhere else with her, it could have remained his affair. But to force the rest of us, all friends or colleagues of Mary, into collusion with him was, we thought, at best unkind.

Mary and I had to pick our way very carefully through our conversations when she came to stay. She could not talk much about Vivien, under the circumstances, and I had to avoid discussion of John's activities during her absence. It was not a happy situation and the rest of us began accepting invitations to stay elsewhere as the atmosphere slowly deteriorated.

It had been such fun until then, despite the hazards of rehearsals. There was excitement in the air as we drew nearer and nearer to the common goal of *A Taste of Honey*'s opening night. John brought a disruptive element into our group; the flaunting of Francine seemed deliberately provocative, and designed to humiliate Mary who was enjoying a flourishing, independent career. Most of their time together, when Mary did come over, was spent engaging in quarrels, which left her tearful and sometimes hysterical.

There was a night when she jumped, fully clothed, into the pool, after claiming that she had swallowed half a bottle of pills. John, who was drinking heavily, refused to do anything about it, saying she was just making a scene, and was probably lying about the pills. I was dubbed 'the Girl Guide' from then on after I went with a friend and fished Mary out of the pool, and put her into the shower, and finally, still sobbing, into her bed. As I was trying to persuade John to go in and see her, Tony came back from a meeting; the pair of them began whooping with laughter as John related the night's events. (Men are from Mars, Women are from Venus.) Tony, of course, loved dramas like that which 'jolted people out of their complacency'; but he was genuinely fond of Mary and he, at least, did go in to see if she was still breathing.

Christopher Isherwood noted in his diaries that August that he found Osborne conceited and 'grand' on first acquaintance though admitted he liked him better when he got to know him. But he was dismayed by John's treatment of his wife and considered Mary a masochist who probably liked it. Judging by what I had seen, I doubt very much that she enjoyed it. She probably just happened to be very much in love. It was pointless to wonder whether it was his extraordinary success that had changed him. He had been such fun to act with during our first few months at the Royal Court. He enjoyed acting and was articulate and witty with quite a camp sense of humour, appearing to be a kindly, compassionate and rather shy sort of man. Only his comments about hating his mother should have given one pause for thought.

'I remember him when he had holes in his socks,' said the stage doorkeeper of the Royal Court Theatre years later when John rolled up in his Rolls-Royce with his fourth wife, Jill Bennett. His subsequent treatment of Jill, both in life and in print, surpassed in its malevolence anything that was currently being inflicted on Mary Ure. And Jocelyn and I were both to become targets in the years still lying ahead.

We opened *A Taste of Honey* successfully at the Biltmore Theater in Los Angeles; then after two uneventful weeks in Cincinnati, our only pre-Broadway date and where David Merrick had hoped for riots, we set off, with high hopes, for New York.

Eight

New York, New York

New York is an awe-inspiring city and the first time I walked down its most famous street, Fifth Avenue, I had to keep pinching myself to make sure I wasn't dreaming. I can find no better way to describe its effect on me than to quote the words of Theodore Dreiser, writing back in 1929:

Nowhere is there anything like it. So strong. So immense. So elate. Its lilt! Its power to hurry the blood in one's veins. To make one sing, to make one weep ... Winey, electric! What beauty. What impressiveness! ... a callous, money seeking and unsentimental city, as one looks here and there. But lyric too. And spendthrift ... to this hour I cannot step out of my door save with a thrill responsive to it all. Its grandeur, mystery, glory ...

And E.B. White, writing in 1949; said: 'The city is like poetry; it compresses all life, all races and breeds, into a small island and adds music and the accompaniment of internal engines.'

Having absorbed its frenzied nature, the people in the streets took great pride in their city, despite its occasional brutality and the high level of anger behind the steering wheels of its taxi-cabs. Their confidence in themselves, and in the fact that they were New Yorkers, gave them an ease and friendliness which was infectious. That afternoon, as I walked down Fifth Avenue I was wearing a beautiful new velvet coat with a full, swirling back to it, purchased on my first visit to Bergdorf-

Goodman earlier in the morning. A gorgeous tall black girl, obviously a model, swung past me and called out, 'Love your coat.' That sent my spirits soaring and I thought how different life was over here, nobody would do that in London. I reached Saks Fifth Avenue and went to find jeans to send home as a present to my young niece. As I held up a pair of small pink jeans, size 6, a nearby New Yorker caught my eye and called out, 'No dear. Take a look at yourself and say no.' That too, I thought, is New York.

It was 1958, and I was rehearsing *The Chairs* with Eli Wallach who was a member of Lee Strasberg's Method Studio for Actors; he took me there one morning to watch them at work in class. During a break we went into a side room to get coffee and he introduced me to a serious-looking young woman in a raincoat with shortish hair which was dyed blonde but already going dark at the roots. She wore no make-up, appeared to be alone, and seemed rather nervous and shy. I had no idea who she was, until he said, 'Marilyn,' and I realized that I was meeting the sex-goddess Monroe, who had discarded her Hollywood image for New York and was studying along with other actors at the Studio. I would meet her again, briefly, in Los Angeles after she came with Strasberg to the first night of *A Taste of Honey*. There in Hollywood, she was back in full warpaint as the Monroe she had invented for the cinema, dressed in a skin-tight shimmering dress, giggling and pouting and blowing kisses to ardent admirers.

When I returned to New York in 1960 the Algonquin Hotel was the favourite place for English actors to stay, and I'm afraid I still have the key to Suite 808. In the middle of theatreland, and still basking in the glow of its past fame with the Round Table, the Algonquin's restaurant was as fashionable for after-theatre suppers as Sardi's, though Sardi's was always the place for opening-night parties. It was also the place where you learnt around midnight, as the first reviews came in, whether your play was going to run or not. If the restaurant grew suddenly quieter and people began to leave surreptitiously, it meant that the early notices were not good and they were too embarrassed to come and say goodnight. Commercial producers, knowing little of the dread in an actor's heart, would make their farewells in businesslike fashion: 'Well, it was not our lucky night, I give it six weeks.' (Or sometimes less – there are plays on Broadway which have closed on the second night.) Happily *A Taste of Honey* was wonderfully received on its first night and the audience gave us a standing ovation. The patrons at Sardi's gave us another when we arrived for the obligatory party, though of course they were mostly the same people who had been at the theatre. We didn't have any dread in our hearts that night; and the restaurant remained full and in celebratory mood as the first paeans of praise poured in from the critics.

'The evening's treasure is Miss Plowright's haunting performance,' said Howard Taubman in the *New York Times*.

And Walter Kerr of the *New York Herald Tribune* added:

When this brilliant actress is shuddering with the shrill gibberish of hysteria the passage becomes as frightening as it is moving. But our interest is not centred on her sorrows. It is riveted to the restless and inexplicable gaiety that overtakes her as she swings backward from a flight of rickety stairs like a clockwork doll and to the droll frisky tease she becomes as she takes a floor mop to her pliant male nurse.

Walter Kerr ended his notice with: 'The play is fresh in its accents, funny in its perceptions, somehow wistful beneath the caterwauling . . . and oh, my goodness, it is talented.'

Larry couldn't come to the first night (he had seen the play in Los Angeles) as he was dress-rehearsing *Becket*, which was opening the next night. And our two plays were reviewed together in *Newsweek* with an introductory comment on our private life, which was inevitable, given the circumstances.

TWOSOME TRIUMPHANT
The reliable arm of coincidence brought two of England's finest actors to Broadway last week when Joan Plowright's A Taste of Honey *and Sir*

Laurence Olivier's Becket *opened on successive evenings. Although it is generally accepted that the couple will marry when Olivier's divorce from actress Vivien Leigh is final, they have been wary of appearing together in public. However, as noted in the reviews below, they have been appearing separately to great effect.*

The *Newsweek* critic noted at the end of his review: 'Miss Plowright is also currently on view as Laurence Olivier's daughter in the screen version of *The Entertainer* but it is *A Taste of Honey* that shows her as one of the finest young actresses anywhere.'

The nights when acting is enjoyable should be savoured to the full, Peggy Ashcroft once told me, because they don't come along very often. The feeling you have inside you that the part has moved under your skin and into your bloodstream, and you know exactly how to get it across to the audience. It is a quietly exultant sensation and you can't wait to get on the stage; there is no feeling of apprehension – nerves, yes – but nerves that are on edge because of excitement and the challenge of a new audience. And those are the nights of 'lift-off' when you feel you are flying, and the twin necessities of technique and inspiration have melded together so completely that the living character on the stage is an entity by itself, and no one can tell by what means it was, or is being, created. And, oh, how rare an occasion it is to feel so utterly at ease and to know that the audience, too, is abuzz with excitement and ready to welcome you with open arms; and that all around you are actors sharing that same knowledge: Angela Lansbury as the wanton Mother who abandons her daughter to marry a ne'er-do-well (but finally returns); Nigel Davenport as her husband; Billy Dee Williams as the romantic Negro sailor who sails away, not knowing Jo is pregnant; and Andrew Ray as her only friend, the gay art student who moves in to cook and housekeep and look after her until she has her baby. The sweet smell of success lingered for quite a while; and I recognized that the part of Jo was as life-saving in New York as Beatie (*Roots*) had been in

London. It established my separate identity as an actress in a way which could not have been achieved after all the personal publicity if I had only been 'currently on view as Laurence Olivier's daughter in *The Entertainer*'.

A separate identity is what Nicole Kidman is now seeking to maintain, the papers tell us this morning (2 February 2001), as her marriage to Scientologist Tom Cruise comes to an end. Among other difficulties, her reluctance to enter whole-heartedly into his religion was apparently as much of a problem as the inequality of their professional status in Hollywood. 'It was very tough for me for those years just to be seen as Mrs Tom Cruise,' she said. 'Don't get me wrong. I don't think being married to someone you love is a burden, but being judged in a particular way, that is something I don't like.' And it is something I would have to battle with, or accept, when I became Lady Olivier. Not that I think Mr Tom Cruise occupies the same position on Mount Olympus as Laurence Olivier, but as a megastar, he is certainly a force to be reckoned with, and the predicament of the ladies remains the same. I am reminded of Mistress Millamant's reluctance to give up her freedom, way back in Congreve's lifetime (1700), and the conditions she laid down before she would consent 'to dwindle into a wife'.

But before I was to 'dwindle' later that year, there were the glittering prizes to be enjoyed: the New York Critics Award, and the Tony Award for Best Actress on Broadway and a second Tony Award for Best Play.

And there was time to relax now that our plays were up and running, and to enjoy the city, and meet old friends and make new ones. Weekends with the Burtons in their house on Staten Island; visits to Sneeden's Landing to lunch with the first lady of American theatre, Katharine Cornell; an evening with Sir William Walton whose new symphony was being given its first performance at Carnegie Hall; and a wonderful dinner party for Margot Fonteyn who had just given her farewell performance as Giselle. We were playing that night and had been unable to see it but I had queued many times in previous years to watch her dance. To me she had been the most exquisite and exciting prima ballerina I had ever seen. It was a cold February that year and the snow lay two feet deep on the streets; I had bought my first ever mink coat to keep warm. Furs were not yet taboo and everybody was wearing one – except, that is, for Margot Fonteyn. As we left the restaurant that night she stroked my mink. 'I had one once,' she said wistfully, 'but it got worn out.' Such are the rewards for consummate artistry in England, I thought.

The composer William Walton lived in Ischia, and his wife, Susana, had built three villas at the bottom of the garden to rent out and earn them an income. He had explained one night what a precarious existence composers led and how little he was paid for an orchestral performance of his work. I was as shocked by that as I had been to discover that Fonteyn could not afford to buy another fur coat. Perhaps it was naive of me to have assumed that greatness was necessarily accompanied by at least a modicum of wealth.

We were married at last on 17 March 1961, St Patrick's Day, and no small date in the American calendar, a day when New York City would be busy with its own celebrations. The press had been waiting around at various strategic places (like the New York Registry Office) ever since the announcement on 3 March of the Decrees Absolute which officially ended our previous marriages. In Noël Coward's opinion we 'behaved impeccably' in allowing ourselves to be the ones accused of adultery, given that Roger was also waiting impatiently to remarry, and Vivien's extramarital affairs had been 'widely discussed across two continents'. However, the divorce courts demanded a guilty party and an innocent one, and so it was simpler for Larry and me to be cited in both cases. But oh what an awful business it is. At least we were spared the attendance at court which our partners had to endure, and were determined for everybody's sake to be married as quietly as possible.

Elaborate preparations were made with the help of Arnold Weissberger, our lawyer and great friend, for a clandestine marriage outside New York; and we spent our pre-wedding night with friends, Nedda and Josh Logan, at their house in Connecticut. After our respective shows that night, we went our separate ways and succeeded in losing the attentions of ever-vigilant reporters. I went back to Angela Lansbury's house, ostensibly for supper, and Larry practised the same deception with his co-star in *Becket*, Anthony Quinn. Leaving our friends' houses by the back doors, where our cars were waiting, we drove separately to the Logans' house, and were married inconspicuously in Wilton, Connecticut, the next morning.

We returned to a New York still reeling from the parades, littered with shamrocks, green hats and inebriated Irishmen singing 'Danny Boy' with varying degrees of accuracy, and slipped, unnoticed, into our theatres for the evening performance. Richard Burton (who was playing in *Camelot*) and his wife Sybil, gave a party for us that night at their house where we celebrated privately with a few close friends. Sybil and Lauren Bacall, now married to Jason Robards, had arranged for a three-tiered wedding cake to be delivered and it was that which gave rise to the first rumours. The event was widely reported the next morning.

'At the party I just remember how in love with her Larry was,' Lauren Bacall said to Sean Mathias. 'He looked at her with such adoration. I remember that because I'm such a sentimental slob myself. He was thrilled that it had been accomplished.'

The next thing Larry wanted so very much to accomplish was to start a family. Not only for my sake, though he knew how I longed to have a child, but also for his own. We had stayed several times with John and Mary Mills during our courtship and he had told me how much and for how long he had envied them their family life. With great dedication and a lot of laughter we sought advice from the best doctor and gynaecologist we could find; I came home with my ovulation charts, and Larry arranged to have a fertility test. We went together to Dr Bill Herzig's surgery to learn the results two days later. The waiting room was quite full that morning but Dr Bill came to the door of his consulting room himself, and called us in first. He held the door open and as we went through he said in his booming voice, 'Sir Laurence, the sperm's no good,' and then closed the door before giving the reason, thus leaving a lot of interested people to mull over that piece of information in the waiting room.

Once inside we were told that for some reason (which I can't remember now), when the sperm sample reached the laboratory none of them was alive and kicking. But Dr Bill was very reassuring when he saw how badly affected Larry was by the news, telling him that the test was not valid and arranged for another on the premises the following day. This time Larry rang me at home the minute he heard the good news. 'Millions of the little buggers,' he said with great satisfaction, his confidence now restored. Although *A Taste of Honey* was scheduled to run for at least another six months, we paid no heed to the fact that if I became pregnant, I might have to come out of the play before then.

With tremendous enthusiasm Larry insisted on employing the old method of holding me upside down on the bed so that 'none of the little buggers can escape'. Then, still gripping my ankles, he leapt up and down on the bed, declaiming simultaneously an apologetic speech to my producer, David Merrick: 'I can't tell you how sorry I am, David – I wouldn't have had this happen for the world – it's the last thing I would dream of doing to a fellow manager – it was just a stroke of bad luck, dear boy – God knows we took enough precautions,' and then we would both collapse on the pillows, out of breath and nearly choking with laughter.

There was much jubilation when we were told that I had conceived, and I began my weekly visits to Irving C. Fischer, my gynaecologist and my guide and mentor. He was passionately committed to the belief that with knowledge and training women would be able to approach childbirth without the slightest fear, and most of them would be able to watch their child being born without the help of drugs. I learnt how to put myself into a deep state of relaxation as we set about discovering my threshold of pain. He taught me self-hypnotism, and as I sat there one day, totally relaxed and with my eyes closed, he lifted up my hand, and pricked it. Quickly I said, 'I felt that,' in case, thinking I was in a semi-conscious state, he might try something more painful. He merely said, 'Of course you did, but it was not unbearable, was it?' A few minutes later, when we had finished the exercise and were talking, I was suddenly shocked to see that there was a large needle piercing through folds of skin on my hand, which I had no idea was there.

Mr Fischer cared passionately about bringing babies into the world in their own time. 'Don't be like those actresses who have a Caesarean for their own convenience,' he warned me. And he gave me the sweetest advice about fathers and husbands. 'When the baby has finished feeding, place him on your husband's chest so that he associates feelings of contentment with the smell of his father's skin, as well as that of his mother.'

Then Irving Fischer came to the play and saw me as the reluctantly pregnant Josephine, flinging myself around in a hysterical outburst. 'I don't want this baby – I'll kill it – I don't want to be a mother!' He was very perturbed, and told me he thought it was dangerous and unwise to go on doing this particular play. I tried to explain that those were Jo's emotions, not mine – that acting was a craft – that the character's emotions don't stay with me after I've expressed them. 'But you have to believe it when you say it,' he said. 'And each time the outburst occurs, the whole of your nervous system, mind and body is engaged in that negativity.' He said that I should not be sending that message to my subconscious each night, and twice on Thursdays and Saturdays. I hadn't thought about it in those terms at all, but whether it was coincidence or not, a few days later there was evidence that the baby might not be safe, and I was whisked into Mount Sinai Hospital and out of the play.

After three days all was pronounced well with the baby, and

we now felt truly apologetic towards David Merrick. And after Larry contacted George Devine in London, Frances Cuka came out to New York and took back her part. Mr Fischer predicted that the baby would be born on 2 December 1961, which indeed he was, New York time, but of course it was 3 December in England. He would be christened Richard Kerr (his father's second name) in the cathedral at Chichester, where another infant prodigy awaited our arrival.

A letter had arrived in New York one day from Leslie Evershed Martin, a leading optician in Chichester. He was responsible for a plan to build an open-stage theatre in his town, modelled on the Stratford (Ontario) Festival theatre run by Tyrone Guthrie. He had been advised to start at the top when looking for a man to run it, and with his tongue in his cheek he had approached Laurence Olivier. There are those times in life when something comes out of the blue and you are astonished to realize that it is exactly what you've been looking for. All Larry's quandaries about what to do next were swept aside as he embraced the opportunity to be in at the beginning of the life of a new theatre. And to develop a company of actors to occupy it.

Nine

....

Back to England

Chichester was not too far from Brighton where we had chosen to live when we came back to England. Our house in the Regency Royal Crescent, overlooking the sea, was still being restructured and decorated; so we were encamped in the adjoining Royal Crescent Hotel for a time. Brighton had always been a favourite touring date for actors; and its Royal Pavilion, built originally by the Prince of Wales in 1787, is a reminder of those days when the town was a second home for London society, as well as fashionable artists, writers and actors. Jane Austen talks of it in *Pride and Prejudice*: 'a visit to Brighton comprised every possibility of earthly happiness.' The sea air has a special tang to it, and we thought it a healthier place to bring up children than London. And it was also a complete break from the lives we had lived before. The train service to London was exemplary; the glorious Brighton Belle could transport you to Victoria Station within one hour, and provide breakfast, lunch or dinner in its ornate carriages, along the way.

Larry was travelling daily to London for meetings, though I was reluctant to go out much because of the attention my condition attracted from the press. But I did go with him for dinner one night with Jocelyn Herbert and George Devine who talked to me about a play by Samuel Beckett, called *Happy Days*. He described it as a marathon monologue about a buxom lady called Winnie who is buried 'up to her diddies' in sand. He thought it was an extraordinary piece of work and said, jokingly, that it was surely a most suitable role for a pregnant actress. Both he and the author wanted to première the play in London. But after that initial scare in New York, I was not prepared to take any more risks by working again too soon. When he sent the script to me I realized what a wonderful, funny and quite devastating play it was, and longed to be able to act the role of Winnie one day. George told me that Beckett, who knew Ionesco and had seen *The Chairs*, was prepared to wait until after I had had the baby. Plans were tentatively made for the production the following year, in October 1962, but by then I was unexpectedly pregnant again. And Beckett, who had already waited one year, wrote sardonically, 'Perhaps we should decide to postpone production till she is past child-bearing – or the Baronet beyond engendering.' His patience was quite naturally at an end, and they went ahead without me. And I lost the chance to play one of the most extraordinary parts ever written for a woman.

But on reading later of the demands he made in rehearsals, I think we might have come into conflict. I would have found it difficult to submit with total obedience to the rhythms and inflections he imposed on all the actresses who played the part. He wanted it performed as he heard it in his head; and did not want any delineation of character or any emotional depth. Brenda Bruce, who finally played it at the Royal Court, was reduced to tears when he placed a metronome on the stage and told her to deliver the lines in accordance with its ticking. And Jocelyn Herbert, who was both his designer and a close friend, had to plead with him finally to stay away from rehearsals. Later in 1974, Peggy Ashcroft, too, would rebel against such restrictions; she had accepted the part with her own ideas on how to play it. But he would eventually find an English actress he was happy with – Billie Whitelaw, who was willing to give herself over entirely to the style of playing he required, and they became good friends. But that was all in the future, and we are still in 1961.

We moved into our new home just in time for Richard's

birth, which Larry attended, causing quite a lot of comment in the newspapers. It was not the custom then for husbands to be present at the birth of their children. He also insisted on being woken during the night every time I fed the baby; and we obeyed Mr Fischer's instructions about putting him on his father's chest so that he felt included in the ritual. The monthly nurse would bring him into our bedroom promptly at 2 a.m. and again at 6 a.m., and on one occasion Larry said rather wistfully, 'If you could see the look on your face when that baby comes towards you ... it's the sort of look you used to give only to me.' When he had to go away for ten days I wrote to reassure him that he was still uppermost in my mind.

My dearest darling,

I don't think you realize quite how much I miss you when you are not with me – baby or no baby! As I go around this house and see all the little (and big) ideas we've worked out together I feel your love for me pouring out of every crack in the paintwork, steaming out of every radiator, smiling out of all those beautiful cupboards and gleaming from the bonzac candles. It is a house so full of love and fun, my darling – but oh it needs you in it too . . .

In the summer of 1961 we had visited Chichester to take our first look at the site of the theatre-to-be in Oaklands Park. We stood in a large field and stared at a huge, muddy hole in the ground where six drainpipes were sticking into the air, marking the six points of the hexagon which was to be the outline of the theatre. We had seen photographs of the architect's model, so we knew that the open-thrust stage would house the audience on three sides but would not be completely 'in the round', which had been a relief.

Less than a year later we would be rehearsing in the newly completed Festival Theatre, with a company which included Michael Redgrave, Sybil Thorndike, John Neville, Keith Michell, Rosemary Harris, Alan Howard, Robert Lang and Robin Phillips.

When Larry told me that he was going to direct the three opening plays himself, and also play in two of them, I was aghast. But having been privy to his doubts and confusions in New York, I suppose I had forgotten his huge appetite for work, his need to challenge himself and take risks, his ambition, audacity and the sense of mission which was such a source of his powers of leadership. 'We can't all be Larry; but some of us could have tried a bit harder,' Robert Morley wrote to me once, when Larry was ill. The first two plays, *The Chances* and Ford's *The Broken Heart*, were not really successful – in fact *The Broken Heart* was something of a disaster in terms of critical reaction. Tynan was the most damning of them all with his 'open letter' to Larry which ended: 'Does the fault lie in the play, in the theatre or in you, its Artistic Director? ... Within a fortnight you will have directed three plays and appeared in two leading parts. It is too much.'

I hid the *Observer* with Ken's notice that Sunday – Larry didn't ask for it – he had stopped reading them after the first two or three bad ones. I could hardly denounce Tynan for saying the workload 'is too much' as it had been my own first reaction when Larry took it on. Shortly afterwards Tynan wrote to Larry saying that despite his review on Sunday, he was applying for the post of dramaturge at the NT. It was a brave and risky thing to do in the circumstances. Larry then read the offending article, was enraged by Tynan's 'colossal cheek' and refused to countenance the idea. I pleaded Tynan's case; his genuine passion for the theatre, his wide knowledge of European drama, and his close contact with important contemporary writers. All of which surely balanced his need to shock and, in his own words, 'rouse tempers, goad and lacerate, raise whirlwinds'. Larry said he would think it over. Despite the notices the audiences still came and appeared to enjoy themselves. Everything now hung on the third play, *Uncle Vanya*.

I was by now pregnant again with our second child. My Brighton gynaecologist had been appalled when he came to the theatre and saw me dancing a country jig and rushing around the auditorium in *The Chances*. I was released from the dancing bits on his strict instructions – and began rehearsals as Sonya in *Uncle Vanya*, telling the costume designer that my clothes must be expandable.

Larry was punch-drunk from the barrage of critical attacks but said to me that he had slept well before the first night of *Vanya*. 'Like a man in the condemned cell, I spent a night untroubled by hope.' But I think he knew somewhere inside himself that his production of the Chekhov play was very, very special. And so it proved to be. And it saved his bacon in the circumstances; it had just been announced that he was to be appointed Director of Britain's National Theatre.

Uncle Vanya inspired such ecstatic notices that it came back for the second season in 1963, and in the *Financial Times*, T. C. Worsley wrote, 'Here is a living work of art so perfect in every conceivable shade of detail, that those who are lucky enough to get to see it, are privileged.' And Harold Hobson wrote in the *Sunday Times* that it was 'now the admitted master achievement in British twentieth-century theatre'. Comparing the company with the Berliner Ensemble and the Moscow Arts Theatre he added that they may

rival the Chichester company in cohesion and co-operation, in dedication to the ideal of playing as a single force, a united organization. But neither of those companies, which are deservedly famous, includes within this unity individual players of the genius of Sybil Thorndike, Michael Redgrave, Joan Plowright and Sir Laurence himself . . . If Uncle Vanya is an example of what, in spirit and execution, we may expect from the National Theatre, of which Sir Laurence is the Director, then that organization will confound all its critics.

That second Chichester season also brought another christening – of Tamsin Agnes (after Larry's mother) Margaret (after mine), who was born on 10 January 1963. She was a beautiful nine and a half pound baby who gave us all much joy. Apart, that is, from the thirteen-month-old Richard who regarded her as something of an intruder on his 'only child' kingdom. But he grew more welcoming as time went by.

It also brought about my first performances as Saint Joan; I would play the part again in the Assembly Rooms at the Edinburgh Festival, and finally at the Old Vic, when the production joined the National Theatre repertoire. John Dexter, who directed, had strong ideas about the play. Joan must not be seen as the saintly victim, he insisted, nor the representatives of the Church as merely oppressive and doctrinaire. They were acting in accordance with the law and order of their time, and genuinely trying to get her to see the error of her ways. And Joan, we agreed, is not just a simple heroic figure in shining armour but also a difficult girl with ideas above her station. She is the daughter of a farmer with all the strength and native shrewdness of her peasant origins. And though she is uneducated and unable to write her name, she is fired with a passionate religious fervour, and an unshakeable conviction that she has been 'chosen'. This gives her the energy and the extraordinary courage to rush in where angels fear to tread. And it was her innocence and simplicity, her innate goodness and sincerity which touched the hearts of people who might otherwise have found her presumptuous, pushy and thoroughly dislikable. It was her belief that she had her own pipeline to God and did not need to be instructed by the Church which got her into so much trouble.

Whether her voices actually exist, or are imagined, we could not decide. And whether she is divinely inspired, or just believes that she is, makes no difference to the way she must be played. 'She was a very odd creature,' said Sybil Thorndike, who had done a deal of research when she had created the part in 1924. 'There was no monthly cycle you know, she never had a period, and never any experience of sex.' Shakespeare gave us a different version of course, though brief and not based on fact or proper research. And no one knows for certain how she spoke, though Shaw makes use of poetic licence to give her very pertinent things to say. And finally, it is Shaw's Saint Joan that the actress must invest with truth and reality, and it is *his* eloquence that she must deliver with total belief. It would become one of those career highlights that actors remember with great affection. But the anti-heroic nature of my performance, which Dexter and I both agreed on, was carried a bit too far to begin with. And I was fighting shy of the rhetoric in the 'light your fires' speech at the end of the trial scene. But during the run we abandoned a bit of our reticence, realizing that Joan needs a heroic outburst of eloquence before succumbing to her terror at the prospect of the fire.

'I never ever feel happy about the way I've played the trial scene,' I said to Dame Sybil.

'Oh, my dear,' she said, 'you never will.'

On my first night she gave me the illustrated volume *Jeanne d'Arc* by H. Wallon, published in Paris in 1876, which Shaw had given to her on her first night, 24 March 1924. She said that she had kept it until she saw a new 'Joan' who represented her own generation in the same way that, she, Sybil, had represented hers. And it is for me to hand on when I see the performance which epitomizes its own generation in the twenty-first century.

Saint Joan was played memorably a few years later by Eileen Atkins; though as she and I are more or less the same generation (I am a little older), her performance still belongs to the twentieth century.

Ten

At the Malthouse

Our Malthouse in West Sussex was partly Elizabethan (small part) and partly 1960s extensions, designed by a friendly architect. It was bought originally to act as a halfway house between Brighton and Chichester when the Festival Theatre first opened there. But it assumed a greater importance in our lives as a country hideaway with paddock, small orchard, and land that we could cultivate and keep in touch with the earth. Larry created a beautiful lime walk, shrubbery and rose garden, and was never more at peace with the world than when he was clipping hedges and nurturing and pruning his roses. In time we added a tennis court and indoor swimming pool, and built wings on either side of the original cottage to house a growing family and friends. Like Topsy, it just grew and grew.

Far from the madding crowd, and beside the banks of the River Adur, it has provided us with some of our happiest days in summer and winter alike. Saturday mornings began with the sensual pleasures of a shopping trip to Storrington, a nearby small town with a wonderful delicatessen, called Eastbrooks. There we savoured the delights of a multitude of different hams, and French cheeses and pâtés, smoked salmon and caviar, and sipped a small glass of the latest wine recommended by the proprietor. Next stop was the fishmonger where we could purchase fresh cod or halibut or plaice, caught earlier that morning in Brighton or Worthing. Then, drawn by the scent of newly baked bread, we all descended upon the Storrington bakery to choose rolls and croissants and brioches and mouth-watering chocolate cakes for the children. On the way home we would stop at the farm shop to find fresh vegetables and fruit, and test melons and avocados for ripeness and readiness. And, once back home we would hand it all over for the approval of Jean Wilson, our lovely young cook–housekeeper who came from the Scottish Highlands.

Friends would come and stay and declare themselves enchanted with it, despite the hazards (power cuts and plumbing disasters) of rather isolated country living.

David Niven experienced one such weekend when a mal-functioning cesspool forced everyone out into the garden because the bathrooms had become unusable.

St Jean Cap Ferrat, France   *Saturday*

My darling People,

   Having been brought up hearing on all sides that the most hideous crime was to fail to thank host and hostess for one weekend before the next one came along, you will appreciate why this little effort is causing me some nervous indigestion having failed largely to get in under the wire.

   The past week of filming has been horrendous and the speed so great that we are now two and a half days ahead, so I had no time to put pen to paper – forgive me.

   I had such a lovely time with you . . . the whole thing – house, people, children, pony, cesspool, was perfection. (I feel quite odd in the Connaught not padding along at midnight in pouring rain in order to piss on FDR's feet in Grosvenor Square.)

   . . . Very hot here and horribly crowded. One child has an ear infection, the other has been pinched by an Arab boatman, the Portuguese maid has scratched the Italian cook and the Afghan hound has been sick on the Aubusson – I can't wait for the peace and quiet of Elstree Studios!!

   All my fondest love and so many, many thanks.

   Niv

I remembered Larry eyeing the Aubusson with a professional interest when we stayed with David and his wife Hjordis in 1961. I was five months' pregnant with our first child, Richard, and practically a prisoner owing to my reluctance to allow the reporters encamped around the hotel to take pictures of my protruding belly. The invitation to St Jean Cap Ferrat seemed to offer a blessed escape but the interest in my condition was not, we discovered, confined to our own shores. There were daily cries of 'Espions! Espions!' from Niven's two sons who had appointed themselves protectors of our privacy. As we fled indoors they took hose-pipes in hand, and sluiced the bushes surrounding their garden, scoring direct hits on hordes of paparazzi who leapt screaming from their hiding places, uttering curses in several different languages and demanding payment for ruined photographic equipment. Some must have followed us from England if David's memory and attempt at recreating an accent is reliable: 'A million lovely memories, and thousands more not yet of age – but none can surpass the reporter from the *Daily Express* in our early days on this Cap ... "David – yeu've or'lways 'ad a very noice relationsip wiv the press ... please stand aside mate bicus we're goin' ter get a picture of that bulge no matter wot." '

The bulge proved to be a safe topic of conversation the night the Nivens invited their friends, Prince Rainier and Princess Grace of Monaco, to dinner. The Nivens, of course, called them Grace and Rainier, but Larry and I, who were quite excited at the thought of meeting them, decided that we should be properly respectful and address them as Sir and Ma'am. There was a certain amount of constraint in the air, for we didn't really have much in common apart from Hollywood and babies. Larry didn't play golf – for which Rainier had a passion; we didn't own a villa in the South of France; we didn't attend society balls or the Red Cross Gala; and we knew very little about the Grimaldi dynasty. Rainier and Grace had brought along an Arab sheikh who was their current house guest and who had not the slightest interest in the theatre, or films, or having babies; and we, of course, knew next to nothing about the present state of his oil fields.

David kept things going in his own inimitable way at the dinner table and Grace talked sweetly to me about her children, and the glorious food and wine helped us all to feel that we had done our best under difficult circumstances. But we met our Waterloo over coffee in the drawing room. After the niceties of who wanted black or white, and who did or did not take sugar, and some comments on how pretty the garden looked through the french windows, there was a lull. And Rainier fell fast asleep on the sofa and began to snore. His friend the sheikh sat beside him, impervious to the snorting and whistling and the social dilemma it presented. The rest of us sipped our coffee without speaking and avoided each other's eyes, trying to control a mounting hysteria, and wondered who, apart from His Serene Highness, would dare to break the silence. Princess Grace, who could have done it, seemed paralysed. Then Larry, who was seated next to her, decided to come to the rescue and asked loudly, 'Have you ever played Detroit, Ma'am?' Niven bolted from the room on the pretext of fetching more coffee. Grace looked surprised at the idea that she might have played Detroit, but was grateful for any distraction from the shattering noise still coming from the sofa. When Niven returned, Larry was telling Grace about the film he had made with Marilyn Monroe. Suddenly aware that its title, *The Prince and the Showgirl*, was perhaps too near the knuckle, he told her that its original title, as a play, had been *The Sleeping Prince*. Niven shot out of the room again and I followed him as Larry realized, too late, that neither title could be a winner that night.

Let it be said in all fairness, and with gratitude, that we enjoyed ourselves enormously two nights later when Their Serene Highnesses took us to an open-air restaurant, where the roasting spits, the gypsy fiddlers and the dancing all around us broke the ice at last, and conversation flowed with ease and merriment throughout the rest of the night.

Back at the Malthouse one wintery Sunday afternoon some years later, when gales blowing across our part of West Sussex had caused an inconvenient power failure, we were preparing by candlelight to return to London. We had said goodbye to the children who were being driven back to Bedales, and the housekeeper had gone back to her cottage up the road. I was in the bath and Larry, flashlight in hand, was searching the airing cupboard for underwear and socks, when there was a sudden and unexpected loud knocking at the door. Clad only in his bathrobe he groped his way down the stairs to see who was there.

Minutes later he called up the stairs, 'Joanie, there are two people here with a white Alsatian puppy.'

'What?' I shouted.

'It's a present from John Osborne and they want to leave it with us.'

'Wha-at!'

'I've asked them in for a cup of tea.'

When I stumbled down to the sitting room, Larry was crouched on the floor, trying to heat a saucepan of water on the dying embers of the wood fire. I could barely see the faces of our visitors, but they sounded nice people as they explained the kind of rigorous training and constant supervision the Alsatian puppy would need.

Now living the life of a country squire, Osborne seemed to have forgotten the nomadic pattern of an actor's life; we were both rehearsing next morning for projects which would keep us busy for several weeks. Our visitors ignored the problems this posed and said how disappointed John would be as he had gone to such trouble to arrange this delightful surprise for Sir Laurence.

'How very kind of him,' Larry murmured half-heartedly. Out of politeness, he then wondered aloud about the possibility of our housekeeper as trainer, though he knew perfectly well that she adored her cat, and both disliked and was frightened of dogs.

At that moment our car arrived and the puppy, making a last frantic effort to escape his owner's arms, knocked over two of the remaining three candles and demolished the tea cups, still sitting, unfilled, on the floor.

'What do you think, darling?' said my husband, desperate to escape and trying to shift the responsibility for Osborne's disappointment on to me.

'It's your decision, darling,' I said. 'You do what you think best,' and I excused myself on the grounds of unfinished packing.

In another of his periodical fits of remorse, Osborne had previously sent the original, handwritten, draft of *The Entertainer* to Larry after penning a bilious attack on him and the National Theatre in the *Evening Standard*. These missives never came with any apology, just a card saying 'Love, John'. I forget which 'knife-in-the-back' broadside occasioned the gift of the Alsatian puppy but I was, of course, blamed obliquely by John in some later article where he complained: 'He [LO] was not allowed to keep it.'

Jubilee Weekend Diary

It is Monday, 6 June 1977, and we have a lunch date with Harry Andrews out at Robertsbridge in Sussex. The day looks most unpromising, wet and windy. I think of all those Jubilee celebrations tonight, the bonfires to be lit, and the street parties to be held all over the country. And I wonder yet again what on earth has happened to the English summer.

We are all scurrying around trying to decide what to wear. Tamsin had planned a sun-frock with a lovely straw hat and is keenly disappointed. I am in a panic because my Jean Muir trouser-suit has not come back from the cleaners. Julie-Kate changes from blue dress to green dress to jeans and then back again. Richard announces that he has a sore throat and doesn't think he ought to go – and anyway should do some revision for O levels next week. Then he proceeds to sit idly in front of the TV intending to watch cricket. At 11.30 a.m., which is our supposed setting-out time, Richard announces that perhaps he will come after all but doesn't know what to wear. Tamsin is now in jeans but has no shoes and so takes mine; Julie-Kate is back in the green dress but hysterical as to whether clogs, sandals or flip-flops are most appropriate. I settle for a green silk suit – and Larry comes downstairs in nondescript trousers, sweater and ill-matching jacket . . . He went for a morning swim and, suddenly realizing the time, snatched up the first things he could get his hands on. He seethes impatiently as the time slips away. At twelve noon he phones Harry to say we shall be late.

We get there about 1.15 p.m. It is a lovely little house with a pretty garden. Poor Harry and Basil and Jean had been looking forward to lunch on the patio outside. Instead they have lit the log fire as it is now really very cold. We have a lovely lunch with turkey and strawberries and then embark on a trip to visit Joyce Redman and her family in their remote country cottage two miles away. Another log fire has been lit as their house is extremely cold – this is not surprising as a large window in one bedroom is left permanently open because swallows have built a nest just above the curtain rod and Joyce will not have them disturbed. We all troop up to see the nest – she stands on a chair and holds a mirror over it so that we can see the eggs. But the eggs turn out to be baby birds, which must have hatched that very morning. Jubilee babies!

Eleven

Birth of the National Theatre

The foundation stone for the building of Britain's National Theatre was laid by the Queen Mother on Friday, 13 July 1951. But it would take many years before any government could be persuaded to allocate funds to build it. Larry had long been a member of an eminent council formed to involve itself in that persuasion, though only in an advisory capacity, not as a director designate. By 1961 there was still no building and no plans or commitment to start on one; but there was more support for the idea of a National Theatre – and plans were made to start the organization without waiting for the new building. Both Stratford and the Old Vic had been mooted as possible nesting-places, with the Old Vic being more favoured as it was in London. Then the idea of a merger between the two theatres was entertained for some time, and Larry was unofficially approached by Lord Chandos who sounded him out about running the venture. If the merger was acceptable, Larry intended to leave Peter Hall in charge of Stratford and ask George Devine to run the Old Vic, whilst presiding over the whole himself, and acting for each of them in both theatres. But it was not to be. Peter Hall was running Stratford very successfully; he was acquiring the Aldwych as a second theatre in London and had no intention of becoming Larry's number two. In fact he considered his organization to be already the equivalent of a national theatre and began gathering support for the achievement of that ambition.

The merger fell through and finally, after a lot of machin-ations, it was announced that the National Theatre would open at the Old Vic in August 1963 and that Laurence Olivier was to be its Director.

Larry approached his awesome task with a knowledge of all that it would entail, and with a mixture of pride, apprehension and genuine humility. Such a position needed, as John Elsom wrote, 'a theatrical Hercules, who could carry like Atlas a world of responsibility'. He would also have to carry a load of sniping and criticism and comparisons with Peter Hall when the Arts Council refused Hall's demands for further subsidy. Depicted in the press as jealous rivals who were bitterly opposed to each other, the two men would have to try and repair that image and their relationship, as much for their own sake as for that of the rest of the profession.

I had written to Peter after a particularly unpleasant article in some paper, and after financial worries, overwork and illness had laid him low at Stratford. He was grateful for my letter which he said had

. . . lightened the beginning of a ghastly fortnight when I was examining budgets with Governors and anxiously negotiating with the Arts Council! All this is why I'm late replying.

I'm very much better now and back in the ring. However, we are now at the end of the road. Unless persons in high places can help us, we shall be finished at the beginning of 1965 and Stratford will have a new director. This is no dramatics, but financial fact! But I'm glad that the issue is so clear.

I won't go on. Your letter showed a profound understanding of our problems. And believe me I understand very well all that you are going through with the pressure of a vast repertory to mount. But do believe me: I know that it is in everybody's advantage in the theatre that the NT has started so well. So I'm glad.

I would so much value a chance of frank talk over a meal with you and

Larry. Could you come to my house in London one evening after a show or when you are free. You name a time.

Love,

Peter

The pressure on all of us at the time was such that the desired meeting never took place. And though the competitive spirit remained, the antagonistic attitude was dissipated as the Arts Council was persuaded to increase Stratford's subsidy, and the work of both companies was being well received.

Peter O'Toole played the Prince of Denmark in Larry's inaugural production of *Hamlet*, and with him were Michael Redgrave as Claudius, Diana Wynyard as Gertrude, Rosemary Harris as Ophelia and Derek Jacobi as Laertes. Our *Uncle Vanya* designer, the Irishman Sean Kenny, was persuaded to do the sets for *Hamlet*, which was quite an achievement on Larry's part. Sean had once been asked, along with other leading designers, what he would like to do at the National Theatre when it opened. He had replied in well-known belligerent fashion, 'Put a bomb under it.'

Larry wanted some reconstruction of the Old Vic stage and the addition of a forestage before the company moved in. Sean was commissioned to build a new revolving stage, which was used to great effect in *Hamlet* when it behaved itself properly. But there were nights when it moved round so slowly that the trumpets heralding Claudius's entry were compelled to play the same piece seven times before Michael Redgrave eventually revolved into view.

My first two roles for the National were in the two successes from Chichester, *Uncle Vanya* and *Saint Joan*, and I then teamed up again with John Dexter for *Hobson's Choice*, with Frank Finlay as Willie Mossop.

Redgrave was to play Hobson and as we had had such a rapport as Vanya and Sonya, I couldn't wait to work with him again. I remembered my student days when I had nearly hit him in the chest with my chair, how much I had loved his

Hamlet back then, and how he had been instrumental in getting me my first film part. The film was *Time Without Pity*, in which he was starring, and he had brought his director, Joseph Losey, to see me acting at the Royal Court. In the film I played the murdered girl's sister and had one good scene with Redgrave; I remember him saying to me that we would talk about the scene but not rehearse it – acting needed to be more spontaneous for films.

We had got to know each other better when he and Rachel had invited us to stay with them during those difficult pre-marriage days. Rachel was a close friend of Vivien's and had previously interceded on her behalf with Larry. She had suggested that nobody would mind if he spent most of his time with me as the mistress as long as he remained officially bound to his wife. Rachel had come to terms with the compromises necessary in her own marriage, and was not prepared for Larry's anger that she should have so totally misunderstood the seriousness of his intentions. But nobody could have been kinder and more generous when she realized the depth of our relationship, and his desire to remarry.

Michael had been so wonderful as Vanya and Claudius but he never seemed very comfortable as Hobson. Once or twice in performance he would cut ten pages or so, or suddenly start saying lines from a scene ahead and we would have to steer him back to the present one. But it happens to everyone occasionally, and no one thought anything of it.

It is probably true that Ralph Richardson, who was first asked to play it, would have been more appropriately cast as the North Country businessman, Hobson. And it would also have been fascinating to see him as Halvard Solness in *The Master Builder*. I never saw him play *Uncle Vanya* with Larry in their earlier Old Vic season, and for me, nobody could have matched Redgrave's superb performance in that Chekhov play. But Ralph was offered all three parts one night in Chelsea when he came on his motorbike to have dinner with Larry and me. He seemed interested and was in genial mood all evening, and then roared off on his back-firing Harley Davidson, saying he would think it over. He finally decided against it. Larry thought it was because he could not accept the fact that theirs was no longer an equal partnership – Larry was the Director of the National, and Ralph would be only a member of the company, albeit a star. His wife Meriel told me later that the parts weren't good enough. But Michael Redgrave obviously didn't think so.

Hobson's Choice was another success and during its run an article appeared in *Plays and Players* to remind me, lest I should forget, that I was not just an actress but also Olivier's wife.

Among the spray and the roaring, the shuddering masts and slapping tackle of Orson Welles's Moby Dick, *way back in June 1955, I remember a small, frightened, half-demented creature with eyes like boot-buttons – the doomed cabin-boy Pip. This in fact was my first sight of Joan Plowright, and I'm pleased to think that (unlike at least one far more eminent critic) I spotted the talent at once. Here was a face and a voice that were like themselves and no one else, that meant something real. Here was more than a routine display of pathos, and it hurt. In the eight or nine years that followed, poor Pip was to become in turn the herald angel of the new Royal Court wave, Lady Olivier, and leading lady of our new National Theatre . . . One thing needs saying at this point. Miss Plowright's marriage to our greatest actor, the man who was to found the Chichester Festival and become the National Theatre's first director, was by no means bound to be to her professional advantage. For one thing, it made her, willy-nilly, a sort of Establishment figure, faintly awesome to the profession instead of just one of them – the fact that she's entirely un-grand and unpretentious, and that her attitude certainly hasn't changed, doesn't alter this. For another, it could have drawn her into unwelcome prominence in more ambitious parts than she would otherwise have risked. When Vivien Leigh was Lady Olivier, she found herself playing Lady Macbeth, Cleopatra, roles which – for all Sir Laurence's devoted tutelage – were frankly beyond her charming, quite unclassical talents. Miss Plowright, more substantially gifted anyway, has so far been shielded from this danger.*

If it seems unkind to quote one man's opinion on the two Lady Oliviers (and we have both suffered worse), it is intended to show the judgemental attitude which existed towards any actress still practising her craft whilst married to Laurence Olivier. And however 'ungrand and unpretentious' I remained, there was no escaping the fact that I was in a position to exchange pillow-talk with the boss. And I was highly sensitive to the resentment that could cause. Though the article goes on to say 'Joan Plowright isn't yet anywhere near the limit of her powers,' and suggests classical roles I could conceivably play, he has already put a dampener on my 'risk-taking', which is such an irrepressible part of the true actor's make-up. (It is why Al Pacino wanted to play Richard III, and Dustin Hoffman came to London to play Shylock, and Kelsey Grammer of *Frasier* wanted to play Macbeth.) And he has made public my private fears about nepotism and 'the actor-manager and his wife'.

Larry had a story about the well-known actor-manager, Donald Wolfit, whom he naturally disliked after a belittling remark Wolfit made one day at the Garrick Club. It happened during the season at the Old Vic, when Larry was playing his celebrated Richard III, and also the smaller part of the Button Moulder in *Peer Gynt*. Wolfit, himself a successful Richard III, had put a hand on Larry's shoulder and said loudly, 'I liked your Button Moulder,' and then moved on. The story Larry told was of Wolfit being rudely interrupted during one of his notorious curtain speeches:

'Next week I shall be undertaking the role of Macbeth, and my wife ...'

'Your wife is an old bag,' shouted a voice from the gallery.

'Nevertheless,' continued Wolfit, unperturbed, 'my wife, Miss XY, will be playing the role of Lady Macbeth.'

I thought nostalgically of my risk-taking days at Nottingham Rep where I could say, 'Well, they think I can do it, so on their heads be it,' and then dive in at the deep end and sometimes miraculously survive. Yet at the same time I knew that giving birth to my children had been more momentous than any act of creation on the stage. And though I would never for a moment contemplate giving it up, I recognized that acting was no longer, as it used to be, my entire reason for living.

The next two leading ladies at the National Theatre, Maggie Smith and Geraldine McEwan, joined the company expressly to take risks, to develop their talent and extend their range, both having made their initial success in comedy. We all shared the same dressing room, though we each occupied it separately as we were in different plays. And those walls must have soaked up a whole history of first night nerves, and disappointments as well as the excitement and blessed relief of success. I would attend every first night with Larry when we weren't playing ourselves, and go round at the half-hour with good wishes and flowers. I remember Geraldine lying prostrate on the divan before her opening night in *The White Devil*, and murmuring, 'Oh God, these first nights, Joan.' And Maggie, on the night of *The Beaux' Stratagem*, trying to keep afloat despite antibiotics and painkillers because of an acute ear infection. 'Just let it be over soon,' was all she could manage. It was the day on which her Oscar for *The Prime of Miss Jean Brodie* had been announced and it should have been a night for celebration. And it was the one night that Bill Gaskill allowed her to take a solo curtain call and the audience shouted their bravos. But all she wanted was to get home and go to bed.

It was in Bill Gaskill's revelatory production of *The Recruiting Officer* that Maggie made her bow with the company and acted for the first time with Robert Stephens, whom she would later marry. Restoration comedy was something she could do on her head; it was the next two roles offered which had tempted her more – Desdemona in *Othello* with Olivier and Hilde Wangel in Ibsen's *The Master Builder* with Redgrave.

Othello was a sell-out hit, with Larry's exotic, though controversial, Moor attracting most of the attention. Franco Zeffirelli described the performance to Tynan as 'an anthology of everything that has been discovered about acting in the last three centuries. It's grand and majestic but it's also modern and realistic.' The director was John Dexter and he and Larry had quite a few arguments during rehearsals. Dexter was well known for his abrasive and sarcastic remarks when giving notes; he thought it gingered things up a bit and kept people on their toes. He and I were much too close friends for me to mind his jibes: 'If Her Ladyship has finished her coffee, perhaps we can get on with the rehearsal,' but actors unused to his method and personality could be reduced to a shivering jelly. He had said something to the assembled *Othello* company which so angered Larry that he had warned him 'never to talk to my company like that again'. Dexter had the temerity to say, 'Your company? I thought this was supposed to be the National Theatre company.'

I went to see a run-through after Dexter rang me to talk of his problems and Larry had told me he wasn't sure if he could trust John's judgement. I sent my letter to Birmingham, where they were about to open on tour.

. . . *Just want to send all my love and thoughts and energy to you for your second opening. Don't let any doubts creep in about your Othello; I know this is about the time one begins to bite one's fingernails and think only of the bits one is still dissatisfied with. No harm in that . . . as long as you remember also that in the greater part of the play you are wildly exciting, beautiful, superb and head and shoulders above anyone living today. Don't know about those who went before, but I'm pretty sure you are way above them too!*

Your characterization is fascinating, original and absolutely valid in human terms . . . the split personality of a man who has had to overcome one powerful part of his nature in order to achieve a certain position in the world.

I know your main problem is that of getting the progress of the character through the play to just flow through your bones without having to think about it. Naturally a great deal of that can only come with playing it but maybe a long quiet mull over what you have already created might help to get the shape and feeling clearer in your mind.

Am going to jot down random thoughts and impressions which might ring a bell somewhere and, if they don't, no harm has been done!

(Act III, Scene 3: 'Ha Ha or No . . . No . . . False to me')
*I think it should be agonized doubt sooner than certainty. He says earlier,
'When I doubt, prove.' So, as yet, it is only doubt . . . and he follows the
Farewell content speech with a savage request for proof. All that you do
magnificently anyway and there is nothing more to be said about that.*

*I remember you saying about Brenda de B. that she 'tries to cry' on
stage, whereas in real life one tried to stop crying.*

*I think you are maybe trying to believe Cassio's kisses have been on
her lips, instead of trying to stop yourself believing.*

*I know that Othello's baser, hidden nature probably wants to find
Desdemona guilty, but the 'noble façade' could still struggle this early in
the play to keep up its head a little longer . . . You don't want yet, if it is
humanly possible, to reveal yourself as the naked animal you really are
. . . but you want proof . . . but if you can get proof and still cling
desperately to the last vestiges of the man you once were, it still leaves you
plenty of opportunity in the next scenes with her for the final revelation
of the mad beast.*

*This is probably just something I feel, but I have felt each time I've
seen it that your passion is too great and openly displayed for Maggie to
top it and try and pretend it is a game. If the first part is shouted . . . as
now . . . and then there is an awful effort to be sane and cunning (which
she takes advantage of) and then the rage and pleading break out again
. . . you've still got somewhere to go when you finally lose control completely
with her.*

*Also it would make her rather puzzled 'I ne'er saw this before' when
you have gone off not quite so much like the understatement of the year.*

*No other suggestions, my love. And I bet you don't like those! And
you are probably quite right! Just one of those ideas of people who come
in rather late on a production and don't realize that you discarded all
those ideas weeks ago!*

Oh . . . I do love you.

Joan

Larry opened to mostly rave reviews: 'It is a performance
full of grace, terror, and insolence. I shall dream of its mysteries
for years' (Herbert Kretzmer, *Daily Express*). 'The power,

passion, verisimilitude and pathos of Sir Laurence's per-formance ... will be spoken of with wonder for a long time to come' (Harold Hobson). There were two or three dissenters whose complaints were ignored by the public, and queues for tickets stretched around the block for every performance.

In an article in *Punch* magazine on 10 February 1970, the young satirical writer (and actor), John Wells, offered his own irreverent but affectionate assessment of Larry, after first meeting him:

I remember being impressed first of all by the military glamour of his entrance as he exploded through the double doors of Sean Kenny's old office, scattering a fall-out of staff-officers and dogsbodies, and secondly by the way he called the Irish designer 'Shawnie' – even, I think, 'Shawnie, Darling' – without having his nose smashed flat by a man who occasionally lifts cars on to the pavement with his bare hands ...

His apparently reckless physical abandon, like that of a crutch-happy, microphone-stroking lead singer in a pop group, may well lie at the root of his massive popular acclaim as distinct from his critical success ...

He himself has said that people will be laughing at his interpretations of parts in twenty years' time, and with a piece of unrestrainedly romantic popular entertainment like his West Indian Othello, *as extreme and camp in its fashionable way as the wildest eye-rolling of the silent film stars, he may well be right. But to create any fashion somebody has to go over the top, and he has gone over the top again and again with the courage and apparent invulnerability of a multiple VC in the trenches.*

Some twenty years later, in 1992, Larry would be proved right when a meretricious Channel Four television programme showed the English master of a renowned school encouraging his pupils to laugh at the film of *Othello*.

But an extract from one of many letters sent to me expresses the distaste felt by most people who had seen the programme. 'May I add my name to the I trust scores of people who have contacted you after the quite scandalous *Without Walls* programme concerning your late husband. I found the entire presentation and orientation of the programme unworthy of the subject, even given that it is a series intended to debunk established reputations.' It was the lack of quality of those who were brought in to do the debunking that made it so mean-spirited and ultimately unwatchable. A bespectacled, intellectual lady called Hermione Something spoke contemptuously of Olivier's vanity and, in her opinion, his total misjudgement of Shakespeare's intentions in his plays. Oblivious to her own vanity, she began her next sentence, 'What Shakespeare really meant in this scene ...' as though, like Gwyneth Paltrow in the film, she had actually been in bed with him when he wrote it. I thought of writing to say that Shakespeare wrote for a company of actors and that nobody would queue all night to hear her academic lectures on him. Instead I remembered G.B. Shaw's advice: 'Silence is the most perfect expression of scorn,' and switched her off.

John Wells' article on Larry rounded off: 'He is about to see his life's ambition fulfilled in the building of the seven and a half million pound National Theatre on the South Bank, and perceptive observers describe him dominating the Theatre's temporary premises, supported and impelled by his wife Joan Plowright, with the sensitive pride of a stag dominating its own territory.' The cover of *Punch* had a caricature by Trog of Larry, in crash-helmet, sitting on a fork-lift truck on a building site with St Paul's Cathedral in the background, under the headline: THE MASTER BUILDER.

I don't know if the allusion to Ibsen's play *The Master Builder* was intended or not, but Larry and I had played in it together in 1964. It was a production which began to rival the Scottish Play for its history of misfortunes. Diana Wynyard, who was cast to play in it with Redgrave and Maggie Smith, became ill after a week of rehearsals, and tragically died shortly afterwards in hospital. Celia Johnson came in to give a beautiful performance as Mrs Solness but she and Maggie had a difficult time in rehearsal with Michael Redgrave, who was suffering from the same uncertainty about his lines which had begun in

Hobson's Choice. After a very shaky first night, there was a concerted attack by critics from which Maggie suffered as much as Michael. At the time no one suspected that his problems might stem from the onset of Parkinson's disease, which would be diagnosed much later. Whilst things improved as they played their allotted number of performances, Michael was unhappy and did not wish to continue into the next booking period. It was an expensive production and, though he was already overworked, Larry decided to take over the part of Solness and keep the play in the repertoire. Maggie was playing in *Othello* and was about to start rehearsals for Noël Coward's *Hay Fever* with Dame Edith Evans.

And so I was cast to play Hilde Wangel opposite Larry for the new opening, after which Maggie and I would alternate in the part, according to availability.

Larry and I went off to Ischia for a week to study the play, and took a pedalo out to sea each day in order to get some exercise at the same time as learning our lines. Our rehearsal time in London was limited as he was still playing Othello and overseeing new productions, and constantly being called away to deal with one crisis or another.

There was a frantic SOS from Noël Coward, who was directing his own play in Manchester, and who wanted Larry to come there and fire his leading lady, the famous Dame Edith Evans. She couldn't remember her lines, he complained, and refused to do much as regards make-up and appearance as the glamorous Judith Bliss; he said she 'looked 105 on stage'. During the pauses in performances caused by her forgetfulness, she was apt to look piercingly at each of the actors around her and then declare loudly, 'It's not my turn.' Somehow Larry persuaded Coward to be patient and Dame Edith to put on her false eyelashes, and he detailed someone to go round to hear her lines each day. He came back exhausted.

Then Maggie's agent sent a message to say that she ought to be allowed to play the first night of *The Master Builder* opposite Larry when it opened in London instead of me. As she would be opening *Hay Fever* in London the same week that the Ibsen play opened on tour in Leeds, there would naturally be little time for her to rehearse with Larry, and he was already worried enough about his own debut in the play. Planning the repertoire for London and on tour was like fitting together the pieces of a jigsaw puzzle, and it was as much to do with economics as making sure that everyone in the company was happy. Actors under contract were expected to go where they were needed without making too much of a fuss about it, but that meant that the management could sometimes ride roughshod over personal feelings without even noticing. And Maggie could hardly be described as a 'contract player'; she had starred in the West End before joining the company. Although critics would be invited to both actresses' first nights as Hilde Wangel, one on the Tuesday and one on the following Friday, the first performance with Larry as Solness was bound to have more of an impact. And Maggie felt, quite rightly, that she should be part of that occasion, and perhaps that she should have been given the opportunity without having to ask for it whatever inconvenience it might cause.

She had come to stay for a weekend in Brighton after those earlier bad reviews with Redgrave, and she had told me that she had written to thank the one critic who supported her, saying that without him she might have thrown herself off Waterloo Bridge. It was of immense importance to her that she should set the record straight and show them what she could really do with Hilde Wangel.

Whatever Larry's feelings about it were, they would be obliterated three days later when I suffered a miscarriage and all the well-laid plans went awry. I was in the early stages of a third pregnancy but I had carried on acting for the first four months during the previous one, without any problem. Only five weeks before I had confided to my diary: 'Feel it is certain now that I am expecting a baby. Great joy!' But on a later date, 20 October, there is a drawing of a black box in my diary and inside it are the words, 'LOST BABY.' I was in the Whitehaven

Nursing Home in Brighton where my first two children had been born, and where, on the day after Tamsin arrived, Dora Bryan had come into my room. She had just lost her own baby but wanted to see mine and hold her for a minute. I remember thinking how brave she was and asking her there and then to be a godmother to Tamsin. Recalling that day I knew I should count my blessings; my diary entry reads: 'Taking stock and getting under control. My darling distraught L. left this morning for Manchester – can't see him now 'til Sunday. Begged to be allowed to go home and be with Richard and Tamsin. Arrived home 6.30 p.m. and hugged and hugged them.'

A nightmare time ensued for Larry with his concern for me hovering over rehearsals, which had to continue with the understudy, Jeanne Hepple, and the prospect of a first night only four days away. For the first time in his life he was assailed by stage fright and the urge to run out of the theatre and catch the first bus that came along, no matter where it was going. But the show went on. After a few days I was back in the saddle and took over again from Jeanne Hepple; and for the final week in Oxford Maggie took over some performances from me; Larry didn't know whether he was on his head or his heels. But their London opening was a success and Maggie conquered the critics on her second time around. And they were mostly welcoming when I played it with Larry on the following Friday. And Noël Coward, who was back on his pedestal after *Hay Fever*'s success, came to see us acting together and sent flowers and his card:

My darlings,
   Thank you both for a great evening in the theatre.
   I am still grovelling at your feet.
   Love, love, love,
   Noelie

The aura of rivalry which was built up around Maggie and me and which we tried to control, was, I suppose, inevitable in the circumstances, even though, as actresses, we were so totally different and there were only a few parts we would safely share.

The saga continued when a TV company wanted to broadcast excerpts from the repertoire which were to include Maggie and Robert Stephens in *The Recruiting Officer*, and Larry and me in *The Master Builder*. The original plan had been for me to do an excerpt from *Saint Joan*, but as some of the cast were unavailable, I was asked to do Hilde Wangel instead. I was happy to accept and gave the matter no more thought. Then came a message from Maggie's agent, saying that if *The Master Builder* was to be broadcast, then it was she who should play the part.

Larry couldn't bring himself to make the necessary phone call to me, so it was an embarrassed George Rowbottom (the Manager) who rang and explained the situation. I realized that it had never occurred to me to ask how Maggie felt about it. But, appreciating the reasons behind the request, I told him I would withdraw from the programme. The broadcast would be the first time that the work at the National Theatre reached a much wider audience. And it was not fair that for her only appearance Maggie would be mostly in disguise and sporting a black, curly moustache. But there was a further issue at stake, which I understood very well. It would look as though she had again been relegated to the sphere of comedy only and her protest and indignation were mainly on that score. After all, Hilde Wangel was her part originally. Although I felt a bit miffed at being put out of the programme, I couldn't help admiring the steely determination that had brought it about, because I recognized that I, too, would be capable of fighting as fiercely for something I felt to be equally right and just. And finally, neither she nor I really knew whether the TV company, or Larry himself, had designated who should appear in what, and ... 'Aye, there's the rub,' I found myself echoing Hamlet. And I suddenly realized how complacent I must have seemed with my children and my lovely home, and the famous husband who had provided them and who was looking after my pro-fessional interests into the bargain.

The next day Maggie thanked me in a strangled voice on the phone and I asked her to come to Brighton as she said she needed to talk. We had a sort of unspoken agreement to separate our professional relationship (not made easier with Larry standing in the middle) from a more personal one as two women friends with complicated lives and quite a few problems in common. She and Robert Stephens had fallen in love and had started an affair; she came to say that she felt she ought to leave the company as soon as her present commitments were ended. She was beginning to feel uneasy with certain actors in the company who knew, and were fond of, Robert's wife, Tarn Bassett. She hadn't known until I told her that Tarn was Tamsin's godmother and often came to stay with her daughter, Lucy; so it was not easy for any of us. Larry came back that night and stayed up late giving sympathetic advice, his irritation with her forgotten in the face of her obvious distress. Naturally he didn't want her to leave; she was a star he couldn't afford to lose. Privately he said to me that it might be just a theatrical romance, but he didn't help matters by casting them opposite each other again for Zeffirelli's production of *Much Ado About Nothing*. Their liaison had to be kept secret, much as ours had been, for both were still living with their present partners. Maggie had been preparing to marry the writer, Beverley Cross, as soon as his divorce came through; and they had seemed so happily suited before the present complications had arisen. And indeed, at the end of that year, on Christmas Eve 1964, my diary notes: 'Maggie and Beverley arrived for Christmas. Spent the evening wrapping presents after dinner and pulling Mrs F— [cook] to pieces. She'll have to go.' Mrs F— was on approval for three months and it was not her cooking that was the problem, but her manner. (I had also started missing some of my clothes, which had been discovered wrapped around a few of our prize ornaments and hidden in her wardrobe upstairs.) Maggie and Beverley gave me a beautiful book of costume designs, with both their names inscribed, which had to be put away for a long time, after they parted, and only brought out again some fourteen years later when they got back together again.

Christmas morning was spent playing with the children and unwrapping presents; and at noon there were more guests for caviar and Christmas drinks: Terence Rattigan and Sir John and Katy Clements, our neighbours, Cuthbert Worsley, the critic, Enid Bagnold from Rottingdean, the Mackenzies (our doctors), and Albert Finney and Norman Rossington. My diary doesn't tell me what Albert and Norman were doing in Brighton on Christmas Day (they can't have been in pantomime) but they were still in the house for dinner that night, along with Maggie and Bev, and Terry Rattigan. Next day, on Boxing Day, we all went down the road for lunch at 'Terry's Terrible House', which was Larry's favourite way of describing Rattigan's Brighton home. On the seafront but also on a corner, it caught the wind from all sides and as the front door opened straight into the sitting room, when gales were high, guests would be blown in with such force that they frequently cannoned into small pieces of furniture before being brought to a halt by a large sofa. Chandeliers would shake and rattle and Terry would need a deal of assistance to get the door closed again in the teeth of the gale.

We received an SOS from Terry another time when Rex Harrison and Rachel Roberts were due to dine with him. They were in an extremely combative stage of their marriage, and Terry was desperate for support, saying that he couldn't cope with them alone. I only remember some hair-raisingly embarrassing remarks from a manic Rachel who paced the floor, describing the inadequacy of their lovemaking and accusing Rex of being merely a voyeur. Another evening was spent with Terry as guests, along with Joe Orton and Kenneth Halliwell, who were destined to meet such a violent death together. There was no inkling of that savagery to come when we met them. In fact they were so polite and well behaved that it was difficult to reconcile the Joe presented to us that night with the one who wrote those outrageous and wildly funny plays.

But we had many happy nights with friends in our own house, which Tony Hopkins described as 'Liberty Hall', and where we often entertained the casts of plays visiting the Theatre Royal. Douglas Fairbanks Jnr. was one such visitor whom we very nearly missed but caught just in time, which resulted in a thank you letter overflowing with charm and gratitude.

The Royal Crescent Hotel, Brighton

Dearest both of you –

That was the most gloriously happy – and delicious surprise last night. I'd almost given up hope of seeing you, those enchanting progeny and the fabled house I'd heard about and longed to see for ages. I resisted the temptation of ringing you for fear of putting you on a spot so soon after your return (no Radie, I!!) The theatre manager had reported to me he'd passed on the details of my temporary existence – but when Friday evening's curtain rose and nary a word, I was very sad. Then, lo – (and, at a later time of course, behold!) – there you all *were – out front. I didn't know until the second act – and by that time we had been grumpy about the relatively undemonstrative and sober audience, and had determined to push on and get it over with as quickly as possible. When word was passed that the Olivier ménage were in the 'House seats' (where else, for Gawd's sake?) we tried, belatedly, to pull up our bootstraps, jockstraps and bras (I'm getting so overweight and aged, I need a 'bra' more than any female in the company!) and got on with it.*

Then the happy reunion and all that sort of stuff backstage – to be followed by the great and glorious supper at the Olivier Arms (J. Plowright, Prop.) – washed fore and aft by the best usquebaugh and wine, and accompanied by a visit which, as far as your most comparatively humble servant is concerned, was the *most agreeable hour (two hours? three hours? more? I've no longer any recollection of how long I kept you both up – and whereas manners and a decent respect for the welfare of friends should have made me considerate I am proud to say that I had such a* marvellous *time – my best in ages – that I don't really care!).*

The escorting of my person safely home, through the blustering Force

10 (12?) gale, with his Lordship protecting me from another pneumonia by covering me with half his coat (and his own head with the goddamndest Holmesian deerstalker I've seen since William Gillette – no, later – Basil Rathbone!), was, I'm sure, a sight not only to behold but one to move the most frigid heart. I only hope the poor lad, being my senior, managed to return himself to his own hearth and home (not having had any panic enquiries, I assume all's now well!). In my happy state of don't-give-a-damn drunkenness, I momentarily considered turning about and seeing him home. Something, I forget what, discouraged me.

Now, we face our last night, and we travelling mountebanks, we Merry Andrews, go our separate ways – but I, the privileged one, leave with a heartful of gratitude, and not a little envy. What a dear and precious family you all are. Darling Joanie, thank you again (it's about the first time we've just sat about and nattered) and you, dearest Larry lad, my most grateful blessings –

Ever thine –

D

PS My love and XXXs to those wonderful young 'uns! God damn it, I did enjoy it all so!

At the beginning of 1965, I received a surprise letter from Vivien who had recently purchased a house in Sussex, not far from Brighton.

Tickerage Mill   *16 February 1965*

Dear Joan,

I have been meaning to write to you for some time, but somehow one puts off difficult things and this is a difficult letter to write. I have felt how much more pleasant it would be if we could all meet. During the past years I have been working and travelling abroad but now I mean to stay here. I do think what is always an awkward situation could be eased by one private meeting. I hope you will agree. I have mentioned it to Larry but imagine he is too occupied to have given it much thought ... May I suggest that you come here for lunch or dinner on either a Monday or a Friday. After rehearsals start on 8 March, of course I can only be here over a short weekend but as I shall invite no one else perhaps that might suit you better. The drive only takes about forty minutes and it would seem to me it would be pleasanter to meet in the country rather than London. I hope very much to hear from you. I was very sad for you when you lost your baby.

Yours ever,
Vivien

In more normal circumstances it would have seemed a reasonable request, but our circumstances were not normal; and the uncertainty about possible recurrences of her irrational behaviour made it difficult to know how to respond. Larry considered it to be a disturbing intrusion on his new life; we had little enough time anyway to spend as a family, he said, and what on earth could we safely talk about? We didn't wish to be unkind, and so he sought advice from her doctor on how best to deal with the situation. The doctor advised strongly against it, explaining that such meetings could only exacerbate the manic phase of the illness, which was not yet totally under control.

Larry's sister-in-law, Hester, who had been an onlooker during the difficult days at Notley, where her husband, Dickie (Larry's brother), had died, came to stay with us at Brighton one weekend. After his death she had married the doctor who attended him and had moved with her family to live in Devon. Her happiness and new life there were destined not to last very long before she became a widow for the second time.

Larry had asked Hester to come to Brighton after her new husband died and when she arrived, alone, I asked her about her children, saying there was plenty of room for them too, if she would like them to come. She said she thought they were quite happy where they were and, looking at me rather oddly, told me they were with her neighbours in the next house along the road. She was obviously waiting for me to make some comment but as none was forthcoming, she added by way of further explanation, 'They're with Roger . . . didn't you know?'

By some extraordinary quirk of fate, Larry's nieces were being cared for by my first husband and his wife and family, who had lived next door to Hester for some time, quite unbeknown to me. Apparently she thought that Larry's older sister, Sybille, would have told us. I remember Sybille saying once that it was a pity we couldn't go down to Devon with the children to visit Hester, adding, 'But I suppose the trouble is Donald.' As Sybille's memory was by then somewhat faulty, I had never bothered to enquire about 'Donald', and therefore had no idea that she had got the name wrong, and actually meant my ex-husband.

There would of course have been no trouble with Roger, and I wished afterwards that we might have been able to go and visit them all in Devon. But weekends with our children were so precious, and the journey down south so long, that I'm afraid it was never attempted.

There would come a time when the Brighton Belle ceased to run and travelling back and forth to the Old Vic became less enjoyable. We rented a three-bedroom flat in Roebuck House in Victoria as our pied à terre in London. Close to the station and barely twenty minutes away from the Old Vic, it was also useful for business meetings, entertaining and first night parties. Its only drawback was the noise from the flat above us which belonged to Peter Sellers. He was obviously obliged to change the decor every time he changed his wives, so the peaceful interludes never lasted very long.

Twelve
....

Moscow, Berlin and
Dinner with Gore Vidal

In 1965 the National Theatre was to undertake its first overseas tour starting in Moscow with *Othello, Love for Love* and *Hobson's Choice*. And it would be the first foreign company to act in the Kremlevsky Theatre, inside the Kremlin walls, which had been originally built for Stalin thirty years before. I had relinquished my part in *Hobson's Choice* to Billie Whitelaw, and was there as Lady Olivier in order to take over some of the duties that Larry would have neither the time nor the energy to perform. He was playing Othello, and Tattle in *Love for Love*, as well as supervising the 'get-in', the lighting and dress rehearsals of the three productions. And there were innumerable receptions and visits to places of national interest planned by the ever hospitable Russians. I had been coached by the exiled White Russian, Moura Budberg, in a speech in Russian expressing gratitude for our warm reception and admiration for all things Russian, which could hopefully cover most events.

Someone from the Foreign Office came to lay down some rules to the company before we left. We must take no Western literature in with us, not even a newspaper; and we must wear no jewellery other than watches, wedding or engagement rings. The Moscow airport was in pitch darkness, apart from landing lights, when we touched down. And then across the runway came two lorry-loads of actors and dancers, carrying huge torches and flowers, to greet us with tears in their eyes and to welcome us to their country. They had no idea who any of us were in the darkness, and it was the wardrobe mistress, a flamboyant dresser, who was presented with the largest bouquet. Once inside the airport we were interviewed for the Russian television news programme by a crew composed entirely of women, including the director. Transported to the huge Ukraine Hotel, we felt rather like refugees in transit. Luggage was lying about all over the place and there were no porters or bell-boys to offer assistance. You had to hunt for your suitcases, drag them to the lift yourself and then find your own room. At one floor of the Ukraine the lift never stopped, and we were told that it was staffed entirely by KGB officials who recorded everything that was said in the rooms. Believing the chandeliers in the dining room to be similarly bugged, the English actors amused themselves by directing uncomplimentary remarks about the food towards them, and adding for the benefit of the listening KGB, 'Did you get that, Vladimir? Could you pass it on . . .'

I was given an interpreter from the Ministry of Culture, a highly intelligent blonde girl called Nina, with a lovely sense of humour. She was not, she told me, a member of the Party. Apparently such membership was not compulsory in order to hold a position in that particular Ministry. One of her favourite authors was Oscar Wilde, who was banned in Russia, I thought, but Nina told me that you could get round anything if you were a college student and said you were doing a thesis on 'decadent Western literature'.

She came with me to the theatre on the first morning of rehearsal where a deal of confusion reigned and Larry was near to losing his temper. The stagehands seemed too overawed by their historical surroundings to agree to make necessary adjustments when the scenery didn't fit properly onto the stage. 'Is there a Russian word for "yes"?' I asked Nina after we had left. 'All we've heard so far is "Niet, Niet"!' Nina laughed and answered in the same vein, 'Oh well, if a Russian says "yes" it means there's work to do.' We were in the lift at the Ukraine at the same time as the English journalist, Barry Norman; her remark was reported light-heartedly in our *Daily Mail* the following day. And Nina didn't turn up the next morning. She came back a little subdued two days later to go with me to a lavish reception for the company, where leading dancers from the Bolshoi Ballet, opera singers, folk singers, circus acts and two brilliant magicians gave us such a stunning afternoon's entertainment that we were left feeling both humbled and very privileged. We had nothing to offer in return – except my little speech, learnt parrot-fashion from Moura Budberg, and couched in very old-fashioned Russian they told me later; but it pleased them that I had tried. Next morning at the hotel I was still in my bathrobe when there was a knock at the door and the two magicians from that show burst into my room. Full of fun and mischief they whirled around me, performing a variety of astonishing tricks, talking in Russian all the time, obviously asking me questions some of the time, and totally ignoring my constant pleas of 'I don't understand.' Finally they gave up and departed as quickly as they had arrived. 'They were sent to find out if you speak Russian well,' I was told later. 'Somewhere along the line you would have revealed it if you did; now they can be satisfied that your speech was a one-off.'

The opening night of *Othello* was a fantastic experience with the audience surging down at the end to throw flowers onto the stage, and erupting into clamorous shouts when Larry took his solo calls. And the critics echoed their enthusiasm. One of the reviews was written by the Professor of English at Moscow University, and he invited Larry and me, and Ken Tynan, to dine with him and his wife in their apartment. He was a likeable man, very intelligent and widely read, and not totally committed, we felt, to the Communist regime, though he was guarded in his comments about its deficiencies, and ready with a polite but uncompromising counter-attack on capitalist values. Hanging on a wall in the main room (which was sitting room, dining room and son's bedroom) was what looked like a framed fragment of charred paper. He had no qualms about explaining its significance when we expressed our curiosity. It was taken from the remains of paintings that had been burnt on orders from the Communist government. The work of non-conformist, free-thinking or dissident artists, they were considered too dangerous for public consumption. He explained that he, and a number of other highly regarded members of the intelligentsia, had chosen this way of expressing their disapproval of the government's action. Their protest resulted in an agreement that such paintings would be preserved in future in a private art gallery, in the Scientists' Pavilion, available to a selected few but not accessible to the general public. This had been accomplished, he told us, mainly because members of Russia's scientific elite had made known their belief: 'Where the artist goes today, the scientist goes tomorrow.'

From Russia we moved to West Berlin for a week, during which we defected to the East side of the Wall to watch a matinée performance by the celebrated Berliner Ensemble, and to meet Brecht's widow, the actress Helene Weigel. Our bus-load of actors was halted at the Wall in the no-man's-land between East and West. And the armed guards who came on board and demanded passports seemed to regard us with a great deal of suspicion. We were kept there for half an hour or so with the actors growing restless and beginning to chant, 'Why are we waiting?' Then a slight figure appeared suddenly from the East side gates and hurried across the ground towards our bus. It was Helene Weigel who had heard the singing and knew that if we aroused the anger of the guards, we might never be allowed in. She appealed to us to be patient and not to provoke them with further singing. The English actors, who had never had to endure living under a totalitarian regime, or in occupied territory, felt suddenly ashamed that they had caused her such anxiety. We greatly admired her as an actress, who was renowned for her stunning performance as Mother Courage in Brecht's play of that name, which had been seen in London during the World Theatre Season. After her husband's death, she had continued to run the Ensemble; the performance we saw that afternoon was a memorable theatrical experience and the highlight of our visit to Germany.

Some thirty years later I would return to Berlin after the Wall had come down and East and West had been reunited. The year was 1999 and my diary recorded the events.

It was the last September of the twentieth century and the sixtieth anniversary of the Second World War. I was in Berlin to make a film and had quite forgotten the significance of the date, until I woke up in the Kempinski Hotel and pictures appeared on the German television of this devastated city at the end of 1944. They showed old newsreels of the mad Adolf strutting his stuff in front of rapturous crowds shouting, 'Heil Hitler,' in the earlier days of the war. Then it was announced that the German Chancellor, Herr Schröder, had rushed over to Poland to lay wreaths and urge the Polish people 'not to bear grudges'. Elsewhere in the world, grudges were being borne with a vengeance in the Balkans, in Russia and in India, and the foolish hopes that Hiroshima and its legacy would prove a lasting deterrent to future wars had been extinguished long ago.

The rebuilt Berlin is a thriving metropolis once again with wide tree-lined avenues and no high-rise buildings to blot out the sun. And visible everywhere in the city are the cranes, symbols of the building going on and still to come. The young Germans we worked with had not been born when Hitler was in power. 'We learnt in school about Germany's sad history,' they said; and to them Hitler was a monster from the pages of their history books, along with Stalin who, as one of them pointed out, actually killed more people than Hitler. But their condemnation of the evil done in Hitler's name was as vehement as our own. The theatre seemed no longer as important as it used to be, and only the Berliner Ensemble, in what was previously East Berlin, retained its high reputation.

Three weeks earlier, before coming to Germany, I had been on holiday in Italy, staying at Marajen Chinigo's beautiful villa,

Torre di Cività. A converted old monastery, it occupies a wonderful position halfway up between Amalfi and Ravello, with views of the sea on three sides, and the mountains on the fourth. And near the top, at Ravello, and overlooking Torre di Cività is the famous Villa Rondinaia, owned by Gore Vidal. We had been introduced by mutual friends and he and his partner, Howard Austen, had invited my friend and me to dinner. 'Are you ambulatory?' he had asked on the phone, meaning that there was quite a walk and some steps to climb before reaching his villa. And no other means of getting there.

I had sent them a postcard from Berlin as we had talked that night of *I Am a Camera* and the days of Auden and Isherwood. 'Renewed thanks for a glorious evening out,' I wrote, remembering the significance of that dinner. After drinks on their terrace with its spectacular view from the Amalfi coastline across the sea to Salerno, we had gone to the Sasso Hotel for dinner. We had wined and dined and Howard had sung at the piano for other guests (and invited me to join him), and then we had ambled out onto the cobbled stones with 'vine leaves in our hair'.

During the course of that memorable evening we had talked about Larry and the proliferation of speculative biographies which had appeared after his death in 1989. There had been some silly and unproved allegations of a homosexual affair with a named actor (conveniently dead), which I knew to be untrue, and Gore took the opportunity to confirm their silliness. 'I hope you didn't believe that nonsense about your husband and Danny Kaye; I assure you it is not true.' I asked if I could quote him as I took him to be the ultimate authority on such matters, and he said yes, of course I could. As it happens, other gay friends had laughed the idea to scorn, including Silvio Narizzano, who directed Larry in *Cat on a Hot Tin Roof*, and who wrote to our son Richard, stating categorically, like Mr Vidal, that it was nonsense. And reports by careless biographers that Larry had admitted to relationships of that kind are equally untrue.

There can be love of a man for a man, or a woman for a woman, which has nothing to do with a sexual relationship. And it can sometimes be more permanent and sustaining. Such loving friendships remain unassailed by fading passion or amorous jealousies; they can enrich our enjoyment of life, and be called on for unconditional support at those times when it is most needed.

Larry tended to shower almost everyone he knew with endearments and demonstrative terms of address. In the same way as the macho Sean Kenny had to put up with 'Shawnie, darling', and our son Richard had to endure 'Dickie-Wickie' for a short time, there is a published letter addressing his supposed arch-enemy, Peter Hall, as 'My dear Peterkins'. And Larry could say, 'I adored Danny Kaye,' in exactly the same way as he said, 'I adored old Ralphie,' without anyone suspecting Ralph Richardson of harbouring carnal desires for his own sex. No man, alive or dead, has ever claimed to have slept with Larry, though the kiss-and-tell merchants of the female sex have tumbled over themselves to boast of a night or two, here or there.

And no man ever wrote the graphic kind of letters which used to arrive weekly from two extravagantly amorous ladies, and which we would read in bed over our breakfast trays. There was the older woman who believed that they were spiritually destined for each other, but informed him that spiritual fulfilment could only be achieved by indulging in a kind of acrobatic physical union, which she described in detail. Then there was the young actress who offered herself tied to the bedposts or whatever, and was equally imaginative in her descriptions of desired scenarios which they could act out together. It was stirring stuff, even at breakfast. But then the older woman turned up at the theatre when he was playing, and shouted at him from the dress circle. And the young actress turned up on his doorstep, clad only in a raincoat, which she dropped to the floor and then stood, naked and tearful, protesting her love for him. That sudden escalation in the pursuit was not as amusing as the letters had been, but it certainly added spice to life. And after all, half the women in the world had fallen in love with him as Heathcliff, or Henry V, or even Richard III, so it was hardly surprising.

In his autobiography Larry thanked collectively those ladies who had been kind to him in an hour of need at some time or other during his life. He had no more to say than that about any of them and neither have I. I have never felt the need to be judgemental about sex between consenting adults. But it is unnecessary and irresponsible to leave falsehoods to posterity. In Larry's case it merely draws red herrings across the trail of an already very complex man.

It was my son Richard who encouraged me to read Rainer Maria Rilke, his favourite poet. And I discovered Rilke's deeply felt, thought-provoking, forward-looking and beautifully expressed concepts of love and marriage in his *Letters to a Young Poet*. For me they have never been bettered.

Thirteen
....

Life Continues at the National

I had been away from the theatre for eighteen months, pregnant for nine of them and then recovering from the difficult birth of our third child, Julie-Kate. It was on 27 July 1966 that our beautiful daughter was born by Caesarean operation. She had fought a fierce battle to survive after complications which might have carried off a lesser spirit and she weighed only four and a half pounds. When she was put into my arms, briefly, her little face looked like an angry red apple. She was rushed off to the Children's Hospital in Brighton to be put into an incubator for a few days; and my only news of her came from Larry who visited her daily. I was not recovering properly from the Caesarean, and there was much concern about the possible reasons, and speculation about another operation. And then a sweet West Indian doctor, who came from the Children's Hospital to talk to me about Julie-Kate, formed his own opinion of my malaise. 'She's lying there staring at all those telegrams and flowers in the room – but there's no baby,' he told them. 'We must get the baby back here as soon as possible and let her look after it herself.' Two days later it was judged safe to bring Julie-Kate to me and we both began to regain our health and strength together.

Three days later I received another letter from Vivien:

July 1966

Dear Joan,

I am so glad you have been able to overcome the many difficulties and congratulate you on your latest arrival – I hope you can find it within yourself to answer this letter in your hand as you once did – a long time ago.

Yours sincerely,
Vivien Olivier

I had no recollection of the letter from 'a long time ago' but of course I wrote back immediately to thank her for her kindness.

The rest of that year I remained absorbed in my children's lives and knew nothing until much later of Bill Gaskill's letter and the invitation to play Masha at the Royal Court.

Royal Court Theatre   *23 November 1966*

Dear Larry,

I thought I should tell you that I went to see Lord Goodman yesterday with some of our Committee. We talked very informally about our repertory and whether the Arts Council had had any objection to our entering the classical field. Goodman was very reassuring about this and, as you probably know, is very much for more revivals of Shakespeare in particular. I asked him quite frankly about Three Sisters *and he didn't seem at all worried about the possibility of two productions and said that it was never the Arts Council's business to dictate repertory . . .*

Even so, I must ask you whether you do still plan to go ahead with your production. I have scheduled ours for late February. My main reason for asking is, if there is any chance of your dropping the idea, I would still very much like Joan to come and play Masha for us and, if you decide not to do it, it would be a pity for her to lose the opportunity . . .

Love,
Bill

In an extract from his reply, Larry wrote:

I must tell you that I have no choice but to go forward definitely with my production of The Three Sisters. *This at the moment looks like being in July.*

I am awfully sorry of course to disappoint you about Joanie, but as you know she has been very seriously ill and I am most anxious that she should have sufficient getting better time. The date of your opening would be just about the time that she must rehearse for us here, in fact a little before this date if possible, and it is, I am afraid, too much to expect of her health that she should be required to play Masha every night for four weeks while she was rehearsing something else.

Gaskill's invitation had been very tempting to me; I would have loved to have gone back and continued my association with the Royal Court. It would have alleviated some of the burden I carried as the 'Director's Wife' at the National. Larry, however, was adamant that I should wait and do it with him. We finally started rehearsing it in May 1967.

In the weeks preceding rehearsals he had begun to seem more worried and preoccupied than usual; and I was being woken three or four times in the night when he left our bed to change wringing-wet nightshirts. He feared that something might be wrong but was reluctant to go and find out. We had begun rehearsing *Three Sisters*, a play that we both loved passionately and which he had long wanted to direct, and he couldn't bear the thought of anything interfering with the work.

I finally persuaded him to have some tests and we were both rocked back on our heels by the news that he had prostate cancer. We rallied after the initial shock and kept each other afloat with optimistic determination to beat it. He took advice on available treatments and finally opted to go as a guinea pig for hyperbaric oxygen irradiation at St Thomas's Hospital. He took odd days off from rehearsals to go for the treatments, which obviously left him feeling very low; and I grew more and more anxious about his depleted strength. Glen Byam Shaw, who had directed him in Strindberg's *The Dance of Death*, offered to come in and take over rehearsals if need be.

We were in the final week before opening, when Larry woke me one night in Brighton, breathing with great difficulty, and asked me to get the doctor. By early morning, we were in the car on our way to St Thomas's where they had been warned that he had contracted pneumonia. It was a journey I shall never forget. He would suddenly gasp instructions to the driver to take a certain turning and drive through a small village or past a church or the windmills we had visited with the children. I realized that he was envisaging it as a possible last journey and I wanted to take him into my arms and tell him to stop it; but I knew I must respect his need to do it, and just smile and keep saying, 'Yes, darling, I remember.'

As we were nearing St Thomas's, he suddenly directed the driver to go to the nearby Old Vic. There was hardly anybody about in the theatre at that time in the morning, but Larry said he wanted to see whoever was there. Harry, the theatre care-taker, rounded up a small band of carpenters, electricians, and someone from the props department, and Larry shook hands with each of them and thanked them for their work. They could see that he was very ill and all of them looked frightened to death, and Harry kept whispering over my shoulder, 'You must get him out of here.' Between us we managed to persuade him back to the car, and thence to the hospital. At St Thomas's they were ready and waiting, and were wonderfully comforting and reassuring. I could at last let flow the tears I had been holding back all through that panicky journey. The next inev-itable step was the breaking of the news to everyone at the theatre, and subsequently the rest of the world. He would not be able to perform as announced, for the next booking period, and the public had to know the reason why.

Rehearsals that day for *The Three Sisters* were charged with a special emotion. We all knew that the best thing we could do for him, and for ourselves, was to try and make his production as near to perfection as possible. The escape from reality afforded by work on a great play is a blessing that all actors acknowledge and embrace with gratitude. The age-old injunction to 'leave your troubles at the stage door' is a harsh, but beneficial discipline, when there are only three days to go before opening night.

No one at the National wanted the responsibility of chairing the necessary press conference, which had been arranged for that evening. As I came out of rehearsal they asked me if I would do it. I was given various nervous instructions to keep it 'contained', 'don't give out too much', 'keep it optimistic' and a final whispered order: 'Don't sit in Larry's chair or it'll look as if you're taking over.' The conference was in Larry's office and it was crammed full of press.

'They told me not to sit in Larry's chair,' I said as I went in, 'but there doesn't seem to be anywhere else.' And I took my place behind his desk. They were kind and sympathetic but there were questions they had to ask. I was too tired to hedge and circumvent. I simply told them the truth, which turned out to be the best thing to do. In return they reported it without sensationalism and I received the following letter, which I sent to my father, knowing how much it would please him.

Daily Express   *3 July 1967*

Dear Miss Plowright,

I would like to send you lots of luck for tonight's opening. Many of us in Fleet Street will be cheering for you and willing it all to be an extra-special success.

If I might add this: your handling of us newspapermen that Tuesday evening when you talked to us was superb. In all my experience I had honestly never witnessed a press conference conducted with such courage and such sense. It was both moving and impressive.

With every good wish,
Yours sincerely,
John Crueseman

After the illness had been announced, Vivien had been kind enough to send me a sweet card showing her concern.

June 20

You must forgive me writing to you, Joan, but of course you are constantly in my mind and I send you my sympathy, and, if you will accept it, my fond thoughts – Take courage, which I'm sure you have,

    Ever,
    Vivien

That opening night was bound to have a more personal significance than any other, as Ronald Bryden wrote in the *Observer*: 'The end of Chekhov's *Three Sisters* is always moving, but last Tuesday at the Old Vic it seemed specially so. For the first time, with their director in hospital and only one actor over forty in a major role, Sir Laurence Olivier's young ensemble had brought off a complex, full-scale world masterpiece. The take-off for which we'd waited four years had arrived. The National company was of age, standing alone.'

There was Robert Stephens as Masha's lover, the philosophizing philanderer Vershinin; Anthony Hopkins as her brother, Andrei, with his early promise and ultimate regret for a life of wasted intelligence; Derek Jacobi as Tusenbach, who loses his life fighting a pointless duel for love of the youngest sister, Louise Purnell's Irina. All of us that night were imbued with such a heightened sympathy for the men and women we were playing; for their discovery that life may not turn out for the best, that men and women can sometime wreck their own chances, and that 'happiness may last a summer, but work lasts till death.' When Bryden said of my Masha, 'It is a performance well beyond anything she has given so far,' it was perhaps to do with life imitating art (or vice versa) or simply that I had grown up with a vengeance in the last three years.

Immediately after the first night, Robert Stephens and I, and some of the other actors, went to Larry's hospital room with bottles of champagne to celebrate what was happily a very successful opening. And with his iron will and lion's courage, my husband was soon on his feet again.

But it soon became clear that there were difficulties ahead.

Carlton Tower Place, London SW1   *7 July 1967*

The Viscount Chandos, DSO, MC

PERSONAL

Dear Joan,

As you may imagine, Larry and his health are never long out of my mind, and I am simply delighted that he appears to be going on well.

For obvious reasons, I am very loath to bother him at this moment with any problems about the future. That is why I am writing to you, as I said I should, when I was in any difficulty in the National Theatre.

These are the facts:

(1) Larry's contract runs out next summer, and we should like to renew it, with any 'get-out' clause which he likes to suggest. We, of course, do not want any powers on our side to terminate.

(2) I recall a conversation, when Larry first accepted the job, when he said that he must have two Associate Directors. At the present moment he has none.

I am haunted by what has happened to Anthony Quayle, and others at Stratford, and now by the pretty serious illness of Peter Hall – although he has much more assistance on the artistic side than Larry . . . let me know what you think.

It was a malign fate which prevented me from being at the first night *of* The Three Sisters. *It seems to me a tremendous feather in Larry's cap, and the notices are marvellous. I am straining at the leash to come and see it, and you would blush if you had heard what everybody has said about your own performance. I am getting positively alarmed about the unbroken series of successes.

Yours ever
Oliver

Chandos needn't have worried; there was a bumpy ride ahead, which was caused mainly by the mounting of an all-male *As You Like It.* It was to have been directed by John Dexter who came into conflict with Larry about his ideas for the production.

There was an unholy row and, much to my sorrow, Dexter left the National for New York, where he was to become Artistic Director of the Metropolitan Opera.

Dexter and William Gaskill had been the two brilliant associates with whom Larry had begun his reign at the National. When George Devine declined the offer to join Larry there, he did the next best thing and gave him two of his most prized directors. Together, they made a formidable trio. Gaskill had left however in July 1965 to become Devine's successor at the Royal Court. As Larry said, 'The Lord giveth, and the Lord taketh away.' Now Dexter was going, and they were both to be sorely missed. The ultimately successful *As You Like It* was sent on tour abroad, taking most of the leading actors with it. And instead of the careful planning of the first seasons, there was an ad-hoc, hit-and-miss repertoire ahead, influenced mainly, it must be said, by Ken Tynan.

He and Martin Esslin (Head of BBC Radio Drama) had been members of an international jury that had awarded first prize to a new play, *The Advertisement* by Natalia Ginzburg. Esslin asked me to record the play for the BBC, and Tynan suggested it for the National; they planned for the broadcast and the opening night at the theatre to take place simultaneously. A double whammy, they thought. It needed only one supporting male actor and offered a virtuoso role for the leading actress. After I read it, I was dubious about its suitability for the National, and asked if I could send it to Gaskill as a possible new play to do at the Royal Court. Everyone was furious at the suggestion. 'Why should my discoveries go to the Royal Court?' fumed Tynan. And Larry felt that my leaving the National to go back to the Court would somehow reflect very badly on him. Neither of them paid any heed to my nervousness about hogging the stage in a huge leading part shortly after I had complained in various press articles about the shortage of parts for women. I didn't read the notices but the publisher Hamish Hamilton obviously did:

Hamilton Terrace, London NW8   *25 September 1968*

Dear Joan,

I hate that little bearded bastard, Irving Wardle, more than ever today. The evening was a triumph, not only for you personally, but also for the play which will have a huge success. So I hope you've had enough experience of the bloody critics to shrug them off now . . .

Many congratulations and much love to you both.

Jamie

Well . . . it wasn't all that much of a success; and most critics complained that it was on at the wrong place.

The bumpy ride continued with Larry running things by himself until Frank Dunlop came on board as Associate Director and founder of The Young Vic. He would be responsible for several successful productions and help with the administration, but much of his energy ultimately had to go into running The Young Vic. By 1970 the National was on a winning streak again but, in the interim, problems of a personal and professional nature were still a cause for concern. I am reminded of some of them by a snippet of news in the *Daily Mail* this morning, 17 March 2000, that caused me a certain amount of wry amusement.

Former editor of the Sunday Times *Harold Evans, seventy-one, calls from New York to discuss his wedding night nineteen years ago. Friends say he spent it in the bar of the Algonquin Hotel, New York, with foreign correspondent Murray Sayle, while his wife, Tina Brown, forty-six, editor of* Talk *magazine, flew to London. But Mr Evans says: 'I woke in the Algonquin next morning alongside Tina, not Murray Sayle. Murray is not very good about times. We had drinks the following day. I'd like it on the record because the papers here repeat everything you say.'*

It took me back some thirty years to a time when Mr Evans was on the other side of the fence. It was during his tenure as Editor that the *Sunday Times* printed extracts from a gossipy book about Larry, written by Virginia Fairweather, an ex-member of staff whom he had been compelled to replace. It was the sort of unpleasant 'through-the-keyhole' stuff that could be ignored if it appeared in a more down-market tabloid; but many people were outraged to find the *Sunday Times* stooping so low. Larry was naturally upset by it but seemed wearily resigned to the fact that disappointed people would wreak their vengeance upon him. Not yet used to living life in a goldfish bowl, I was more indignant on his behalf. The detailed descriptions of our house, our bedroom and his-and-hers bathroom, which we had designed together with such love and enjoyment, were now exposed to public view and I felt it was an unwarranted violation of our privacy. Larry was now living quite a modest life of enormous responsibility and dedication to the National Theatre, with a young family in the background. It was not the stuff of gossip columns and I felt it was unfair of Evans to subject him to that sort of treatment.

On the Monday following I attended a meeting of the Arts Council Drama Panel, whose chairman happened to be J. W. Lambert, Literary Editor of Mr Evans' paper. Sensing the atmosphere in the room, he felt obliged to open the meeting with a kind of apology: 'I would just like to say that I am not responsible for everything that is printed in the *Sunday Times*.' As Larry and I had talked of writing to the Editor to put certain things 'on the record', I asked Mr Lambert if I could quote him. Naturally he said he would rather I didn't so I respected his wishes. By Tuesday, Larry said he felt self-conscious about making a protest on his own behalf: 'There is no sound so hollow as that of an actor trying to justify himself.' When I offered to do it for him, he suggested that I ask brother David (then Managing Director of Granada TV and who knew and liked Evans) what, if anything, we should do. David said that I should write and let him know how we felt, but keep it cool. I sent off my letter and was invited to a meeting in the Editor's office. I don't know what I expected to come of it, and as I neared the *Times* building, the phrase 'fools rush in' kept reverberating in my head. But I was still fired with what I felt was righteous indignation, and it carried me through the group of grinning employees on the ground floor.

Harry Evans put on a wonderful show. There was a lot of 'mea culpa' and pleading guilty, though asking for certain mitigating circumstances to be taken into consideration. It was apparently a desperate, last minute, substitution. The article intended for that page (something to do with tobacco manufacturers) was almost on the presses when it was judged to be extremely libellous and the extract from the book was all they had. He fetched in two or three of his staff to confess that they, too, had found it most distasteful and thought it should not have been published in their newspaper. It was all so democratic and honourably honest that the wind was taken right out of my sails. Totally at a loss, I found myself thanking them all profusely before I left; but I've no idea as to whether or not they all burst out laughing the minute the door had closed behind me.

Perhaps they didn't. We have now grown so used to the dishonesty and callousness of *most* of the press that it is difficult to remember a time when standards were higher, and honesty, integrity and a strict regard for the truth prevailed. Of course there was still plenty of gossip to be enjoyed, and unsubstantiated rumours, but you knew where to find them then; they were not indistinguishable from news reporting, as they are today.

We were further provoked when our children's school asked if they should acquire Mrs Fairweather's offending book for their library. Extracts from it having been published in the *Sunday Times*, they assumed, erroneously, that it was, as it claimed, an authentic record of Larry and the National Theatre at work.

I felt a sudden twinge of sympathy for Lord Chandos who had fought so hard to prevent the play *Soldiers* by Hochhuth from being presented at the National Theatre. It imputed certain actions to Winston Churchill during the Second World War and concerned the death of the Polish leader, Sikorski. No evidence could be produced to suggest that the accusations had any truth behind them; it was 'theatre of supposition' only. The play was championed by Tynan and Dexter, and though Larry disliked it, he became embroiled in fierce rows with Chandos and the Board on matters of principle and what amounted to censorship. The Board, however, were not preventing it from being shown elsewhere; they were simply adamant that it should not go on at the National Theatre. Chandos's argument that 'whatever was printed in *The Times*, or put on at the National Theatre was presumed both here and abroad to have been sanctioned by all the authorities concerned' fell on deaf ears.

In chastened mood I wrote to him after our similar, if much more trivial, experience. Though we appeared to be poles apart politically, I liked and respected him; he had proved to be a staunch friend in need, and his enthusiasm and dedication to the National Theatre was boundless. I ended my letter with: 'It is Foulweather that blows nobody any good,' and added a postscript: 'As a penance I absolve you from attending a performance of *Rites*. There are things coming up which you will personally enjoy more!' *Rites* was a new play by Maureen Duffy, a modern and riveting reworking of Euripides' *The Bacchae*, which I had directed in a short Writers' Workshop Season at the Jeannetta Cochrane Theatre. And, with *Macrune's Guevara*, directed by Robert Stephens, *Rites* had transferred to the Old Vic. It starred Geraldine McEwan in a frighteningly funny and powerful performance and was set uncompromisingly in the ladies' lavatory at Charing Cross Station.

His reply was as follows:

18 June 1969

Dear Joan,
    Thank you for your very amusing letter.

I think you are right in supposing that people do weigh the written word – generally in profound ignorance of the issues which are raised. This leads them to think that what is in a respectable newspaper, especially The Times, *is as near the truth as can be found.*

The dangers of the 'documentary', theatre are still greater, because in stage productions, devices are often employed to give verisimilitude. The actor who played Winston in Soldiers *gave a sort of Bransby Williams imitation of him; make-up as near as possible like him, slurred speech, cigar, etc., etc.*

I think it is sad that the dead have no redress against libel and slander. I don't think the enormity of the false evidence against Winston, and the rest of his colleagues, is yet quite realized.

Thank you for your absolution about Rites. *As a miserable sinner, I shall see if I can't go, although, as I said to Arnold Goodman, 'Scene: A Forest Glade' is perhaps more suitable for an old square, or rather cube such as*

Yours ever
Oliver

My part of the Workshop Season had included plays by Margaret Drabble, Shena Mackay and Gillian Freeman, as well as Maureen Duffy. The motive behind it was to try and encourage more women to write for the theatre, and to provide parts for the younger actresses like Jane Lapotaire and Anna Carteret who didn't have enough to do. There are usually around ten good parts for men in a classical drama, and not more than three for women. And there is only so much you can learn from watching the leading players.

It was an enlightening experience for me to go round and discuss the ideas with Drabble and Mackay at home. Both writers had to conduct a conversation about the project in pauses between the feeding or restraining of energetic small children who whooped and shrieked and clambered over us on the sofas. I suppose they somehow found time to write at night and I was full of admiration for their acceptance of the limits imposed on the nurturing of their talent.

The four one-act plays made for a fascinating evening and were much enjoyed, though they were not received with a great deal of enthusiasm by male critics. And the writers returned to their novels and didn't write for the theatre again.

Fourteen

Ingmar Bergman and *Hedda*

After a patchy two years of trial and error Tynan redeemed himself with the suggestion that Ingmar Bergman be invited to direct his own celebrated version of *Hedda Gabler* with the company, including Maggie Smith, Robert Stephens and Jeremy Brett. He agreed to come, after a lunch with Larry, and the theatre was abuzz with excitement. His films were greatly admired and everyone wanted to know how he worked and what he did to draw such searing performances from his actors. Larry had been told that everything was in hand to welcome his arrival but in the event Ingmar made a some what cataclysmic entry into our life during one weekend in May 1970.

We were due to attend a concert given by Daniel Barenboim and Jacqueline du Pré at the Brighton Festival and were looking forward to meeting them again. Only two days previously we had watched them battling with an officious British Railways conductor over the safety and well-being of Miss du Pré's very precious cello. Barenboim had purchased a first-class ticket for the cello and it was nestling beside them in the carriage, doing nobody any harm, when the official demanded that it should be removed forthwith and dumped in the luggage van.

After a successful but contentious struggle with officialdom, we had agreed to meet in more harmonious surroundings on Sunday night; but urgent phone calls from London requesting Larry's presence put an end to that reunion. Ingmar Bergman had arrived and expressed unqualified disapproval of his hotel accommodation near London's bustling Oxford Street. He was now threatening to return to Sweden.

Extremely sensitive to noise and newly arrived from the peace of his remote island home, he was appalled at the bedlam around him in London. He was moved immediately to another hotel, which pleased him no better; his control snapped and he started throwing chairs at the wall.

Cancelling our seats for the first night of the Comédie Française at the Aldwych on Monday night, we moved Ingmar into our flat in Roebuck House. He arrived with his designer, Mago, and as Larry poured the drinks, I opened the sliding glass doors to show Ingmar the balcony. Putting his hand under my elbow, he moved me out onto it and, without preamble, said how traumatic it must be to have become 'a lady of the Establishment' after being a rebel at the Royal Court. I tried to deny the trauma and claim that I didn't consider myself to be part of the Establishment, but he was clearly genuinely intrigued by the situation and went on delving for some time. I had the feeling that he was waiting for me to admit that I could be standing on quicksand. Nobody I have ever met in my life has asked me such deeply personal questions after only ten minutes' acquaintance. Afterwards I realized that to him it was simply a natural way of behaving with actors, and it made me long to work with him one day.

I showed him his room; cleared our desk for him to resume work on an important film script, which the invitation to direct *Hedda* had interrupted; gave him a small dinner party, and then left to join Larry at a dress rehearsal of *Back to Methuselah* at the Old Vic. (Another emergency call!)

In the rush of the evening, I had neglected to tell Ingmar that our rather ancient little Irish housekeeper, Christy, lived in, and would also be sleeping in the flat.

It had become difficult over the years for Christy to lift her chin very far from her chest, owing to curvature of the spine and a pronounced dowager's hump; she was very round, and very short and spoke with a delightful Irish accent, which was fairly unintelligible except to the initiated. Larry had inherited her from Roger Furse, the designer, who had gone to live on a Greek island. She dwelt quietly in the kitchen when there were people about, venturing out occasionally to offer a little sustenance if she thought it might be needed.

But Ingmar had no idea that she was there. Under the impression that he was alone, he had settled down to his writing at the desk, when she materialized unexpectedly to ask if he would like 'a cuppa and a bit of bread and butter'. Startled, and uncomprehending, he had tried to dismiss her from the flat, and from his mind.

Two hours later she had re-emerged, with a bread knife in her hand, to enquire cryptically if she could make him a 'jam omelette', her favourite offering. To Ingmar's bemused mind she seemed, at midnight, to have taken on all the dark imagery and menace of a Norwegian troll; and he admitted later that he had been genuinely frightened by the knife into believing that she had some malignant purpose in mind. He had fled to his bedroom and tried to lock the door. As the key did not seem to fit the lock, he became increasingly apprehensive that dark forces were at work; and when I rang just after midnight (12.15 a.m.) to say that we had missed the last train to Brighton and would have to return for the night, he was a nervous wreck, muttering, 'Thank God, thank God, thank God,' incoherently on the phone.

Christy had naturally gone to bed after Ingmar appeared to have retired for the night, however hastily; and it was Ingmar himself who welcomed us thankfully at the door. He was in a state of intense agitation and confessed that if 'she' had re-appeared again before we had got back, he might easily have leapt off the sixteenth-floor balcony.

We soothed and comforted; I explained that Christy was the dearest, most wonderful creature in the world; but that I would remove her next day and get a butler if that was what he wished. Grateful for company and needing to wind down, he began asking us probing questions about our personal relationship, in work and in life; whether we were jealous of each other; whether we took holidays together or separately; all the while looking piercingly at us, each in turn, as though intent on catching us out if we told lies. Reticently English, we murmured and stammered and evaded, unused to such uninhibited soul-baring; we were also very tired. He confided to us his own and Liv Ullman's difficulties and gave us the unwelcome news that if she arrived, as she might, in London the next day, he would have to leave the country immediately. I made some camomile tea to calm our nerves, and, for the first time that evening, the two men came much closer together when the conversation suddenly evolved into a discussion on the subject of guilt. Both, they discovered, had been brought up by clergymen, and they spoke intimately of childhood terrors and of how they had carried their guilt into adult life.

When we parted for the night, I promised to be up at seven in the morning to eat breakfast with Ingmar and guard him from Christy; but as it was already 3 a.m., I naturally overslept. Rushing out in a dressing gown at 8.30 a.m., I found him, also in dressing gown, eating his yoghurt, at peace with the world, declaring that he had a 'very good relationship with Christy' and would have no one but her to look after him.

As was his custom Larry attended the first rehearsal of *Hedda*. Knowing the problems which would be encountered as regards lighting etc. in the Cambridge Theatre, he insisted on giving practical advice and moving the furniture about.

'Furniture is not to me important,' Ingmar demurred. 'Furniture is not going to speak.' Next day he ordered the door to be locked for his rehearsals, and with a gentle smile said to Maggie Smith, 'Sir L. does not love *Hedda*, Sir L. loves the furniture.'

His rehearsal hours were from 11 a.m. to 3.30 p.m. with no smoking allowed, doors locked and no lunch break, though people could bring their own food if needed. Rehearsals were conducted at such a concentrated pitch of nervous energy that both he and his actors were exhausted by 3.30 p.m. The company were at his feet with admiration for the detailed insight he gave them into their characters; Maggie Smith said that he was the only director she had worked with so far who really understood women.

Knowing his favourite relaxation was listening to classical music we had invited him to Brighton for the weekend, with the treat of a Barenboim and Arthur Rubinstein concert. He had accepted. When I met him after rehearsal on Friday he looked pale and distressed, and asked if we could go back to the flat to talk. He spoke of inner ear trouble, which caused him to lose balance, both physically and mentally, if he did too much; he had to have regular hours and rests and not too much company for too much time. He was trying gently and haltingly to withdraw from a weekend which he knew had been planned for his benefit, but which, after a week of intensive rehearsal, he could no longer face. He admitted that he was nervous of telling his troubles to Larry who was so 'vital – so much life force'. (Three years later Larry would suffer the same inner ear condition.) I ordered food for the weekend, told Christy to look after him at the flat and everyone else to leave him alone.

By Monday he was totally recovered, apologized for 'being a nuisance' and said he was grateful for our understanding. He showed a generous interest in other work at the National Theatre, watching *The Three Sisters* on film because he had been bowled over by the previous Chekhov play, *Uncle Vanya*, and giving unstinting praise. I was playing Rosaline in *Love's Labour's Lost* during his *Hedda* rehearsals and he came to see it with Garson Kanin and Ruth Gordon, who were staying with us overnight; he seemed delighted with it, describing it as 'warm, and sensual, with much elegance'. Then, after a pause, he said, 'I should not say it is a boring play.' Garson, Ruth and I spent a lot of time trying to decipher that remark.

He seemed surprised that we had done two shows that day; such a thing was not allowed by the Actors' Guild in Sweden. He was equally surprised that we were not prepared to cancel three sold-out performances of *The Merchant of Venice* at the

Cambridge Theatre, when he encountered dress rehearsal problems with *Hedda Gabler*. But he left us with a hypnotic production, which added to the National Theatre's prestige and ensured full houses at the Cambridge Theatre, in tandem with *The Merchant*, for many weeks.

Fifteen

Jonathan Miller and *The Merchant*

The Merchant of Venice had cropped up from time to time in planning meetings over the last five years, usually, I presume, because it was one of the few Shakespeares not announced by the Royal Shakespeare Company.

An intermittent pushing and shoving by Tynan about Larry's Shylock had met with little enthusiasm. Even when Tynan tried public persuasion by courtesy of the *Daily Telegraph*, and expounded his own conception of Olivier's Shylock as a sort of Greek shipping owner like Onassis, Larry's response was limited to a few ribald comments in our bathroom.

Neither of us, even then, realized the depth of Ken's ambition to direct in the theatre. Though he later admitted to me a passionate desire to direct *King Lear*, I only learnt after his death that he had secretly nursed those ambitions throughout his years at the National Theatre. Undaunted by Larry's lack of interest, Ken shifted gear and started telling me that I should play Portia. Suspecting that I was being used as bait to tempt Larry to change his mind, I said I wasn't interested and the matter was dropped.

It finally surfaced again when efforts were being made to entice another actor of Larry's calibre and authority into the company. Shylock was to be used as bait, together with a Peter Shaffer play in the offing, though unfinished, called *The Battle of Shrivings*. It was hoped that Alec Guinness or Paul Scofield might like to have a go at it, and tentative negotiations were begun. With the possibility of another actor as Shylock, I felt in more positive mood about Portia.

Playing opposite my husband was something I had determined to avoid during the first years of the National Theatre. It is perfectly acceptable for a married couple to star opposite each other in the commercial theatre, but unwise in a government-subsidised company, where the husband is also the Artistic Director. It opens the door to hidden resentment, and accusatory remarks about nepotism and 'the actor-manager and his wife'. Perhaps I was also mindful of George Devine's stern injunction some nine years earlier: 'Marry him if you must, but don't act with him too often, or he will destroy you.'

Safe in the knowledge that Alec Guinness was now considering Shylock, I was blissfully unaware of the possibility of any such danger, and began my research into past productions and Portias, alighting in the process on James Agate's disenchantment, expressed in his book *Brief Chronicles*: 'I feel about Portia's pleadings, subterfuges, and skittishness as Mr Bennet did about Mary's singing – "That will do extremely well, child. You have delighted us long enough." ' He then makes the point about 'the wholesale miscarriage of the moral in this play, in which Shakespeare asks us to condemn Jewish spleen, which has reason behind it, and applaud Christian malignity, which has none.'

One weekend in Brighton I had a conversation with Rosemary Harris, a close friend and great actress, who was about to play Portia for Ellis Rabb, her then husband, and his company in New York. We shared our feeling that the play was difficult to mount nowadays with any degree of credibility unless, perhaps, its setting were to be moved to another period, and Portia could be presented as a highly intelligent woman rebelling against the restrictions of life in a gilded cage.

Encouraged by several glasses of wine, we threw caution, tradition and Shakespeare's poetry to the winds and made out a case against her for our own amusement. She is, we decided, maliciously arrogant in her remarks about her suitors, and positively racist when referring to the dark–skinned Morocco's failure: 'Let all of his complexion choose me so.' Though madly in love with Bassanio, we continued, she is fully aware of his homosexual relationship with Antonio, but clever enough to accept that if she can't beat them, she will join them. 'You are welcome notwithstanding,' she says finally to Antonio when he is still hanging about the house at the end.

She can be quite nasty, we agreed, when flaunting her financial superiority over Bassanio: 'Since you are dear bought, I will love you dear.' She is also quite vengeful in the besting of Shylock, calling him 'an alien', seizing all his goods, forcing him to his knees in public and finally divesting him of his birthright and religion. Then, flushed with success, and bereft of any of that quality of mercy she has urged on other people, she looks around, twinkling-eyed, for another victim to sharpen her wits on. Skilfully defrauding Bassanio of the ring she bade him never to part with, she sets off merrily to Belmont, looking forward to another session of baiting, outwitting and thoroughly discomforting the male sex. It was, we decided, her revenge on her father for landing her with that unforgivable lottery for her destiny.

Larry was interested and amused by our complaints and told Tynan about the discussion. He seized on it immediately with great enthusiasm and suggested Jonathan Miller as possible director. Jonathan had just done rather revolutionary productions of the classics at Nottingham and had the advantage of being Jewish 'but not going the whole hog'.

Larry and I met him for dinner; it was not easy at first as both men were remembering Jonathan's uncomplimentary, and published, remarks about Larry's Othello. That was balanced by Larry not having liked Jonathan's *The Seagull*, which we discussed politely. As we began to throw ideas around, Jonathan leapt ahead of us and began talking at breakneck speed about the emergence of the Rothschild dynasty two centuries before.

He threw in a brief lecture on Disraeli, some pertinent reminiscences about his grandfather, and, as we were soon to leave for Ischia, gave us the *Confessions of Zeno* as holiday reading.

A lunch was arranged with Alec Guinness before we went away, to see how he felt about such a new kind of production. Larry had to leave early for a rehearsal, so it was Ken Tynan and I who talked with Alec and gave him the gist of the ideas under discussion.

In the interim, before Jonathan had officially accepted the offer, I had a letter from Ken Tynan which ought to have made me recognize how much he wanted to be a director.

Dear Joan,

I think I may be going mad, but bear with me a minute.

Portia is 'a rich heiress', living with a companion. She can't have been at Belmont all that long, or somebody would have chosen the right casket. What is her background? Why doesn't she seem to know anybody (except Bassanio)? Where does she come from?

I think her father was an American millionaire, from one of the Western states. (He may even have made his money mining lead.) He brought his daughter up to be virginal, tough-minded and thrifty. He sent her to Bryn Mawr, where she majored in Law. But: he did not teach her anything about sex or men. They travelled in Europe during his later years and after his death she decided to settle there.

Like so many American heiresses, then and now, she falls for the first Italian adventurer she meets. Her book-learning is no use at all when she looks at Bassanio and inwardly melts. She feels alien to these sophisticated Europeans – even to the upper-class Englishman Falconbridge, whom she can't understand because of his impenetrable Etonian accent (she even mimics it when she says 'he understands not me, nor I him').

In this world, less intellectual than hers, but infinitely more experienced, she is, indeed, as she confesses, 'an unlesson'd girl, unschool'd, unpractis'd'. With her wide eyes wide open, she seizes a man who represents all that her daddy would have hated – one of those scented goddamned dagos – perhaps partly because Daddy would have hated him.

I'm not suggesting a broad Yankee accent, of course. All you'd need is the faintest hint of a Kate Hepburn twang. And perhaps an old American sampler on the wall and one or two other touches in the set to suggest that the girl who's taken Belmont for the summer is an American.

Tell me if I'm dotty.

Meanwhile, love,

Ken

'Oh my goodness,' I thought; it's a difficult enough task already playing Portia at Britain's National Theatre, without risking wholesale slaughter by turning her into an American. Lively ideas, though, and perfectly possible for an American production with Miss Hepburn herself in the role.

Meanwhile Alec, having thought it over, decided against it.

Dear Joan,

Here is the Butler book on the Sonnets, sent with my admiration and affection, and apologies that I shall not be your Shylock. (I am writing to Larry at the same time.)

I think all your ideas are lively and worthwhile, but I have just reread the play and hate it. I cannot throw off schoolboy associations, with shades of Henry Baynton as a sort of Holman-Hunt sinister Light of the World Shylock . . .

It could well be, and fascinatingly, a director's piece – but that doesn't interest me as a performer.

Sorry to disappoint you.

Love,

Alec

And thus Larry, who had been surreptitiously looking at portraits of Disraeli and the Rothschild dynasty, stepped into the breach and said he would play Shylock. And thus I, who had been officially engaged to play Portia with someone else, had to push George Devine's grim admonition to the back of my mind and just get on with it.

Notes in Rehearsal from my Diary

Jonathan gave a brilliant opening discourse and rehearsals had begun in March with all contributions from actors gratefully received. There had been talk of one actor playing all three suitors, Bassanio, Morocco and Arragon, an idea culled from the source story from which Shakespeare took his plot; but it was soon abandoned.

Jonathan also suggested that Portia could just (though remotely) be connected to the Dark Lady of the Sonnets who came between Shakespeare and his friend or, in this case, Antonio and Bassanio. In the source story the Antonio figure is the young man's godfather; so we all think that if Shakespeare had intended Antonio to be paternal in feeling, he could easily have made him Bassanio's godfather. He didn't, so it's another kind of love, we say. Jonathan talks about Portia and Bassanio and their entourage as a sort of jet set or, to be more precise, the Jackie Kennedy set.

We have an idea about starting with Portia in bed and reluctant to get up to meet the next batch of suitors. One look at Julia Trevelyan Oman's set makes that impossible, so we substitute looking at their photographs . . .

The trial scene is instantly exciting and consistent in conception, and is one solid thing to hold onto. Everybody understands their function in it and it only needs to be run through for timing, reactions and confidence to grow.

But other scenes are still in a state of flux. Charlie Kay wavers between a cloak-twirling bullfighter and a senile old prince as Arragon; Tom Baker tries a kind of Peter Sellers Morocco, which works hilariously for two days, then people stop laughing; so he goes for a more fiery, pseudo-civilized, Oxford-educated Moor type.

Portia and Bassanio caused difficulties for Jeremy Brett and me; are they equally and truly in love? Is it just that they would make a 'nice pair', each able to lead their own lives? How do we cope with the change in Jonathan's satirical version of the casket scene from farce, or high camp, to a deeply felt and poetic love scene? We finally agree that Portia herself can send up the first two suitors, and deliberately engage the two wicked singing ladies to relieve her own boredom; but we also agree that she takes Bassanio's scene in deadly earnest, for she is deliriously in love for the first time in her life.

Julia and Jonathan have come up with the idea of Portia in a riding habit for the casket scene. It suggests that she's taken Bassanio riding to delay his choice of the casket and because she looks good (and sexy) on a horse, also because the Amazonian women of that time wore similar costumes, not to mention the emergence of the first cycling lady, Mrs Bloomer. It identifies Portia with the women trying to free themselves from the prison of ultra-delicate femininity in dress and in life; and it seems a logical lead into the man's disguise she adopts in the trial scene.

Jonathan goes on talking vaguely about Jackie Kennedy, until I suggest, quite mildly, that perhaps he ought to get her in to play it. He smiles and promises not to mention it again as we both agree that she would be the last woman in the world to fall in love with a penniless man.

My own Portia is beginning to take shape in my mind and I have moved away from those cynical ideas first expressed in Brighton. Now I see her as rueful and wry, ironic and provocative, and prone to ecstasy when she falls helplessly in love. She cannot hide her intelligence and wit, however much it is expected of her, and sometimes it just leaps out and it hurts. It is given full rein in the trial scene where I wanted her to be totally disguised as a young man, dark hair (Portia is blonde), brown face and all. But there is no time to change wig, costume and make-up back into Portia for the last scene. Shakespeare's plays, like T. S. Eliot's humankind, cannot stand too much reality. So I had to make do with just the hair.

Jonathan encourages this Portia who will later be described by one critic as a 'Henry James heroine' and who will remind Sir Kenneth Clark of Edith Wharton.

Even Tynan has come round to it, though he would prefer a bit more bite at the end:

In the last scene, by the way, she seems to have recovered her balance a little. She's almost the old mocking Portia of her first appearance. Perhaps from now on this is how she will treat him – as her intellectual inferior, the butt of her jokes. Perhaps she will reserve her ecstasies for the bedroom – and punish him in public for thus abasing her.

Love,

Ken

Devine's warning has disappeared from my mind; I am enjoying acting with Larry, though it has to be said that in these roles, we are not so much playing opposite each other as against each other!

He, in the meantime, has acquired an extraordinary accent, an alarming set of false teeth and is experimenting with a nose. Jonathan begs him to stop. They had quite a tussle for some days, and things were a bit difficult at home, as I adored working with Jonathan, but knew that Larry was resenting his criticism. (He came round finally to Jonathan's way of thinking, and with gratitude, as he has acknowledged in his book *On Acting*).

Jonathan comes up with a disturbing idea about Jessica and Lorenzo. Taking us through their famous love scene – 'The moon shines bright: in such a night as this, When the sweet wind did gently kiss the trees . . .' – he informs us that each one of the great love affairs quoted ended in disaster.

He decides to end his production with Lorenzo going into the house arm in arm with his Christian chums to party, whilst Jessica is left alone outside with Shylock's letter in her hand. It is a radical departure from the usual fairytale ending, and provides a poignant reminder of the ruined Shylock, who normally disappears from the play in Act IV.

The resulting production was described by a colleague and great actor, Paul Scofield, in a letter after we had opened.

My dear Larry,

How difficult it is in dressing rooms – to make genuine excitement sound different from ordinary politeness without giving too much of a performance.

So I feel I didn't really express my sense of the uniqueness of last night's performance – from the production, from you and from Joan – the entire evening.

It looked beautiful. I loved the sets and costumes – the women all looked lovely, the pace and rhythm of the performance was breathtaking and I just didn't notice the passages I usually find unendurable (in this play, I mean). Your own conception was astonishing (you always manage to surprise). Shylock was someone we knew and had talked to (Monty Berman?), both commonplace and with dignity – but pathetic and dangerous and all so light and subtle – like a sky changing so fast that you only just have time to imprint the shapes of the clouds on your mind's eye.

Joan is 'formidable' (with a French accent) – in the first place her Portia is very endearing which is no mean achievement, she is needle-sharp accurate in her wit, she has a beautifully serious authority in the Trial Scene. I think it's the balance of comedy and high seriousness performed with complete originality that she brings off so impeccably. And she used her eyes and her backbone so marvellously!

Please forgive all this – but really I felt so happy to be in the business –

I meant to congratulate you last night on your new honour – and then forgot. Please accept congratulations now – it's theatrical history and most exciting and deserved.

Much love to you both from us both,
Paul

It is to Miller's credit that the buzz that surrounded his production ensured that it continued to play to full houses, despite Larry's sudden disappearance from the cast when he became ill.

Sixteen

Difficult Phase at the National

Larry had been becoming more and more overtaxed and was also worrying about the new building with its three theatres to fill (subsequently the Olivier, the Lyttelton, and the Cottesloe).

The cold war, which had existed between him and Lord Chandos since the Hochhuth debacle, was proving most unhelpful to discussions and planning for the new theatre. I was sent back and forth between their offices as an intermediary until Lord Goodman came to the rescue with an invitation to meet on neutral ground at his flat. Either deliberately or accidentally, Arnold Goodman himself was late; so that when we arrived, Chandos was sitting alone, sipping a sherry that had been provided by the butler. In an atmosphere of icy politeness we chose our drinks, commenting on the quality of Arnold's sherry and the impressive paintings on his walls. Then we got down to business as Arnold arrived to give his usual dispassionate advice.

Larry asked for two more house directors as well as Frank Dunlop, and a Consultant Advisory Committee to deal with the move into the new theatres. Chandos agreed to one more house director but refused another £5000 for a second one because, as he said, 'After all, you've got Joan.'

Arnold interposed with the quiet and knowledgeable statement: 'Joan may have a life of her own she wants to lead.'

Chandos looked taken aback; the idea had obviously never occurred to him, and Larry looked a little flushed. I had recently asked for leave of absence to do a West End play for H. M. Tennent, which he had violently opposed, shouting a lot in the bathroom and threatening to resign if I left him to carry on at the National by himself.

'Irving could never have done it without Bram Stoker,' he had yelled, frothing at the mouth with an excess of toothpaste. Not being as well versed as my husband in the story of Henry Irving's life, I had no idea of the part played in it by Mr Stoker; but it was not hard to guess that he had been very supportive. I was aware only that when I had set out with such passion on my journey as an actress, it was not with the intention of becoming somebody's Bram Stoker, however eminent and much-beloved that Somebody might be. I think I may have said this in the bathroom with some spirit, as a diary entry leads me to believe that we weren't on speaking terms the next day.

It was probably his remorse about keeping me from other work which caused him to make unsuitable suggestions about my appointment as an Associate. I told him often enough that it was not a wise move. I could go on helping as I had done from the beginning – in the way Peggy Ashcroft's advice was sought by George Devine at the Court, and later by Peter Hall when she was at Stratford. But I also had three young children who needed my time and energy and would sometimes have to take precedence over my work at the theatre. I had my own private word with Chandos to make quite clear the fact that I considered my position difficult enough as an actress in the company, without adding the burden of any official status.

I had suggested at the time that it would be more appropriate to ask Robert Stephens to be an Associate Director. He was liked and respected by the company, and he and Maggie had become a successful, and popular, acting couple, as well as an invaluable draw at the box office. It seemed only fair that they should be included in the artistic planning for the company. After all, I always knew what was going on, through Larry, and because meetings were often conducted in Brighton. Robert had been duly appointed in 1969; but after they eventually married in 1967, when Maggie was pregnant with their first child, they had left the National for two years to pursue film careers. Maggie was to win an Oscar for her performance as Miss Jean Brodie, but Robert was not so lucky with the film, *The Private Life of Sherlock Holmes*. He suffered a breakdown at the end of shooting and was taken to hospital. When he recovered they were both welcomed back to the National to star successfully in *The Beaux' Stratagem* and *Hedda Gabler*; but the balance between them was altered and some difficulties in the marriage became apparent. Robert seemed under great pressure to establish a firmer ground for his own formidable talents, and his behaviour became somewhat erratic.

All this added to Larry's other problems. I knew that I was the only one he really trusted, and that he desperately needed such a confidante. At the same time I suspected that the threat to resign if I left cloaked a deeper fear that he had lost his own passion for the job. And that added to my growing disquiet about his health and state of mind. All his life he had been single-mindedly prepared to do anything he really wanted to do, with or without any particular wife in attendance. But his great sense of duty still prevailed, plus the understandable desire to lead the company into the new building before he retired.

Ultimately, the decision as to whether to go or to stay was taken out of my hands. There had been a reconciliation with John Dexter in the summer, which made us all very happy, and he was returning to the National to direct Thomas Heywood's *A Woman Killed with Kindness*, a play of his own choice. He stated firmly that he would only do it with either Vanessa Redgrave or me as Anne Frankford. As I was still holding onto the possibility of the West End play at that time, I wrote off forthwith to Vanessa to tell her that Larry would be writing to her with the official offer. Owing to Vanessa's extraordinarily busy life, the letter took a long time to reach her. And by then Larry was suddenly in hospital again, having had to leave the successful *Merchant of Venice* production which had been playing to packed houses since April. She wrote to me at the National:

18 September 1970

Dear Joan,

I was amazed and so very sorry to read in the papers of Larry's illness. I do hope he is feeling better.

It would be lovely to meet you again and see your lovely children; I thoroughly enjoyed the evening we spent with you and the strange Weissburgers. I had no idea of their history, and thought that Mrs Weissburger was Arnold's wife. This gave some of their conversation a very surreal flavour.

I'm sorry I have been such a time answering Larry's sweet letter about A Woman Killed with Kindness. *I think the play is very strange and very nice, and would love to play Anne. I would also very much like a chance to work with John properly.*

The main problem is that I am fixed up until the end of May. I wonder when you were thinking of putting the play on. Would you let me know. Anyway, I was very pleased to get Larry's letter, and please thank him for me properly.

Yours,

Vanessa

Unfortunately, Dexter's production was planned to open in March 1971; and so with Vanessa unavailable and Larry not well again, I abandoned the idea of leaving the company for the present, and agreed to stay for *A Woman Killed with Kindness* opposite Anthony Hopkins.

I was still playing in *The Merchant of Venice*, though now without Larry as Shylock, and was grateful when it came out of the repertory for four weeks, and I could join him at home for a much-needed break.

Seventeen

Nyerere and the Burtons

On 29 September 1970 Larry called a press conference to say that doctors had advised him not to act for twelve months though he would still be running the theatre.

Then we both went off to a health farm to recuperate for two weeks, and discovered how unwise it is to embark on fasting or a strict diet when you are sharing. Our breakfast tray supported two small plates, one with five grapes on it and one with four. A great deal of self-sacrifice was called for: 'You have it', and 'No, no, you have it'; and the thought that lunch and dinner times might cause similar anguish almost made us move into separate rooms.

We came back to find we had been invited by Prime Minister Edward Heath to dine at Chequers with President Nyerere and his Foreign Minister from Tanzania.

We were dreadfully late arriving because of the usual British Railways Sunday delays and a disapproving lady in Wrens uniform told us they had all gone into dinner ten minutes before. I had taken the precaution of looking up Julius Nyerere in *Who's Who*, so we were forearmed with the knowledge that among other accomplishments, he had actually translated *Julius Caesar* into Swahili blank verse. I found myself seated next to his Foreign Minister, who had played Brutus in the same play and who was as delighted as I was relieved to be able to discuss theatre all night instead of politics.

We had a marvellous time; and Larry's presentation to

President Nyerere of his own marked copy from his first school production of *Julius Caesar* went down very well.

Those sorts of occasions were looked upon as very welcome perks in a job which was becoming daily more burdensome because of anxiety about the future and the obvious need to find and appoint Larry's eventual successor.

On Saturday, 17 October, I played two shows of *The Merchant of Venice*, which had reopened in London with Robert Lang as Shylock, and was met unexpectedly at Brighton Station by Richard Burton's uniformed chauffeur. He informed me that Sir Laurence was awaiting me in a limousine outside. As we approached the car, my husband, always courteous and gentlemanly, but tonight having drunk more than he should, opened the door unsteadily to greet me, and then fell out onto the pavement. The discreet and quick-witted chauffeur scooped him up deftly, and had him back in the car, with the door shut, before any of the curious onlookers had time to recognize who it was. Chafing at having to stay at home while the rest of us were acting, he had leapt at an unexpected invitation to dine with Burton and Elizabeth Taylor who were consoling themselves at their Brighton hotel after an unrewarding experience of their own. They had journeyed to Rottingdean to visit Enid Bagnold, author of Elizabeth's first success, *National Velvet*, under the mistaken impression that they would be spending the evening with her. They found her drowsily under the influence of her own brand of comfort, though making gallant efforts to show interest and entertain them; and they left discreetly at 7.30 p.m. when she fell sound asleep on the sofa.

Back at the Metropole Hotel, Larry joined the Burtons for an evening's carouse and reminiscence during which he suggested that Richard should take his career more seriously and follow him to the National Theatre.

Throughout his early life, Burton had often been hailed as the 'next Olivier' and, despite their divergent paths since those days, Larry still believed in the possibility that his talent and charisma could be harnessed and trained to occupy a position of leadership in the theatre. He was still obsessed with the desire to find an actor to succeed him, rather than an 'academic'.

It was generally conceded, in the first few years, that the National was known as an 'actors' theatre', and the Royal Shakespeare Company as a 'director's theatre'. Both provided some evenings of great excitement but the atmosphere in each was very different; Larry wanted the National to remain an actors' theatre.

The Burtons came to have dinner with us at home the next night; he complaining of a hangover and asking only for tomato juice, and she in a silk trouser suit with scarves wrapped round her neck, which together with her back, was causing her some pain; but both very warm and friendly and sweet to the children. We were joined shortly by André Previn and Mia Farrow, whom I had invited in all innocence the previous week for a relaxing Sunday dinner; not being gifted with second sight, I could not have foreseen that it was going to be transformed into something of a battleground.

There were kisses and reunions all round as they had not seen each other since Mia was married to Frank Sinatra; and we went into dinner talking of other things, in carefree mood.

Between the soup and the fish Richard asked me if I would stay on and help him, as I had helped Larry, if he took over the National Theatre. There was a moment of silence at the table. The Previns looked astonished, as well they might; Larry looked startled, as though aware that things must have gone further the previous night than he had intended (or could remember); and I was left wondering how to explain that it wasn't all going to be as easy as that.

I began in a roundabout, and hopefully humorous, fashion by pointing out what a huge difference it would make to their present lifestyle. Their magnificent yacht was e'en now moored on the Thames at Tower Bridge, the cynosure of all eyes.

Elizabeth was staunchly prepared to give up all luxuries if it would help Richard, and he was most anxious to find out how we thought the rest of the profession would react to the idea. It seemed the moment to explain as gently as possible that the rest of the profession would have very little to do with it; that the theatre was subsidised by the government; that its directorship was a Board appointment; and that names would have to be submitted to them, vetted, probably put on a shortlist and finally rejected if the Board had their own man in mind.

There was a distinct feeling of coldness in the air, and Elizabeth got quite cross with Larry for not telling them that the job was not his to give away.

Upstairs in the bedroom where we ladies retired to break up the tension, she continued to defend her man and chastise mine for his thoughtlessness; she would not allow Richard to face the possibility of rejection: 'He has a very fragile ego,' she said. I have no idea how the men fared in the dining room, though with André to help, who is both wise and witty at such times, I knew they would come to no harm.

When we came down again, they were back in the drawing room where we found Richard in full flow, declaiming his favourite passages from the Bible. André was looking very appreciative, but Larry, I'm afraid, was not. He never enjoyed being upstaged in his own drawing room.

Elizabeth recovered the friendliness that she had arrived with, and we all finished the evening determined to enjoy it, the way actors do after a bad first night. On the way out the Burtons paused in the hall to await the arrival of their armed bodyguard, and were confronted by an old biscuit tin with a jagged slit in the lid and bearing a hurriedly painted label appealing for funds for Oxfam. I had never seen it before and immediately suspected mischief from behind the nursery door. Richard felt obliged to make a generous contribution though he was as suspicious of the tin as I was. Next morning I confronted my own small Richard who had apparently told his sister that the money would come in very handy for extra fireworks; they wouldn't miss it, he had protested, they're very rich – I mean, didn't he buy her that huge diamond?

Metropole   *18 October 1970*

Dear Larry and Joan,

Thank you for an enchanting evening and for your enchanting children and all that stuff but for heaven's sakes there I was going along quite happily until you put terrible ideas into my head (I mean Larry, Joan, not you) and also getting me sloshed two days in a row. We loved your house and Elizabeth adored Joan and so do I and even Mia has changed into a totally different creature since she has come together with André – a very different lady from Mrs Sinatra. We are just about to go off to Hampstead on the Belle and Elizabeth wants to buy the whole of Brighton – which I will try to arrange – so that you can get me sloshed again and again.

Much love from us both,
Richard

Some weeks later Burton wrote again from their yacht, moored in the port of Cavtat, in Dalmatia, Yugoslavia, where he was playing Tito in a film.

Bugger of a thing to do because tho' it's all right to play your occasional 'great man' it's a bit odd to know that he can have a look at the rushes and if displeased have me sent to the tin mines or something. E and I see a lot of him – he has taken a tremendous fancy to the old girl – and he remembers your appearance in Belgrade with admiration. In fact I think we are the only two actors whose names he knows. Despite his seventy-nine years he is as bright as a button and seems, most unusually for a dictator, to be universally adored.

Anent your letter: I had written you a longish letter a longish time ago – asking you to drop any idea of my doing the job. [The letter was lost.] *I had said that I didn't think I had the administrative ability and certainly not the experience and apart from anything else that you were a hard man to follow. In addition to which (and this is strictly confidential) I had overnight as 'twere become pretty deeply involved with the OUDS. You may remember that E and I had made a film of Marlowe's* Faustus *some years ago with the students at the university. Well, though we think* it a goodish film the public wasn't overanxious to see it. We therefore considered it a dead loss and felt terrible as half the loot was to go to Oxford. But suddenly, starting about the middle of last year some clever little man asked if he could sell it in his own way. He showed it only in small cinemas around college campuses and the funny little thing started and continues to make money. In short, Oxford have so far received £150,000. One of the conditions of such a gift was that a Chair of Drama be established at Oxford and a proper theatre built.

Within a few years something should happen there, something concrete I mean, and by that time I think E and I will be ready to come home. In that case I will, if I'm still alive and enthusiastic, have a great deal to do with the form of theatre to be set up but not, repeat not, the enormous responsibility that you have at the National.

In addition, though I am perfectly content to do the odd film and the occasional play and write belles-lettres for E's amusement she is adamant that I must go back to the theatre again, making that the main thing and doing films now and again. And despite protesting a great deal I must confess that there is an intermittent ache in the gums and tremble in the stomach to have a bash again. The bloody woman will drive me to it yet.

Finally, dear old heart, I have always felt, perhaps mistakenly, that my true forte if anything is teaching. I rather fancy myself as one of those Bellocian Dons with a lovely old house and being offensively oracular.

Thank you again milord Larry. E sends special love to you both and those adorable children.

As so do I.

Richard.

Such plans . . . such lovely plans . . . Six years later when I went to Toronto to act opposite Richard in the film of *Equus*, he and Elizabeth were divorced, and Suzy Hunt was the new woman in his life.

Eighteen

More Difficulties at the National

In November 1970 there occurred what Gaskill later described as a palace revolution, caused by the jostling and scrambling for more power that was going on during Larry's recuperative period. As he was debarred from performing, the actors too grew restless and were missing 'that little touch of Larry in the night'. A meeting was held from which I was naturally excluded, and which was apparently instigated by Robert Stephens; it caused some sort of rift in the company. A letter was composed by those who agreed to attend, concerning the difficulties apparent in the administration and asking for reassurance about the future. I presume it was intended for the National Theatre Board. Unfortunately the contents were leaked to the *Evening Standard* (by whom nobody knew) and extracts from the letter appeared in the paper the following day.

'DIFFICULT PHASE AT THE NT' was the headline.

Uproar and consternation followed when the *Sunday Telegraph* took it up, and suggested that Peter Hall and John Clements had been sounded out as possible successors.

Between shows on Saturday, 7 November, Anthony Nicholls, Tom Baker and Robert Lang, representatives of the Liaison Committee, had come to my room, aghast at the consequences of their efforts, and saying that they had actually been trying to help Larry! They asked if they should write to the *Standard* and I suggested that they ignore it, but was touched by their stated intention of writing to the Board, pledging faith, loyalty and trust in their director. Then came the telegram to Larry from another actor in the company, Kenneth Mackintosh:

I WAS SICKENED BY THE STANDARD. THE FAITH, LOVE AND RESPECT OF YOUR FRIENDS OF THE COMPANY ARE IN FACT DEEPENED DURING YOUR ILLNESS.

This seemed to indicate that not everyone could be called a 'friend'. Binkie Beaumont of Tennents, who was also on the National Theatre Board, rang to say that the Board would issue a statement immediately, refuting everything. Then Maggie Smith rang to ask if she could help as she had been a party to the offending letter; I asked her if she would be around with John Dexter at Brighton where I was to be interviewed by Sydney Edwards of the *Standard*, who was a friend and wanted to help.

The three of us presented a united front at lunch: Larry's wife, a supposedly embattled rival actress and an ace director who had been sacked for 'differences' but was coming back to direct at the National. Sydney wrote a warm and witty article about us, and the National in general; everyone felt that harmony had been restored and that, for the time being, the crisis had passed. Maggie and John and I talked into the night about our lives, our marriages, the theatre, how we had all started and where we had all first met. John and I had shared the excitement and steady employment of the Royal Court years; but Maggie had jumped about from revue to straight play, from West End comedy to the Old Vic, and had been discovered and rediscovered more times than she cared to remember. She envied me my more settled life and, para-doxically, I envied her her freedom.

She and Robert were due to leave the company again to appear in *Design for Living* at the Ahmanson Theater in Los Angeles, which would earn them much more money, always a necessity when you have a family. But I knew she was troubled about the future from a personal point of view. Two weeks previously she had come to my dressing room at the theatre with a strange request. It was the afternoon of the National Theatre Board Meeting, which Robert would be attending (and so, of course, would Larry). She asked me to tell Larry not to take any notice of anything Robert might say at that meeting. I learnt later that he had taken the opportunity to seek the Board's approval of his desire to play *Antony and Cleopatra* with Maggie for the new season, early the following year. It was not really a matter for the Board and caused a certain amount of embarrassment. Larry and his other Associates were taken by surprise, as they knew the commitment to Los Angeles was definite, and Maggie had given no indication of when, or indeed whether, she would be returning.

We never mentioned it that night at Brighton; little bouts of madness on the part of husbands (or indeed wives) were to be expected considering the kind of frantic life we were all leading; they were to be dealt with as effectively as possible, and not 'gone on about' to other people. I said they would be much missed and she said she was genuinely sorry to be leaving at a time when they were obviously most needed. And so they left us after a triumphant year and were destined by circumstance not to return.

We gave a huge party at Christmas to cheer everybody up, imbued with such heady feelings of peace and goodwill that we even invited John Osborne. New Year's Eve had to be spent without Larry. He was off to make a bit of money for a week in a Sam Spiegel film. I put him on the Golden Arrow train at 10.30 a.m. and we indulged in one of those movie farewells, him leaning out of the window and me walking along, holding his hand, until we were forced to let go.

It was the first time we had been apart on that particular evening since we were married, not that we ever made a ceremony of it; we usually spent it in bed with a bottle of champagne, watching those wonderfully silly Scots on the TV.

*   *   *

It is Monday, 7 August 2000. At breakfast time this morning it was announced that Sir Alec Guinness had died yesterday; and by teatime we had been told that the broadcaster, Sir Robin Day, had followed him. Maggie Smith and I shared our feelings of great sadness on the phone, and agreed with Noël Coward that we were getting to that stage where, 'One is grateful if one's friends last through lunch.'

Sir Alec was one of the greatest actors of the twentieth century, much loved and much admired, and his death came as a shock to us all.

I played Viola to his Malvolio in a TV film of *Twelfth Night* directed by John Dexter in 1970. He was a brilliant Malvolio, fastidious, supercilious and vain, with a steely disdain for the rowdy Sir Toby Belch and his cronies. When he confronted Olivia in the ridiculous garb that he believed she had requested, he was hysterically funny and more than a little sad; and he endured Malvolio's final humiliation with a touching dignity. I wish I had seen him play it on the stage; Shakespeare is notoriously difficult to transfer to the small screen. It was a starry cast, boasting Ralph Richardson as an exceedingly eccentric Sir Toby Belch, and Tommy Steele plus guitar as Feste; but the acting was a mixture of styles which didn't always gel. However, we were in the hands of Sir Lew, later Lord, Grade who, when told apologetically that one actress was more suitable to Noël Coward than to Shakespeare, replied, 'Thank God. They'll understand that better in Wisconsin.' I played both Viola and her twin brother, Sebastian, which is only possible on the screen with trick photography. In the theatre two actors are necessary as they appear on stage together. I deepened my voice for Sebastian, which worked for some people and was criticized by others, but on the whole we were accounted a success.

Commercial TV was on the downward slope even then as regards highbrow entertainment and *The Times* notice began: 'ATV's television version of *Twelfth Night*, pushed away to the fag-end of Sunday's programmes to minimize the danger it might do to the ratings, had much to commend it.' The film went onto video, however, and Christopher Hampton told me twenty years later that his daughter was studying the play with that video for A levels at her school.

A diary entry, written after the 1970 General Election and before the Shakespeare play was transmitted, reads:

The election is over and Twelfth Night *will soon be over. I class them together as both are shows which were sneaked in during the summer in the hope that not too many people would take much notice. But critical reactions to a play are mercifully short-lived whereas reactions to the Labour Party defeat will go on and on. There was George Brown defeated and robbed of his constituency; the Harold Wilsons leaving Number 10 ignominiously by the back door; the indefatigable Jennie Lee, our Minister of Arts, also booted out like George Brown. It doesn't take long for actors to get going again after a flop, but it may take a few years for politicians to get back into office.*

It was Harold Wilson who had invited Larry to accept a peerage in 1970 and Lord Goodman who went on with the persuasion when Larry seemed reluctant. But Wilson was not to be there on 24 March 1971, when Baron Olivier of Brighton was introduced to the House of Lords. Family and friends and august personages like Lord Mountbatten gathered to watch the ceremony and afterwards to enjoy a splendid lunch.

Lady Hartwell put into words what we all felt; and added her sweet compliments about our two small daughters.

Cowley Street, London SW1   *25 March 1971*

Darling Joan – and Larry,
    We want to express our heartfelt gratitude for the unforgettable – in fact historic – lunch and ceremony which we were both thrilled to be at and deeply touched to be invited to. However proud we have often felt of Larry in the past, at the conclusion of a great performance – we have never felt more proud than yesterday, as we watched him receiving the rightful and fitting accolade for his greatness.

It was truly marvellous and unforgettable and we do thank you both so much for letting us be there.

Much love from us both,

Pam

P.S. *We couldn't get over the beauty of those two girls – you* must *have them painted or drawn.*

I was always amazed by Larry's willpower and ability to absorb suffering and overcome difficulties, and still maintain an exuberant spirit with his plans for the future. We began 1971 with good news. Paul Scofield had delighted everybody by agreeing to join the National Theatre and would make a very successful debut in *The Captain of Köpenick*. It was the kind of boost the company needed and everyone seemed in very good spirits, though there were rumblings underneath of discord to come in the future.

I went into rehearsal with Anthony Hopkins for John Dexter's production of *A Woman Killed with Kindness*. John had the stimulating and sometimes disconcerting habit of making his cast watch their understudies perform the play. He would have rehearsed them meticulously and he allowed a deal of personal freedom within the set framework of his production. It could be quite an eye-opener to watch scenes done completely differently, sometimes catching a mood or nuances which we, the principals, had missed. Derek Jacobi and Louise Purnell were surprised one afternoon to find that their rather strait-laced, sub-plot characters had been turned into an hilarious double act by an oddly assorted, inventive couple who, at that run-through, stole the play.

On the night of our dress rehearsal, Ken Tynan, who usually attended them and gave perceptive though quirky notes, was absent for some reason from this one. Tony Hopkins came back afterwards for supper with Larry and me, and asked if Ken had been in as he wanted to know his reaction. Larry was caught off-guard and said, brusquely, 'He's probably as far away as he can get, he can smell a flop a mile off.' It was so uncharacteristically tactless, on the night before we were due to open, and in the event it was to prove a wrong forecast, but it left Tony feeling very unnerved and me quite perturbed. It also effectively demolished Dexter and Tynan in one sentence and exposed his feelings of anger towards them. He had been involved in arguments with them about *Tyger*, the controversial musical play by Adrian Mitchell, which they championed and which he thoroughly disliked. Michael Blakemore had come in on their side and Larry felt that he had been coerced into giving in to a majority decision, and was now regretting it. In the event our production was highly praised and so was the acting; Larry controlled his feelings again, and joined in the celebrations.

I was much troubled as I knew now what he really felt and didn't look forward to the future. As I was not involved in *Tyger* and was busy acting in two other productions, I had neither the time nor the energy to concern myself much with judgement on it. I tried to see everybody's point of view and both sides of the argument. I was obviously under heavy fire at home as there is a quote in my diary (from Winston Churchill), which is deeply underlined: 'I do not resent criticism, even when, for the sake of emphasis, it parts for the time with reality.'

Paul Scofield had also agreed to do *Coriolanus* next, with Anthony Page as director – but, for reasons I was not privy to, they suddenly withdrew. As the play had been announced already, and booking leaflets had gone out, it was decided to keep *Coriolanus* in its appointed place in the repertoire – but it was to be an entirely different production.

Christopher Plummer, whom Larry much admired, had been wanting to join the company for some time, and Tynan had seen an exciting Berliner Ensemble version of the play by the two young directors who had succeeded Brecht, Manfred Wekwerth and Joachim Tenschert. They all agreed to come to the National and rehearsals began with everybody feeling very excited about the conjoining of East and West.

But difficulties were soon apparent between the directors

and their leading actor. The East Germans were used to being the boss, used to a disciplined ensemble rarely questioning their moves or motivation. Plummer was a Western civilization star, used to being consulted, treated with respect and having his own ideas about his part incorporated into the production. There was a final flare-up and an ultimatum was delivered by the Germans: 'Either he goes or we go.' They were perfectly willing to leave the already plotted production, the moves, the music and the lighting plot, for somebody else to put on the stage.

But they refused to work any longer with Plummer unless he (a) apologized for his defamatory remarks in front of the whole company, and (b) promised never to argue about anything in the future. It was an impossible situation; no actor of Plummer's stature could be expected to agree to such demands. Larry took it to the company. Should the directors go? Were they unreasonable or difficult to work with? Or should the leading actor go because he couldn't work with them? The majority decision was that the actor should be replaced; the company as a whole respected the East Germans' work and wanted to do the production with them.

A chaotic weekend followed where Christopher had to be asked as politely as possible to step down, and yet persuaded to stay for the other two parts he had agreed to play. He left us in suspense all through Saturday and Sunday morning, saying he would have to think it over. Then, at lunchtime, he rang to say that he would stay.

The only possible actor in the company to take over *Coriolanus* at such short notice was Anthony Hopkins. He had just started gaining recognition after a stunning understudy performance in Larry's part in *The Dance of Death*, and there was no one to touch him for promise and power. He accepted the role and went straight into rehearsals. That caused a further problem as *A Woman Killed with Kindness* was about to go on tour, and no one could be found to replace him.

Another chaotic weekend ensued, with huge reorganization

of the touring schedule, and we went out with *The Merchant of Venice* instead!

And so the great juggernaut went on rolling. In preparation for running two or possibly three theatres in the new building, it was decided to expand into the West End again; the repertoire was still successful despite all the problems and seemed to be wasted just playing at the Old Vic. So the National Theatre also took over the New Theatre for a season of three new productions, the first of which was a new adaptation of Pirandello's *The Rules of the Game* with Paul Scofield and me in the leading roles. Paul's subtlety, intelligence, passion and sardonic humour were wonderfully right for Pirandello, and rehearsals went along at a very enjoyable pace. I was not totally at ease, I confess, in the part of Silla, though I could get away with it from an audience's point of view. The critics proved a harder nut to crack, and though they found much to admire in the production and in Paul's performance, there were some reservations about mine. Ronald Bryden's notice, which began by saying that I had been cast against the grain, then continued: 'Still, it's a skilled and very funny performance ... Preening herself like a bridling osprey, fluttering huge lashes above a great crushed raspberry pout, she flounces through the part like Minnie Mouse imitating one of Bette Davis's sulkier temptresses, keeping the farcical half of the evening spiritedly afloat.'

I realized that I had allowed myself to be flattered into accepting the part despite the fact that, in my own estimation, I was not ideal casting. But Paul himself had joined in the general persuasion, and who could resist the chance to act with the great Scofield? During rehearsal one day, when I asked director Anthony Page if I had made the right choices in a scene, he sought encouragement from David Hare, who had done the translation and had come in to watch. David, who didn't wish to be rude, said apologetically that he couldn't really help because he hadn't envisaged it being played that way, meaning that he too thought I was miscast.

Next into the New Theatre was *Amphitryon 38* with

Geraldine McEwan and Plummer, and they fared not much better. *Danton's Death* with Plummer, directed by Jonathan Miller, followed and made a much better score; and the public were still supportive, despite the critics.

But the stretching of resources was not ultimately successful and those productions which would have played to full houses in the company's recognized home, the Old Vic, did not do so well in an unaccustomed repertoire system in the West End.

With the diminishing of the 'company ideal' (though it was perhaps inevitable), the National seemed to have lost the identity it had established so strongly in the first seven years. Larry had taken leave of absence for short periods in the year to make films, and I had come to the conclusion that my usefulness was at an end. I made the decision to leave and committed myself to Chichester for the following year's tenth anniversary season.

I needed for a while to be just an actress again; to be offered parts and accept or turn them down on their merits and my own desire to do them, instead of allowing myself to be persuaded into things because John Dexter needed an anchor in his cast, or Paul Scofield would rather have me than Vanessa Redgrave, whom I had suggested for *The Rules of the Game*. Larry's illnesses had taken their toll and his ideas about a possible successor had not proved acceptable. I remembered that when he first approached Richard Burton I expressed my doubts about the desirability of having another actor at the head of the organization. The problems of the administrative staff were doubled when the man who made the decisions was rehearsing an arduous and taxing role and could not be disturbed with urgent questions. It had been right for Larry because of his unique position in the theatre, powers of leadership and previous experience in an administrative capacity, but there was no actor alive who could match that record. He was about to become unapproachable again by taking on the role of James Tyrone in *Long Day's Journey into Night*, which would be hugely successful and bring him into closer contact with its director,

The Malthouse, after it had grown like Topsy, and, right, as it was before extensions.

Slaughtering the daffodils.

More scenes at the Malthouse, where the pool was much in evidence, and the goldfish pond proved a place for quieter reflection.

Old friends: left, Larry, with Ralph Richardson, and, below, watching Helen Montagu pouring champagne for John Osborne.

Maggie Smith and Beverley Cross: near neighbours and good friends.

Larry rehearsing *Othello* with Maggie Smith: 'He'll just go on at me about my vowels.'

Franco Zeffirelli rehearsing *Saturday, Sunday, Monday* with Frank Finlay and Larry (standing), me and Gawn Grainger sitting.

As the cover of *Theatre World* saw my St Joan in 1963; with Anthony Hopkins as Petruchio (top right) in *The Taming of the Shrew* – Queen Juliana of the Netherlands' least favourite play; as Hilde Wangel in a blonde wig with Larry as Solness in *The Master Builder* (lower left); and as Jennifer in *The Doctor's Dilemma* with John Neville – testing myself, perhaps, for Cleopatra?

As Arkadina with Helen Mirren as Nina in *The Seagull*; a none-too-smooth transfer to New York of another Eduardo de Filippo play. Below: La Poncia in *The House of Bernarda Alba*; and, as Edith Cavell.

As Lady Pitts, having had one too many in *Daphne Laureola*.

As Alma getting one of her headaches in *The Bed Before Yesterday*.

In *The Merchant of Venice* as Portia, and reminding Kenneth Clark of Edith Wharton, with, left, Jeremy Brett, and right, Derek Jacobi and Anna Carteret.

In *Way of the World* with Maggie Smith.

Michael Blakemore. Michael's name was then put forward as a possible successor, following Albert Finney and the Richards, Burton and Attenborough.

I had no idea that he had ever put *my* name forward, except perhaps in the context of a conversation about Brecht's widow, Helene Weigel, who ran the Berliner Ensemble after her husband's death. He had proposed it rather wistfully one day after I had attended a meeting when he was in hospital, and Kenneth Tynan had said, 'If anybody is to sit in Larry's chair, I suggest it should be Joan.' It was Tynan's way of preventing any of the Associates, Dunlop, Dexter or Blakemore (or even himself), from snatching the opportunity to look as though they were in charge of the proceedings. But Larry had rather approved the idea and quoted the example of Helene Weigel as someone who presided in her husband's name. I had, I thought, made quite clear my unequivocal rejection of the idea. I was in no way equipped and had no desire for such a position; nor was the Berliner Ensemble, created by Brecht to perform his own work, in any way comparable to the National Theatre. I put it down to the effects of illness and wishful thinking, and thought no more about it. I would be at Chichester when I next heard about it and I considered my defection from the National to be a sufficient disclaimer to the rumour. I could hardly say, 'He's at his wit's end and clutching at straws, and please don't take any notice,' which was what I felt, and which was why I knew that leaving the National had been the right thing to do. If I was acting at Chichester we could lead a more tranquil life at the Malthouse, see more of our children and, hopefully, Larry would be able to take a more objective view of his situation, and make the right decision.

I remembered how shocked and grieved we all were when George Devine died in 1965 at the much too early age of fifty-five. He had given so much of himself and his life's energy to the running of the Royal Court Theatre, and I was reminded of his words to me as I sat by his bedside in St George's Hospital: 'It's done for me and I'm not sure it's worth it. Don't let it happen to him. Get him out before it does it to him.'

There is a letter (undated) from John Dexter about the problems encountered during this time. He was taking a short holiday in his place in France, and as yet knew nothing of the names put forward as possible successors. But it describes his personal response to the changing face of the National and his uncertainty about the future.

St Vivien par Villereal, France   *Monday*

Dear Larry,

This letter is really for you and Joan, it might annoy but I hope not. It's a difficult letter to write and I don't want to dictate it to anyone. I need to clear my mind to old friends about work we have shared with some success in the past and in which we all believe. It is always awkward to talk to you directly, Larry, the eminence you have achieved entitles you to respect and a measure of obedience from all of us, and the problem of expressing views which diverge from yours without seeming divisive and disloyal has, in the last year, been more intense than I have ever known it. I told you once in a letter, Larry, that I wanted to see the National Theatre opened as you wanted it to be and that I had no ambition of power beyond that. This was, is, and always will be true. My arse does not fit the seats of the mighty, I like to work in close contact and trust with people with whom I can disagree and still trust and love. The trouble is I can neither trust nor love Ken or Michael. They represent the two poles of dryness and ambition with which I find it difficult to empathize and seem to me to regard the National as a means of self-expression and to be absolutely ruthless in pursuit of their own personal ambitions. For Michael there is an excuse. He has not yet had that degree of international success which he regards as needful to his peace of mind and well-being; I believe he looks to the National as a means of arriving at that end. The problem of the gadfly Kenneth has always been with us though I believe when you and I worked in conjunction with Bill, his impolitic politicking was kept in place. Now he seems to be playing a destructive power game to rules of his own devising. Of course I long for the days when you and Bill and I used to sit down and plan the schedule and our planning bore a close relationship to the humanities involved. Perhaps the organization has grown too big for this to be a valid work pattern, but a lot has gone from the atmosphere around the place. When I came back for Woman Killed *this was the first thing I felt, that expedience and survival had taken the place of close personal interaction . . . George Devine gave a training to both Gaskill and myself that bred a sense of duty and obligation. I am much more of a whore for worldly comfort than for power, Bill I think not at all, and for that reason is the best product of George's teaching.*

I don't like office work, or sitting in the canteen listening to company complaints; I do it because I believe it to be a major part of the work. Nursing the East Germans, or soothing ruffled thespian feathers, or keeping Tony sober, even hearing lines are all part of the function of an Associate and I have tried my best to operate full-time in that area. The reward is certainly not financial and can only come from feeling that one is a vital part of your organization. If you accept that all this is true, what on earth can I do to be useful, there's nothing I can change, the organization rolls on like a mighty juggernaut.

I write to you both as two people I love very much and from whom I seem to be drifting apart . . .

You don't both have to reply, but a few words from one of you will help.

Love always,
John (is it the 'change of life' perhaps?)

I wrote back to him, acknowledging that much of what he said was true, but that the problem of clashing personalities was too delicate to be dealt with in a letter. He knew that I had decided to leave the company for a while, but he himself would make the decision to stay when Larry's successor was ultimately announced.

Nineteen

Taking a Break

I went into 1972 playing Katharina in *The Taming of the Shrew*, happily reunited with Anthony Hopkins as Petruchio, and Jonathan Miller as director. Both of them had taken time off from the National to do other things, and we all rather relished the freedom of being away from the pressure. But as rehearsals progressed Tony seemed unable to escape a certain nervous pressure of his own. His rise to leading man status had been so swift, he knew that much was expected of him, and the responsibility of living up to all that lay heavily upon him.

Performances at Chichester began at 7.30 p.m. and I usually arrived around 5.30 to give myself plenty of time to prepare. One such evening, as I was beginning my make-up, Tony came into my dressing room, fully dressed, made up and ready to go on. I panicked, thinking I had mistaken the time, and after he had left, rang for the Wig Mistress to come immediately. 'What's the hurry?' she asked. When I told her about Tony, she said, 'Oh, don't worry about that, he's been ready and dressed since 3.30 this afternoon.' We had opened five nights previously to generally good notices, but he had been coming in at the same time every afternoon since the first night. He would wander on and off the stage, running through odd scenes by himself, and trying to calm his nervousness about the performance.

He came back with me one Saturday night to spend the weekend at the Malthouse and hopefully to relax a bit in the garden on Sunday. But as Larry was at work pruning his roses, Tony felt he ought to be doing something, and offered to mow the grass. He set about it in such obsessive fashion that when I took them both a drink, the sweat was pouring off his brow as he explained to me the need to keep the lines of mowing absolutely straight because he knew Larry was watching him. I tried to calm him down and say that Larry was completely absorbed in his roses and not paying any attention to the mowing; but I suppose I had forgotten the effect that just his presence could sometimes have on younger actors.

That night, after Larry had gone to bed, Tony and I stayed up talking, and he told me of his recurring nightmare about being an actor.

He comes onto the stage alone to begin a serious speech (as he was currently doing as Petruchio). He faces the audience who are completely silent and looking at him expectantly – he begins his speech and suddenly they start laughing at him – the laughter grows and grows until he is forced to turn tail and flee. 'I know they've found me out,' he said, 'that I'm nothing but a big con-trick.'

I told him of my actor's nightmare, which has afflicted some of my friends as well.

It is the first night of a performance, you have played Acts I and II – and suddenly you are shocked by the realization that you have no idea what the third act is about – you have never seen it, never mind rehearsed it. There is great panic as you rush around, trying to find a script or someone who can tell you what happens in it, so that you can at least improvise something when you have to go on stage. Of course, as it's a nightmare, you hurtle around in a vacuum; there is no one and no script to be found – and as you hear, 'Beginners, please,' the terror explodes and you wake up.

Peter Shaffer, who was keen on analysing dreams, described that one as being really to do with life, not a performance. By the time you've reached forty, the first two acts are more or less over, but what the third act of your life holds, nobody knows.

Tony was due to return to the National to play Macbeth later that year, but the nervous strain had by then reached such a pitch that he was obliged to withdraw from Michael Blakemore's production. I suspect that with his intuitive approach to acting, he felt freer and happier in films, though he would return to the stage in New York and at the National in brilliant form. But a successful film career would take first place and ultimately bring him the coveted Oscar for *Hannibal Lecter*.

I was to play Jennifer Dubedat in *The Doctor's Dilemma* for my second part at Chichester, opposite John Neville and Robin Phillips, both of whom had been with us in the opening season at Chichester in 1962. I had accepted the part as a trial run for some risk-taking I was contemplating – to see how I would be received in a sort of junior 'femme fatale' role. For two years I had been having the carrot of Cleopatra dangled in front of my nose by Jonathan Miller, Tynan and Dexter. When I refused the idea of doing it at the National for the obvious reason of not being, in my own reckoning, the first choice, Jonathan tried to persuade me to do it for him at the Mermaid Theatre. The head of that theatre, Lord Miles, gave me a splendid lunch and a lot of champagne, and claimed that it was his idea in the first place anyway. Buoyed up by all that masculine persuasion, I allowed the prospect to take hold in my mind, and set to work to create a physical look for Jennifer which might take people by surprise. With the help of make-up, beautiful William Morris dresses by Beatrice Dawson, a spectacular wig and rigorous dieting, the gamble appeared to have paid off. 'Astonishingly seductive,' wrote Milton Shulman in the *Evening Standard*, which, though not immensely flattering when you think about it, was certainly a step in the right direction. But what with one thing or another, I lost my nerve the following year and decided to leave it to Glenda.

Twenty

On Being English

A debate raged throughout the year 2000 on our national identity and what being 'English' means now in the twenty-first century. The following letter from John Dexter to Larry in 1972 shows that it has been going on for some considerable time.

The play *Tyger* mentioned by John was Adrian Mitchell's satirical extravaganza with music by Mike Westbrook (in which I was not involved), which was put on by the National Theatre in July 1971. As we have seen Larry disliked it. The Establishment and the government came under fire in it, and a member of the National Theatre Board was heard to say it was 'subversive through and through and left me white and shaking'. It was championed by Tynan, Dexter and Michael Blakemore, by the acting company who had enjoyed playing in it and by a very small band of critics.

St Vivien par Villereal, France

Dear Larry,

I have an idea I'd like to plant in your head. I would like to make a last gesture against the Common Market and do King John. *Wonderful parts for everyone; a perfect company play, and the way I see it, very timely.*

When we had that awful row near the end of Tyger *you asked why we didn't leave England if that's how we felt about it; the point is, I could never leave England and I realize that all my work in the last year has been a reflection of what I feel.* A Woman Killed with Kindness *and* A Good Natured Man *are in a tiny way attempts to remind people what it means to be English, at a time when we are on the edge of losing our national identity altogether.* Tyger *I responded to because it made demands and stated hopes for the future of England.* King John *is as appropriate for* now *as* Henry V *was when you made it; tho' I can't hope to emulate that gigantic originality of concept, I could hope to make* King John *as relevant at this time as* Henry V *was at invasion time. Living down here in the remnants of what was the first English colony to be lost, I am very aware of all the parallels.*

John's letter started me thinking in more personal terms about identity and Englishness. People have sometimes asked if I had any Italian or Spanish blood in my veins, particularly after I had appeared in two of Eduardo de Filippo's plays and Lorca's *The House of Bernarda Alba.* But I have always felt myself to be English to the core, though not in any way the traditional English rose. In his book *Mid Century Drama*, Laurence Kitchin wrote: 'It would seem ungracious, perhaps, to call her a female equivalent of Ralph Richardson although she is the only actress to possess that actor's ripe deliberation.' I didn't find it ungracious, just interesting that I should be compared to a man rather than a woman; and of course there was no one more essentially English than Sir Ralph. Unless of course it was Larry to whom Maggie Smith was once compared by New York's Vincent Canby for her 'elegant theatricality' in *The Prime of Miss Jean Brodie.* Strange that we should both be compared to men, and to those two particular men who managed to sustain a long friendship. Strange, too, to realize that in some ways our friendship mirrored theirs.

When Larry was elevated to the peerage and became a Lord, there was much rejoicing in the profession. But the very English tradition of rewarding achievement with titles can sometimes cause confusion both at home and abroad. The Russians honour their top performers by appointing them 'Peoples' Artist', which is simpler and much easier to comprehend. The titles of

Lord and Lady were somehow still associated in people's minds with courtiers attending on the Queen and belonging by right of birth to the aristocracy. In our case, this could make people who didn't know us, or the system, feel rather awkward in our company and sometimes uncertain as to how they should behave. I was introduced by my daughter's dancing teacher to her pianist, who dropped to the floor in a deep curtsey before I could prevent her, leaving me speechless and feeling a bit of a fraud. In America, before he became a Lord, Larry would find himself addressed as Sir Olivier, which would move later to Lord Laurence, and I progressed from Lady Laurence to Lady Plowright when I began to appear in more films, as though Lady had become a Christian name like Lady Bird Johnson's.

It was not that Larry didn't feel very proud and gratified to be so honoured, but there were certain times in the theatre when it made him uncomfortable. He couldn't bear the thought that, when he was due on stage, he might hear the stage manager's voice summoning him with the words, 'Your call please, Your Lordship.' So he told them to go on calling him Sir Laurence (Larry to his friends and colleagues), which he felt was more friendly and affectionate.

There was another kind of anxiety coupled with an actor's sense of loss, which he expressed in a letter to the *Sunday Times* drama critic, Harold Hobson.

Sunday, 27 June 1971

... Could you be very kind and leave out the 'Lord' when you refer to me in your column?

Should your reference be laudatory (not very much to be expected in view of recent record, I know), it would seem to make grandiose, and take the charm from such words. In the case of the reverse attitude, then it seems to add mockery to the words of blame, and sarcasm to severity.

This I feel is unfair in that I do not believe that this is your intention or that you think it is quite my desert.

The use of the surname only is always pleasing to the artist, suggesting as it does the accolade of the household word, but if you feel this not to be merited in my case, then it would be obliging of you to put my Christian name before it in the normal manner of programme or billing credit.

Please forgive this request.

Yours sincerely,

Larry Olivier

For my part I learnt to cope with the problem of having two identities. Though I remained known as Joan Plowright professionally, people would sometimes be worried that I might be offended to be addressed as Miss Plowright and thus deprived of my illustrious title. It was not a problem with friends and colleagues, who, as we had more or less grown up together, were apt to treat the whole thing with a certain amount of amusement. But there were times when I couldn't help wondering how appropriate it was to reward a lifetime of extraordinary achievement with the same title as that already held by some small boys in their cradle, and before their lives have proved to be of any consequence or not.

I don't know whether Larry had any prophetic dream about his elevation to the peerage, but according to the next letter he certainly did have an early vision of his future memorial service. And it was after that event took place in Westminster Abbey in 1989 that Toby Rowlands, theatre producer and long-time friend, wrote to me:

Millie and I want to thank you so very much for inviting us to your magnificent party. It was an exciting end to one of the most memorable days of my life.

I have so many happy memories of my association with you when our lives came together. I wrote my first theatrical fan letter to you after The Chairs. *The lovely holiday at Daphne and Sam's in Majorca with you and Roger. Parties at the Royal Crescent with you and Larry. How proud I was to be presenting* Saturday, Sunday, Monday *in the West End, and your courage and bravery when Larry became so ill . . . I thought the service was superb and grand and most moving. Larry would have respected and loved it all.*

A story I've never told you. Very early in my days in England, I was invited to dinner at Durham Cottage. I arrived too early. Vivien was still at the theatre and Larry was upstairs resting. I asked the maid not to disturb him, but she did. When he came down and I apologized he said, 'You didn't really disturb me. I wasn't sleeping. I was just lying down and thinking about my funeral: I could see the sun shining through the windows of the Abbey and I felt joyous.' He was only a Mr then and I thought to myself that he was being a bit pretentious. Of course he wasn't and about a quarter to one on Friday the sun did shine through the great rose window.

George Bernard Shaw's Saint Joan is the great part most English actresses want to play at some time in their career, but though it is wonderfully written, she is of course France's heroine, not ours. In 1982 I appeared in a biographical play about a truly English heroine, Edith Cavell, and the letter below came as a poignant reminder of that indomitable lady.

Imperial War Museum   *13 September 2000*

Dear Joan Plowright,

You might be interested to know that at 12.00 noon on Thursday 12 October the Belgian Ambassador is presenting us with the door number from Edith Cavell's prison cell, mess tins used by her and other material to mark the eighty-fifth anniversary of her execution.

If by any chance you happen to be free, it would give us great pleasure if you would be our guest of honour at the event, which will be followed by an informal buffet lunch. I very much hope that you will be able to join us.

With best wishes,
Yours sincerely,
Christopher Dowling

Her statue still stands in St Martin's Place (off Charing Cross Road), but I suspect her history has been largely forgotten by those who walk past it each day. Born in a vicarage in Norfolk, she became a nurse and eventually ran a hospital in Belgium during the German Occupation that began in August 1914. There she tended both the wounded German soldiers and the fugitive English ones who came secretly into her care. Accused of assisting enemy soldiers to escape, she was executed by the Germans and went to her death with the courage that stemmed from her religious belief. She left the world her message: 'Patriotism is not enough. I must have no hatred or bitterness towards anyone.'

I was playing the role of Cavell at Chichester at the same time that the Falklands War was being conducted by Mrs Thatcher, another indomitable Englishwoman, but one who, rightly or wrongly, paid no heed to Edith's words. I remember how perturbed we actors felt at the jingoistic jubilation of the English press when the Argentinian ship, *General Belgrano*, was sunk with much loss of life. The ferocity of a tabloid headline, GOTCHA, celebrating the slaughter, gave an ironic significance to the message I was delivering as Cavell each night in performance. The play was written by Keith Baxter and was very popular with audiences, though received in rather lukewarm fashion by the critics. But the award-winning playwright Robert Bolt was more appreciative.

Hartington Road, London W4   *20 August 1982*

Dear Joan,

... I came last night to see your piece at the Chichester Theatre, and thought it magnificent. The fine line which you had to tread between the wittily felt dialogue, and the strict schooling of your Christian upbringing, was marvellously felt throughout. Congratulations.

I decided against coming to see you as I have had a really enormous stroke ... and there seemed to be such a lot of well-wishers milling round the stage door ...

Love,

Robert

I was grateful to him for coming to see *Cavell* and giving it his seal of approval. It was Robert who wrote about another great Englishman, Sir Thomas More, in his play *A Man for All Seasons*. Sir Thomas also has a statue erected in his memory, on the Embankment in Chelsea. And whenever I pass it I find the resemblance of the face to that of Laurence Olivier quite uncanny. Not that he played the part, of course; it was Paul Scofield's triumph in 1960, which he later repeated in the film, winning the Oscar for Best Actor.

I shall move back now after that digression to Chichester's tenth anniversary season in 1972 and the appointment of Larry's successor at the National.

Twenty-One

Leaving the National

In March 1972 just before Chichester rehearsals began, we went on holiday to Italy. We returned on Friday, 24 March, and that was the day Larry was told that the Board wished to appoint Peter Hall as his successor. We were asked to keep it a secret as nothing had been finalized, and the official announcement would not be made until later in the year. Hall had been approached by Lord Goodman in 1971, after he withdrew from an agreed Covent Garden contract. He was forbidden to tell Larry about it, but apparently could talk freely to Trevor Nunn, John Barton, Peggy Ashcroft, John Goodwin, Peter Brook and other colleagues at Stratford, to ask their advice. So for three months there were quite a few people hugging this privileged information to themselves or passing it on, with more requests for secrecy, to yet other colleagues.

It came as a shock to Larry to discover that so much had gone on behind his back and for so long; he felt that his years of dedicated service deserved better treatment, and he would never really forgive them, however hard he tried. I know that Lord Goodman and Sir Max Rayne feared what Tynan and Larry's other Associates might do to oppose Hall's appointment publicly if they were given the time and opportunity. Though ironically enough, all of them, except Tynan, would readily agree to work with Peter Hall in the future. I remember Ken and Kathleen Tynan visiting us that Friday night in Brighton; they had been to see his daughter, Tracy, who was a student at Sussex University. I felt that we should be allowed to tell him as it concerned his future so closely, but Larry decided to play by the rules and keep it secret, as Max had requested.

There had been rumours ever since Peter Hall left Covent Garden so abruptly, and John Dexter had asked me point-blank one day if they were true. I had been able to say, quite truthfully at that time, that they were not, as far as I knew. I didn't relish the deception now that we *did* know – it seemed pretty monstrous to have to lie to people we had worked with for eight years and who might or might not be able to stay on when Hall took over.

The pity of it was that Larry could have been finally persuaded to agree to the appointment if he had been properly consulted, given time to digest it and to prepare his colleagues, without all the deception and unpleasantness which followed. When we talked to each other about it we had to admit that Peter was the only properly qualified candidate at the time. And Larry had told me how much he had enjoyed working with him on *Coriolanus* at Stratford. He was a man of immense practicality, and I know that eventually he could have been talked out of the feelings of rivalry and disappointment that 'Stratford had won', if he had been made to feel that his opinion mattered, and if Peter had come himself to ask his blessing. But the fait accompli which he was presented with only exacerbated those feelings. And the outrage of his colleagues, and the company at the Old Vic, when they heard the news, added fuel to the fire.

Peter came to dinner with us to discuss the whole business; to explain why he had not been able to tell Larry himself; to say he was sorry that it had happened that way and that he would not accept the job unless Larry approved him. He said that he had told the Board as much and that nothing had been finalized. After he had gone, Larry and I wondered whether we should tell some of our own colleagues; far too many people were in the know for it to stay out of the press much longer.

We finally decided it was better not to say anything until Larry and Peter met with the Board.

A few days later it broke; there was an unpleasant article in the *Guardian*, which was taken up by the evening papers, and consternation and mutiny at the Old Vic. I was rehearsing at Chichester and could not bring myself to join in Tynan's counter-attacks. He chided me for not being willing to protest against 'this insane mistake'. But I knew that Larry was nearly at the end of his tether and that the decision, though unpopular, had put an end to one of his biggest problems.

On 12 April there was a big party at Windsor Castle, attended by many of our colleagues in films and theatre, and given in honour of the Queen of the Netherlands. I was drafted to sit beside her on a sofa to chat for two minutes, and she was most friendly. But when I said I was about to play in *The Taming of the Shrew*, she was not pleased. Her face clouded over as she described it as 'the one play Shakespeare should not have written'. Other faces were clouded over that night as people discussed the latest article in the *Evening Standard* about the 'takeover row' at the National. Everyone was sympathizing with Larry, from Richard Attenborough to the Snowdons, who asked me what Tynan was going to do about it. And Lord Goodman and Max Rayne were being accused of many things that night, including the suggestion that they had leaked the news to the press themselves in order to hurry things up.

From then on things began to simmer down a bit, though the feeling of outrage persisted for some time at the Old Vic, particularly as 1972 proved to be a very successful year for the present administration. Blakemore's production of *The Front Page*, Jonathan Miller's *The School for Scandal*, and a new play, *Jumpers* by Tom Stoppard, all ensured full houses; and the National Theatre regained its position as one of the finest stage companies in the world. Peter Hall was not due to come in until the summer of 1973 so everybody set to work determined to show that they were perfectly all right without him! However, the die was cast, and in due course Larry and Peter met the press, the official announcement was made, and everybody contrived to look pleased and in good humour about it. And some of the Associates began their own private negotiations with Hall about the future.

In early January 1973 came the news of another delay on the new South Bank building; it would not be ready until 1975. Larry told me he wished to resign that October; it would be ten years exactly from the date he began the National Theatre in October 1963 and he didn't want to wait around for another two years. We decided to give a small dinner party at the flat for Tynan, John Dexter and Administrator Paddy Donnell to tell them, and I rang each of them personally to say we needed to talk. It seemed only right that they should be the first to know this time before either Peter Hall or the Chairman, Max Rayne. Michael Blakemore was not invited, as he was staying on with Peter and so was not affected in the same way. Their reaction was predictable; they would dearly have liked to have gone on under the present regime until the move had been made. Tynan was even hoping that the two years Hall would have to spend on the fringe might put him off altogether, and someone within the organization could be appointed. He went so far as to state that if the Board were making their choice this year instead of last, they would not choose Peter Hall. Whether he had any grounds for such an assertion, I didn't know; perhaps he was referring to the spectacular flop of Peter's recent production of *Via Galactica* in New York. All of them, however, begged Larry to stay at least until April 1974 so that the whole season was in theirs and his hands. (The financial year is from April to April, as is the planning and the actors' contracts.) That sounded reasonable enough, and Larry said he would think it over. We saw them out to the lift and waited as the doors closed upon them. But they must all have been too cast down to remember to press the ground floor button. 'I thought she was just going to give us one of those pep talks about all pulling together,' said Tynan morosely, unaware that the lift hadn't moved, and that we could hear every word. We grinned at each other for the first time that evening and Larry banged on the lift doors and we shouted a loud, 'Goodnight.'

On Friday, 12 January we asked Peter to come for a late dinner at the flat to tell him the news. Larry was playing at the theatre and was not due back at Roebuck House until 11 p.m. Peter came earlier, as he had been taking part in the BBC's *Any Questions?*, which finished at 9.30 p.m. Ringing home to warn his wife that he would be late, he got into trouble for having admitted to the sins of sloth and lust on the radio. We had a drink and I asked him how he would feel about taking over earlier at the National as Larry now didn't want to wait until 1975. He admitted that the delay had made things more difficult for him as he would be hanging around for two years instead of one. But at the same time he thought it would do him a lot of damage, personally, if Larry left and didn't lead the company into the new building.

By the time Larry arrived, Peter had thought out a plan of action. He said that he would be prepared to start working unofficially under Larry in October 1973, then take over in April 1974 and let Larry go off for six months or even a year if he wanted to – as long as he stayed connected with the organization in some official capacity and had made a definite commitment to do a production, or act in one, at the time of the move. He insisted that the date of that production must be announced at the same time as Larry's resignation because otherwise he anticipated a lot of bad feeling. He said that vague statements about Olivier promising to work there 'sometime in the future' would not be believed, and that he, Peter, would be accused of even more skulduggery, intrigue and manipulation than he had been so far.

He then went on to a further development which we had not anticipated and that was the virtual amalgamation of the Royal Shakespeare Company and the National Theatre. He had dined with Trevor Nunn the night before and Trevor had told him that he could foresee no future for the RSC in its present circumstances. They had had a very bad year and apparently Trevor was finding it increasingly difficult to get actors to go to Stratford unless they could be guaranteed a London showing; also the Aldwych Theatre was not proving financially viable. As for the Barbican ... that was 'a lifetime away'.

We began to talk of those days nearly ten years earlier when the National was being formed and of the scheme to join Stratford and the Old Vic into one National Theatre. Then the cry of 'monopoly,' which stopped it, together with those Stratford governors who wished their theatre to stay as a family concern. The press weren't too keen either, if I remember rightly, and neither was the profession. It would have meant only one management instead of two, with totally different preferences in their selection of actors. I said that I thought that objection would still apply today, that Corin Redgrave would start marching, and that I couldn't bear to read the article John Osborne would write about such a merger. Peter replied that after seeing Osborne's play *A Sense of Detachment* he didn't think he cared. He went on to compare Osborne unfavourably with Harold Pinter and said that he would want Pinter on his staff at the National as an Associate Director. Larry then suggested that he, too, would rather be an Associate Director than the 'President', which is what they were trying to make him. To him it suggested a retired old workhorse, who is brought out, with all his medals, on state occasions, and he was resisting it with all his might. But the idea of him trying to pretend he was just one of the boys after all those years as God was, it seemed to me, impossible.

So much was discussed and so many cards were put on the table that it was difficult trying to sum up what, if anything, had been decided. Peter suggested that we assume nothing had been decided until we had slept on it for a week; Larry might suddenly change his mind again, and want to go on as the boss. But I doubted it; once that decision had been made and a great weight had lifted off his shoulders, I didn't think it would be voluntarily taken up again.

In the meantime, during our work at Chichester, I had come into closer contact with Robin Phillips who was taking over the Greenwich Theatre for a year in 1973. I agreed to join his committee of three with Jeremy Brett, and to play Rebecca West, an Ibsen heroine who appealed to me, in *Rosmersholm*. After the summer of 1972, when Larry went to film *Sleuth* with Michael Caine, I had taken myself off to a health farm for three weeks. I was suffering from an overactive thyroid gland condition, caused, doctors said, by stress. It had been pointed out to me one Sunday by Maggie Smith, who had said, 'You are juddering all over, even your toes.' It had not been the dieting so much as the stress which had resulted in my rapid weight loss for the part of Jennifer Dubedat in *The Doctor's Dilemma*. And I felt it necessary to resist until later any attempts to get me back to the National.

'Company theatre', as it was called, at Greenwich was fun. Robin Phillips had a great talent for making everyone feel involved, even to the extent of helping in the redecoration of dressing rooms and bathrooms in the theatre. His main emphasis on roles for women in his first season paid large dividends: Lynn Redgrave joined us to play in *Born Yesterday*, and Mia Farrow played Irina in his *Three Sisters*, both very successful productions. I loved working with him on *Rosmersholm* and playing opposite Jeremy Brett, who was also an ex-National player; and our first night brought excellent reviews: 'An enthralling experience,' wrote Michael Billington in the *Guardian*. If my enthusiasm for the venture and my admiration for Robin's direction of it may seem to be lacking in restraint, it is appropriate in the light of what was to happen next. He was beginning to make his name as a director and had done an innovative production of *Two Gentlemen of Verona* for the Royal Shakespeare Company. But at his dress rehearsal, Peter Hall, the Artistic Director at the time, and his deputy, Trevor Nunn, had been dismayed by what they saw, even considering cancelling the first night. In the event, it opened very successfully but Robin was never asked to work for them again.

In June 1973 Peter Hall, now more or less running the National Theatre, came for dinner with us at Brighton and asked me to consider coming back to the company. I told him I had made a commitment to Robin for the next season at Greenwich. That I was happy working in a more intimate atmosphere, with a smaller company, and where, for a while, I could experiment away from the limelight, and put into practice those ideals of 'company theatre' which he said were no longer viable at the National, but in which I still believed. He suggested that those of us involved with Greenwich could come and do what we were doing under the umbrella of the National. I argued that autonomous small theatres needed to be free to experiment in ways perhaps not envisaged by Peter and his associates, and had no desire to come under such an umbrella. He warned that there wasn't going to be enough money around to keep the smaller theatres open, and he fully expected many to close down.

His main objective that evening was to persuade me to play the lead in J. B. Priestley's *Eden End*, which he was asking Larry to direct. He needed to secure Larry's commitment to the production in time to announce it for the next press release. For me there was a sense of *déjà vu* – the suspicion that I was again being used as bait; and the anticipation of press reports: 'Sir Laurence will direct his wife in . . .' And though I had no wish to put a spanner in the works, I made clear my reluctance as yet to withdraw from my involvement with Robin Phillips.

Peter continued with his persuasion in a letter two days later:

Glyndebourne   *20 June 1973*

My dear Joan,

  Thank you for your hospitality and a most pleasant evening.

  I don't know how far we progressed – I can't easily give up a situation where I believe the best casting for a play and the best director are being abandoned because of public difficulties which I do not believe exist now. But that is my opinion . . .

I shall hope that you and Larry will give it a week or two longer before deciding.

In the meantime, I am sending you the Etherege play, She Would if She Could.

I hope I assuaged some of your unease about the future of the National. It has to be an open situation with a great deal of activity. Otherwise we are making a fortress of culture with a few actors and directors cowering behind the battlements.

I hope you will work there in the new situation.

Yours ever,

Peter

The fact that he had had 'a most pleasant evening' was not recorded in his *Diaries*. 'I sense an antipathy to me which she very nearly masks,' he wrote. And from my remarks about my involvement in company theatre, he deduced: 'I am convinced she did want the succession at the NT.' I would have thought that Dexter and Blakemore could have told him otherwise, if they had been asked. But I think he believed me when I told him later how wrong he was. As he could acknowledge the help that he himself had been given by Peggy Ashcroft, 'Without her I could never have started the RSC,' and not accuse her of wanting his job, I hoped he would recognize that this was a parallel situation. I was a helpmate, not a competitor for the hot seat. Not at the National, or with Robin Phillips or Lindsay Anderson, whom I later joined to form the Lyric Theatre Company. I loved being part of a company, and would do my utmost to help keep it afloat.

Shortly after that Brighton evening and Peter's letter, a meeting was arranged by Robin to discuss plans for the next season at Greenwich. But two days before it took place, he rang in a state of some agitation, saying he needed to talk. And he came down to the Malthouse where he confronted me with his dilemma. He had been offered the Artistic Directorship of the Stratford Ontario Theater in Canada – on Peter Hall's recommendation. It would mean the end of the Greenwich venture. And though we spent the afternoon debating whether Peter had changed his mind about Robin's talent, or simply wanted him out of the country, we both knew that the offer could not be turned down.

And so company theatre at Greenwich came to an end, and Robin went to make his name in Canada where Maggie Smith joined him for four years to work in many of his successful productions.

And I returned to the National (not for *Eden End* initially, which would be in 1974), lured by the prospect of working with Franco Zeffirelli on Eduardo de Filippo's play, *Saturday, Sunday, Monday.*

Having got his own way, Peter has been extremely nice to me in recent years. So that when my children were inviting people to a party for my seventieth birthday, I mentioned his name. 'Peter Hall?' exclaimed my son, who had just returned from a Conference on Forgiveness in Edinburgh. 'Surely that's going too far.'

Of course I should no longer be calling them children. They were now young adults leading busy lives and making waves of their own. After Larry died in 1989 we continued our long tradition of bringing old friends together again for a Christmas party. And a letter from the actor, Ronald Pickup, who was an original member of Larry's National Theatre company for seven years, illustrates how memories of those days are still so deeply treasured:

26 December 1994

. . . I just want to thank you from both Lans and myself for the wonderful party the other night, in the marvellous atmosphere of Tamsin's restaurant.

I am sorry we did not get to talk longer. I can only say that the family atmosphere of your parties reminds me (not that I need reminding) of a time for me – I think for many of us – when 'company' meant something so real and tangible, alive and exciting in the theatre that it has been hard – for me I think impossible – to recreate. I am not being morbid or

defeatist, because being with all those folk the other night was an inspiration
as well as a reminder.

'Tamsin's restaurant' is The Engineer, an historic building designed by Brunel, conceived as a pub restaurant with organic food and a spacious garden, and with paintings by new young artists for sale on its walls. She and Abigail Osborne, an artist friend from Bedales, had been talking of such a venture for two or three years but Tamsin's acting commitments (including a well-received *Antigone* for John Dexter) had prevented her from giving time to the project. It won a Time Out Award in its first year and has remained popular ever since.

In 1990 we embarked on a theatrical family venture together in J.B. Priestley's *Time and the Conways*. It was the author's favourite play and the one he had suggested to Peter Hall for the National Theatre instead of *Eden End*. Concerning the impact of time on the lives of the widowed Mrs Conway and her six children, it starts with a twenty-first birthday party for daughter, Kay, and shoots suddenly into the future when she has a vision of them all as they are twenty years later. I was Mrs Conway, Julie-Kate and Tamsin were two of the daughters, and Richard directed the production. We rehearsed and opened at Theatre Clwyd in Wales, went on a short tour, and finally arrived at the Old Vic in London. We were sympathetically received on the whole and the author's family, and his widow Jacquetta Hawkes, were especially welcoming.

Green Place, Hampshire   *6 December 1990*

Dear Miss Plowright,

This is from all the Priestleys to say how very much we enjoyed my father's play last night. It was the most excellent production, done with great sensitivity and style. Jacquetta told us that it was the best Conways that she had ever seen, and we all now agree.

I was particularly interested, as I must be unique in having, in my early teens, attended rehearsals and first nights, in both productions in

London (wonderful Jean Forbes-Robertson), and in New York (amazing Sybil Thorndike and Jessica Tandy).

Miss Tamsin Olivier as Kay moved me as much as did Jean F-R. She is very gifted.

... I am sending you some flowers from us all by separate delivery; and with our very good wishes to the whole cast, and especially to the director.

Sincerely yours,
Barbara Priestley

John Mills came to the first night and told me afterwards how nervous he and Mary had been, and how relieved they were to find that 'they can all do it'. As the effervescent youngest daughter, Julie-Kate was called upon to do a couple of impersonations, which had made him laugh, and he told her she was a good mimic like her father. Some time afterwards, Billie Whitelaw would write to me about her when they had finished making a film together.

Rose Cottage, Suffolk   *30 July 1990*

Darling Joan,

It was a joy working with Julie-Kate – what a talented, well-centred girl she is.

My love to you. Think of you often ...
Billie

Richard went on to direct three West End productions and then joined Mark Rylance at Shakespeare's Globe Theatre on London's Bankside. Back in 1987 he and I had each directed a play by Sean Mathias at the Edinburgh Festival. Richard's leading lady had been the actress, Jill Bennett, now divorced from John Osborne; and they got on so well that she wrote an unsolicited reference to help him on his way.

London SW3   *29 January 1987*

TO WHOM IT MAY CONCERN
I had the pleasure of working with Richard Olivier on a play called Infidelities. *I found him extraordinarily mature for his age, aware, hard-working, imaginative, kindly, full of brilliant ideas, wonderful on moves and absolutely dedicated to the play – nothing was too much for him.*

I would be delighted to work with him again and I am sure he has a great future.

He is also a very nice man which always makes people work better.

Jill Bennett

It is naturally heartwarming to hear the efforts of one's family praised; particularly in our case where they've had to bear the weight of such an illustrious name. And I have included these fan letters because I agree with everything they say – but as a mother could hardly say such things myself and expect them to be taken without a pinch of salt.

But to return to the time in 1973 when they really were children and accompanied us one evening to a ceremony at Chichester where another theatrical succession was taking place. John Clements' reign at the Festival Theatre was over, and it had been announced that the actor Keith Michell had been appointed as the new Director. Bearing in mind the amount of talented and experienced young directors around (John Dexter, Clifford Williams, Jonathan Miller), all of whom were considered by the Board after Paul Scofield turned it down, the choice caused quite a few raised eyebrows. The farewell ceremony to Sir John took place in a marquee in the grounds of Stansted House, the home of Lord and Lady Bessborough, who were great supporters of the Festival Theatre. During Leslie Evershed Martin's address, which began: 'Sir John has been with us for eight happy years ...' a voice cried out, 'Not long enough.' So the feeling had spread around that some members of the Board were not wholly in agreement and would in fact rather have renewed John's contract for another term.

However, we all behaved in the civilized fashion expected on these occasions. And Larry and I kept catching each other's eye at any references to us in speeches and thinking back to the day when we first arrived at Chichester and looked at a hole in the ground in a field...

Eric Bessborough made the final speech and concluded by inviting as many as could get in to his private chapel for a short service. We were staying on for dinner but had the children with us and the business of getting them into the swimming pool (a treat they had been promised) took longer than we thought so we missed that part of the evening. Having finally got them out and dried, and having ignored their protests about not being invited to dinner, we sent them off home to the Malthouse. It was a nice informal evening, the Bessboroughs having only just returned from holiday and gaily surmounting lack of staff problems. We both agreed later that there was something rather sad about a once great house no longer functioning in the way it was meant to do. Huge rooms with tapestries and ancestral portraits, the Irish Chippendale salvaged from the fire years ago, the beautiful extensive lawns and grounds which could no longer be maintained in the style of days gone by. One felt that the place should be alive with people and children and livestock, and wonderful flowers; but the Bessborough family had grown up and flown the coop, and the place was functional only and a bit of a strain on their resources.

Driving back in the early hours to the Malthouse, Larry and I realized that our country sojourn was over for that year. But what a glorious summer it had been for us, we had never enjoyed the Malthouse so much. The weather had been fabulous, apart from a few odd days; friends had visited, including the John Millses, Edna O'Brien and, in the spirit of 'hatchet-burying', Peter Hall and his wife, Jacky. And we had a happy day with Mia Farrow and André Previn who brought their children and introduced us to Tara, their latest Vietnamese orphan. Larry and I had been marginally involved in the adoption process as we signed a document guaranteeing that the Previns would be good parents (which would cause certain repercussions for me in the future, but that's another story). And good parents they have proved to be, acquiring a country house in Surrey with its own wood at the bottom of the garden which was looked upon as paradise by their children and by ours.

The new pony arrived on Julie-Kate's birthday and grew so fond of us that he spent most of his time trying to get into the garden from the paddock, or into the caravan with the children, and twice trying to get into the kitchen. The pool had been the centre of our existence during the long, hot spell; and we had all taken turns to mow the lawns and the tennis court, tend the flowers and Grandpop's greenhouse, and had never been happier.

In September we started rehearsals for *Saturday, Sunday, Monday*, which would prove to be a sell-out success and move to the West End in 1974. And it was the beginning of a long personal and professional relationship with Franco Zeffirelli, with happy memories of idyllic family holidays at his home Tre Ville in Positano. Originally owned by Diaghilev and overlooking the sea with its own private rock beach, it was for us a paradise on earth. And Larry and I slept in the Blue Room where Nijinsky was said to have done his daily barre practice. It was at Tre Ville that Richard, Tamsin and Julie-Kate first experienced the beauty of southern Italy and were amazed and fascinated by the archaeological remains at Pompeii and Paestum. Franco was an exuberant and generous host and guests would arrive in droves during the summer, often unexpectedly, and extra beds would somehow be found to accommodate them. Julie-Kate's birthday would often be celebrated there on 27 July with a special cake baked by Franco's chef, Ali, and everyone wearing spectacular party hats made from newspapers and lavishly decorated with flowers from the garden.

Saturday, Sunday, Monday was described in the *Guardian* as 'a beautiful production, constantly catching you between laughter and tears'. And the *Telegraph* critic wrote: 'Franco Zeffirelli has not only endowed English actors with Italian mannerisms and excitability. He communicates the passionate integrity and wide-awake humanity of the author, the seventy-three-year-old actor dramatist, Eduardo de Filippo ... All round me I do not know when I have seen so many happy faces in a theatre.' And that spirit pervaded the company of actors too, despite early fears that it was an Italian *Coronation Street* and an explosively angry exit by Franco from the dress rehearsal. He was naturally in a nervous state and unused to the English actors' practice of stopping during a run-through to familiarize themselves with the set, the timing of entrances and to check the position of their chairs. When Frank Finlay moved down right on the stage and discovered that there was no light there, he understandably pointed this out. We had all worked closely together for several years and were like technicians doing research and passing on information to each other. But Franco felt that such concentration on details, and the consequent lack of passion in the playing, in some way displayed arrogance and a disrespectful attitude towards his author. And he stormed out shouting, 'The audience will teach you about this play.' He came back, of course, after a day or two; and he was right about the audience letting us know what a powerful effect it had on them. The first night was an extraordinary experience and the cheers at the end made Franco feel thoroughly vindicated and harmony was restored all round.

We transferred to the Queen's Theatre where there was always a joyful atmosphere, both backstage and in the auditorium, aided and abetted by the exuberance of the Neapolitan songs played at the beginning, the middle and the end. And the smell of the ragout cooking on stage caused a sell-out of sandwiches at the interval.

But that happy time was to be interrupted by illness on the home front. Larry, who had originally played the small but show-stopping part of the *Grandfather* at the Old Vic, did not transfer with it to the West End. And suddenly he was afflicted by swelling in the facial muscles and a general feeling that something was wrong. In October 1974 he went into hospital for tests and some diary notes from November of that year record what happened.

Sunday 24 November 1974

Larry has been in hospital now for six weeks – first two weeks we kept it secret. It was tests only. Results of tests confirmed – dermatomyositis. Consultations with doctors – I am told it is serious – can be fatal – could have cancer in the background but need not necessarily. It is apparently a rare disease and not much is known about it. Treatment prescribed – steroids. For a few days a good response – swelling down and face back to normal. Then the doctor, Joanna Sheldon, called and said she must talk to me. I usually went straight to the hospital each night from the station so it was around midnight when we met there. She said the condition was static – no improvement – he was finding it difficult to swallow. They were not giving up hope but it was serious.

Asked Laurence Evans, our agent, to meet me with a car at the Queen's Theatre and drive me to Brighton so that I could lay everything before him and ask what should be done. Larry wanted to release all details to the press. Doctors against it. I asked Laurence Evans if I should come out of the play. He said firmly that I couldn't – or rather shouldn't until absolutely necessary. We agreed that a press release would not be a good idea because of the children who were not aware of the seriousness of the situation. Also it would make it hard for me in the play – audiences hardly going to feel in the mood to laugh at me if they knew the facts. Evans suggested a quiet release to one paper that he was temporarily in hospital. The doctors agreed to cloak the full facts by calling it myositis – said people could look that up in medical dictionaries and not get very far with speculation. The press took it reasonably quietly though Guardian suspected more – and said it was possible that he was quite ill. Many phone calls at theatre that night – all ignored – and I was told Victor Davis from the Express *was sitting at the stage door determined to see me.*

John Dexter was in my dressing room with me that night. He was visiting from New York where he was now Director of Productions at the Metropolitan Opera. One of the few friends who knew the truth, he had come up with the plan to ask Larry to direct the opera of *Macbeth* at the Met next year. It would give him a goal to work towards in the future, a reason to fight, and John could make a private arrangement with his Board to take over if Larry couldn't do it. John agreed to come with me to the stage door to see Davis and to say that Larry was working on the *Macbeth* opera and that he was 'responding to treatment'.

Dexter saw Sydney Edwards the next night at a party for Pygmalion *and told him about* Macbeth *and asked him to help get the press to 'leave Joan alone – she's got eight shows a week to do'. Sydney printed a marvellous cooling article in the* Standard *saying Larry had accepted to direct* Macbeth *in 1976 and was recovering from myositis in Brighton Hospital. Other papers reprinted more or less what Sydney said and only close friends know the truth. Ralph Richardson, John and Mary Mills, Lilli Palmer and close family have been the only visitors – therefore the only ones to know that he has been fed by stomach tube for the last three weeks.*

As for me – after first asking Frank Finlay and Robin Taylor (Company Manager) if we should cut certain lines in the play (regarding husband, loss of appetite, illness) and finding that they were not as sensitive about it as I am, I decided to grit my teeth and hurl them (lines not teeth) at the audience. Some nights I have not been able to get the lines out properly, which I suppose is a Freudian slip. Then I practised saying them several times into my mirror so that they meant nothing to me any more and I've been able to get by. There were nights when his voice on the phone was so weak I thought he might slip away before I got back. Then two nights ago the voice was suddenly stronger and mental energy back. Today, Sunday, energy is enormous. Mental energy I mean – the body is still weak. But the mental energy almost manic – planning opera, writing books, redecorating our house – he can't sleep because his mind is working overtime. Said to me this morning, 'I feel almost mad – I've felt mad for three days.'

I remember taking the children to see him that afternoon and they were much cheered to find him so lively and it didn't bother them that his conversation veered erratically from one subject to another. After they had gone back to Bedales, I returned to the hospital to find him in a very disturbed state. We had been trying to encourage him to work on a book as well as the opera, and two weeks previously his sister, Sybille, had come to stay, visiting him each day to talk about their childhood. Our secretary had taken in a tape-recorder and things had gone well for a few days. But then he had become bored with the idea. That night in the hospital when I asked how the work was going, he claimed to have finished both projects. 'It's done – finished,' he said about the book. 'All seven volumes.'

'Seven?' I asked, my mind shooting to that other Lawrence's *Seven Pillars of Wisdom.*

'Yes, seven,' he said, at the top of his voice, and then, with staccato delivery, spelt out his name, 'O–L–I–V–I–E–R'. I couldn't make out whether he was just playing me along, or if he believed it. But when he told me that the opera was also planned and ready to go, I went to see the Sister. She told me that the nursing staff had all reported a sudden change in him – he was not himself any more – and she suggested that it might be a side-effect of the treatment which they had not expected. Doctor Sheldon came first thing in the morning to see him and confirm it, and she ordered an immediate reduction in the steroids. Meanwhile at home next morning, two builders arrived at 8.30 a.m. to say that he had ordered iron bars to be erected at every window in the house. They agreed with me that it would look like a prison if they went ahead and I sent them away, saying I would talk it over with him.

After two days he came back to us – he was himself again – and about three days later he rang early in the morning and said, 'I've had scrambled eggs this morning.' He was eating again and the stomach tubes had gone. Nobody knew quite what had caused the turnaround. He would still have to be in hospital for a long recuperative period, but he was over the worst; he had survived and won that particular battle.

Both my brothers came with their families to stay and help over Christmas and provide a more festive atmosphere for our children. We begged the doctors to allow Larry to come out for a few hours on Christmas Day; and though they did not approve, they agreed to it. David and Bob went to fetch him home at 3 p.m. in the afternoon. It was an appropriate day for such a miraculous homecoming, however brief, and it was crowned by the showing of his Shakespeare films on the TV. This of course he said had been planned as a posthumous tribute as everyone expected him to have left the planet by now.

As he had abandoned the idea of the book and couldn't seem to get started on the opera, David began talking about a TV project, which caught Larry's interest immediately. He was to mastermind a series of his own choice of significant twentieth-century plays, which could be prepared whilst he was in the hospital, with helpers coming each day from Granada's drama department. The series would bear his name, and he could select which ones he, himself, wanted to act in or direct; but there would be a team of other directors standing by if necessary. The idea proved to be a life-saver; he was back in harness again, back in charge, full of zest and enthusiasm and couldn't wait to get started. I remember reading an article in one of the Sunday newspapers around that time with the headline, GREAT MEN OUT OF OFFICE HAVE GREAT ILLNESSES. It had named prime ministers and presidents and heads of huge corporations who had suffered such breakdowns; and I felt that it was partly the cause in Larry's case too. But now there was a future to look forward to, and a great load was taken off all our shoulders.

Twenty-Two

After the National

The Granada series took up the next two years and was a successful and rewarding time for Larry; and with his returning strength we were back on an even keel. We acted in two of the TV plays together, James Bridie's *Daphne Laureola* and the filmed version of *Saturday, Sunday, Monday*. And enjoyed weekends with Natalie Wood and Robert Wagner who came over to do *Cat on a Hot Tin Roof* with him.

And I joined Lindsay Anderson, Helen Montagu (producer) and Helen Mirren to form the Lyric Theatre Company. Some of our planning sessions had taken place through the summer of 1975 at the Malthouse, in the garden — where Larry and Derek Granger, his co-producer, were also encamped, working with their Granada colleagues a few yards away. Larry kept a sharp eye on our casting, wandering over frequently to find out which actors were being considered, and telling Lindsay, 'You can't have him, I want him for the Pinter play.'

Lindsay had long wanted to direct *The Seagull*, which was to be our first play, and Helen Mirren and I were excited by the roles of Nina and Madame Arkadina. As I noted in an earlier chapter, the production was much liked, especially by Tennessee Williams, and Helen Mirren added to her growing reputation as one of the finest young actresses of her generation.

And it was the ninety-year-old Ben Travers who provided us with the second play of our season, *The Bed Before Yesterday*. We all thought it was very funny, though perhaps a bit near the knuckle. It concerned a formidable middle-aged lady inter-viewing a possible male lodger, with a view to exploring sex for the first time in her very sheltered life. John Moffatt, a long-time member of Larry's National Theatre Company, played the lodger with his usual brilliance. And I remember Lindsay asking us at one rehearsal to play it like Ibsen. And, oh my goodness, it made us shiver to realize what a very different play it could become: about loneliness, eccentricity, shyness, compromise and anger, with just an occasional burst of hap-piness to keep the people afloat. Of course we didn't play it like that when we opened – but we kept the knowledge of it in our subconscious, so that the comedy was rooted in reality. It was a smash hit and more than justified its choice in the repertoire.

I want to leap forward for a moment to another Chekhov play with Lindsay, *The Cherry Orchard*, which was presented at the Haymarket Theatre in 1983. I played Madame Ranevski, Frank Finlay was Lopakhin, the forerunner of the revo-lutionaries who rises from his peasant origins to take over the estate and chop down the orchard; Leslie Phillips was Gaev, my sensitive but hapless brother, and Bernard (Lord) Miles was the faithful old retainer, Firs. My most vivid recollections of that adventure concern the first week when we opened out of town at Guildford. For though it was all pulled together and made a respectable debut in London, our first performance was a bit of a nightmare. There were monumental technical problems and, due to lack of time, an unfinished set; we had no curtains at the windows, doors didn't fit properly into their frames, and opening and closing them was a precarious business. Entrances and exits were delayed by seconds extending into minutes as baffled actors pushed where they should have pulled, and vice versa. The stage was awash with unpainted walls, lopsided chandeliers and a tiled floor which erupted in unexpected places, causing the actors to trip in mid-sentence and walk with circumspectly careful gait around it. The technical dress rehearsal had not finished, but was abandoned when the half-hour was called and the audience began filling the theatre for the first night. As we prepared to meet our doom, over the tannoy system came the voice of Lindsay Anderson, speaking in grave, sepulchral tones reminiscent of Neville Chamberlain announcing the onset of the Second World War.

'This is your director speaking. As you are aware there are immense technical problems facing us this evening. I ask you to forget the physical aspects of your surroundings – the unfinished set, the lack of curtains, pictures, etc. – the fact that doors may or may not open when you wish to make your entrance. I ask you to believe only in the play, the author and your own poetic imagination. Rest assured that the play will come through as it has in the rehearsal room. Forget the physical shortcomings around you – keep your faith, and we shall give our audience a good account of Chekhov's play.'

We tried to respond to Lindsay's rallying call and struggled through the evening, ignoring the swaying chandeliers and the scenery which shivered and threatened to collapse each time a door was closed too roughly. 'One last look at these walls,' I cried tearfully, towards the end of the play, stumbling around the uneven floor and tripping over the unfinished hem of my huge overcoat, as surreptitious bursts of laughter erupted from the nervous first night audience. 'Oh my sister, my sister,' sobbed Leslie Phillips, burying his head in my shoulder and whispering, 'Oh Christ Almighty – let's get off for God's sake.'

Thankfully we left the stage to Firs, the old servant who is forgotten and left behind and who has the last scene to himself. 'They've locked me in,' wailed Bernard Miles, rattling the handle of a door which promptly swung invitingly open and rendered the closing moments of the play quite meaningless. The audience was as relieved as we were when it came to an end, though they gave us sympathetic applause. Of course we should never have opened, but theatre economics make it compulsory when tickets have been sold. And it is only those companies with large subsidies who can afford to confess 'We are not ready' and turn an audience away.

I would return to the Lyric for *Filumena* in 1977, my second De Filippo play and my third production with Zeffirelli as director. Filumena is an ex-prostitute who has three sons, only one of whom is the son of her lover, Domenico. She is trying to get Domenico to the altar but refuses to tell him which child is his, as she is adamant that all three must be treated equally. De Filippo himself had been an illegitimate child (as had Zeffirelli) and knew what suffering was involved. Franco had told Willis Hall and Keith Waterhouse, who were doing the adaptation, how tough and strong he wanted the play to be. 'Think of it in terms of *Who's Afraid of Virginia Woolf*,' he had said, and left them to work on it through the summer. It was to open in the autumn but meantime the children were home from Bedales, and holidays were upon us.

We all went up to see *Romeo and Juliet* at the Aldwych. The principals, Ian McKellen, Francesca Annis and Michael Pennington, were excellent; some mediocre bits of acting and staging here and there, but oh what a play! And how strengthening Shakespeare always is – and beautiful – and timeless. And how so many other plays fade into insignificance in comparison. Of course there are contemporary plays which have broken new ground and changed the face of theatre, and it was exciting to be a part of that initial revolution. But in the aftermath which followed, there seemed so little new inspiration. And there comes a time when ordinary, domestic plays about ordinary domestic life become a bit deadening. And anyway they work better on the television. Theatre must stimulate the imagination and appeal to all the senses if it is to survive.

I remember feeling a bit like a traitor when I had to acknowledge that I had found the finale of *West Side Story* more moving than a straight production of *Romeo and Juliet*, and Matthew Bourne's male swans more dramatic and touching than the ladies in the traditional *Swan Lake*. On the one hand it was the addition of the music and dance which excited me, and on the other it was the unpredictability, the danger and the innovative nature of the choreography which affected me so strongly.

It was in 1977 that I made my first ever visit to the Old Bailey and I am reminded of it because of the furore today in June 2001 surrounding the early release of the two boys who killed the two-year-old James Bulger eight years ago. They are now aged eighteen, and have been supplied with entirely new identities, so it is hoped that their rehabilitation has been successful, that they are no longer dangerous, and that leading a new and useful life is preferable to them remaining in prison. Many people believe it to be an unwise decision, and the possibility of vengeance being wrought upon them, should they be discovered and identified, is being widely debated in newspapers and on the television.

It has made me wonder what happened to the boy I saw in the dock for murder at the Old Bailey twenty-five years ago. I had been invited to lunch with twenty-six judges by the Sheriff of London. It is their custom each day to invite guests who are then free to watch the court proceedings if they are interested. It was extraordinary to move from my world of acting and make-believe to the reality of that court scene – to an atmosphere of quiet concentration that was not at all dramatic, except for the fact that we were watching a real killer and very real and bewildered people in the jury. And real and world-weary officials at work around the court. 'If you get bored with this one,' whispered the clerk who showed us in, 'I'll put you in Court Two where there's a bit more hammer and tongs.' A rivetingly undramatic defence counsel was pleading with the jury for a verdict of insanity, saying, 'Stephen is a psychopath.' Stephen was a beautiful, well-dressed boy, apparently seventeen years old but looking nearer to an angelic fourteen-year-old, and he was accused of murdering his sister. He seemed quite unperturbed by anything that was said about him, and just sat there, looking rather bored and occasionally asking his attendant for orange juice. I never knew the outcome of the trial, or the sentence. He must be around forty-two years of age now ... wherever he is.

That same night I had dinner with Edna O'Brien, who gave

me a copy of her new book, *Johnny I Hardly Knew You*. And because of where I had been in the morning we suspected telepathy, or intuition or whatever – as her book begins with a woman in the dock for murder. She told me it was about a woman who fell in love with a boy the same age as her son – and later killed him.

I have always enjoyed Edna's writing from way back when I first encountered *The Country Girls* and first began to enjoy her company. And I loved her frank and unfashionable admission that she adores potatoes, which gives us something else in common. She has been a valuable friend and confidante, always sensitive to mood and atmosphere and ready to discuss anything with the utmost candour. And she has made us realize that sometimes the hectic pace of our life left too little time for opening our hearts and soothing our hurts. And I remembered a few lines from a letter that our son, Richard, wrote once on the same subject: 'It is wonderful to have a shared, family conversation about theatre. But it is even better to have open communication about feelings, thoughts, life and the future. Sometimes I think we talk about theatre in order to avoid talking about ourselves, and each other...'

Filumena opened in November 1977 and turned out to be a smash hit. It is a lovely, heart-warming play, and it was revived in the late 1990s with Judi Dench in the title role. With me in Zeffirelli's production, playing the part of the son who is a plumber, was a good-looking but unknown young actor called Pierce Brosnan. Later, as James Bond, he would meet up with the other *Filumena*, Judi, who plays his superior, M, in the Bond films.

In 1978 we were trying to decide whether *Filumena* should go to New York. All the Americans who came to see it in London thought it would be a huge success over there; and Larry was particularly enthusiastic about the idea. He spent a lot of time trying to persuade Franco, who was still uncertain. And he sent his old friend, Ralph Richardson, to see it, who enjoyed it enormously, but in a letter to Larry he expressed some reservations about the move to New York.

Dearest Laurence,

Thank you for your letter – I do hope that Filumena *has the rich reward that it deserves – there is something odd about translated plays in the US. Do you recall that our* Uncle Vanya *did not go extremely well.*

I hear you have been doing some splendid work just now in the film of Waugh's tale.

There is a chap who wants to write a book about me – I do not want him to bother you, if you wish to talk to him no harm of course, but it is not my WISH *that you should.*

Send my love and prayers to Joan.

Always LOVE

EVER

R

As events turned out we would need those prayers when we made the decision to go to New York a year later; and our production, too, 'did not go extremely well'.

The audiences loved it during the previews and New York seemed as welcoming as ever. I stayed at the delightful Wyndham Hotel on 58th Street which had become the favourite place for the English contingent on Broadway. But not, unfortunately for very long this time. Once the critics had expressed their lukewarm reactions, we knew we were in for a very limited run.

But I have always found it exhilarating to work with Franco though we sometimes have flare-ups during the course of it. He gets impatient with my incessant questioning, and worrying at the text, and trying to find what thoughts are going on behind the actual lines. But I need to stock my subconscious with as much knowledge of the character as I can before the brakes are released and the acting juices can begin to flow. And moods, inflections and gestures can start to arise spontaneously and take over by themselves. And I tend to keep on trying to find a better way to do something, even when it's working well. 'Perfection is the enemy of good,' Larry once quoted to me when he, too, lost patience. Franco is not afraid to show emotion in rehearsal if he has been moved by a scene. And he will come up to the actors with tears still on his cheeks and give generous praise. And I remember he and his designer, Raimonda Gaetani, having passionate arguments over the exact shade of green necessary for a chair cover. Raimonda had fought him with equal intensity over the ingredients for the ragout in *Saturday, Sunday, Monday.* And the English actors had learnt a great deal about the Italian temperament from just watching them.

As for *Filumena*, we accepted the fact that certain plays do not survive crossing the Atlantic – in either direction – and returned after six weeks to England.

Back at home, on Thursday, 3 May 1979 another General Election day was upon us. For once we accepted Lady Hartwell's invitation to dine at Cowley Street and watch it on TV. It was upper Tory and upper class, except for occasional interlopers like Tom and Miriam Stoppard, and us, and Lord Goodman. As he had seemed such a close friend of Harold Wilson and Jennie Lee, I was a little surprised to see the latter there. But as Lady Pamela put it, 'You are apolitical, aren't you?'

We talked to Lord Goodman about the terrible state of affairs at the National and the backstage strike that had been going on for six weeks. There were pickets outside the theatre; plays being given in reduced sets or no sets at all and, of course, at reduced prices. Larry could not be brought to care much. Apart from a letter to *The Times* three months earlier, he seemed to be making no offer to help. He still somehow felt unwelcome there and I suspected that he was secretly quite pleased that Peter Hall was having such a dreadful time.

We watched the defeat of Shirley Williams, which seemed shocking; and then the defeat of Jeremy Thorpe, which was more understandable because of his involvement in a legal case due to come before the courts in the near future. Remarks were made about the unsuitability of his standing in this election and Lady Pamela said, 'It's so awful when you own a newspaper ... I mean, I like him so much ... and Marion, she's had such a rotten time, first Harewood, and now this.' I remembered what a lovely dinner companion Thorpe had been at some of those official receptions we attended. And how Tamsin campaigned for him when he was Leader of the Liberal Party. I look at Marion, his wife, and immediately visualize one of my children's first piano books, which bore her name and photograph when she was Marion Harewood and very much to do with the world of music. And I feel great sympathy for both of them.

Mrs Thatcher came on the screen and we marvelled at her for a while. How well she had done, and so on. 'She's had some good men behind her,' someone said, which caused Goodman to warn people not to underestimate her. He added that a great deal of her success was due entirely to her. So ... the first woman was installed at Number 10 Downing Street, but the one that most of my friends thought would be the first, Shirley Williams, had lost her seat.

Twenty-Three

Filming *Equus*

Theatre had played a major part in my life until the late 1970s, and films seemed to have passed me by. So I was naturally delighted when Peter Shaffer and Sidney Lumet came to talk to me about a role in the film of *Equus*, starring Richard Burton. It was nearing the end of Larry's work on the Granada series, and I had just finished playing at the Lyric. I wrote all about it in my diary.

As I boarded the plane to Toronto I suddenly realized it was the first time I'd gone off on my own for years. I used to travel all over the place by myself without a care in the world. Now I worry about family left behind. Will Larry be all right? He's very busy on the Granada project, spending most of the week in Manchester and I know that brother David will have plenty of people rushing around looking after him. I turn and wave to him; he stays until the plane starts to move, then gives a final wave and I am suddenly tearful, feeling I shouldn't be leaving him, but oh, how I want to do this film.

There are flowers from Peter Shaffer and our director, Sidney Lumet, at the hotel, and Harry Andrews and Colin Blakely and Eileen Atkins are there to greet me. Burton is still finishing another film and won't arrive until later. Rehearsals take place in a room in a masonic temple; we sit and read and discuss – very like a theatre rehearsal. Sidney is as dynamic as ever. We had first met in New York during A Taste of Honey, *and he had offered me a film two years previously which I'd turned down because of family commitments. But I'd always wanted to work with him. Peter Firth, playing the Boy, calls me 'Flower' which makes me feel younger and rather with-it; then I discover he calls most people 'Flower'.*

Peter Shaffer is present throughout, charming, courteous and extremely helpful.

He reminds me of a letter I wrote to him after his play, The Battle of Shrivings, *was savaged by the critics. It starred John Gielgud and was first intended for the National Theatre, where it was hoped that Larry and Gielgud could do it together as it had two marvellous parts for actors.* Equus *had been a huge success there and its director, John Dexter and Shaffer were all set to repeat their collaboration with* Shrivings. *Something went wrong between them, and Peter Hall somehow became involved. He tempted Shaffer away with an offer of a West End theatre where his play could be seen eight times a week instead of perhaps only three in the repertoire system at the National. After much lobbying and heartache, Peter Hall won the day. Presumably Gielgud, too, was tempted by the much greater financial reward of the commercial theatre. There was a fixed top salary and no percentage for all leading players at the National Theatre; you went there for the prestige, not the money.*

We were living in Brighton when they came to open the play there and I sent them first night greetings. This was Gielgud's reply:

Wednesday

Dear Joan,

The flowers are so beautiful. It was very sweet and thoughtful of you to send them. I can't help being sorry that the plans fell through for Larry to be in the play too. There seems to be a kind of jinx against us ever making plans to appear together again – which is sad . . .

Love from John

And after the London opening, Shaffer wrote:

Earl's Terrace, London W8   *12 February 1970*

Dear Joan and Larry,

Many thank yous for your telegram. It was indeed kind and generous of you to send it, and I was most touched.

The play has had a rough reception – in some instances a cruel and malicious one – and we all feel a bit battered and unhappy. That kind of pain one can only hope will lessen in time, and go away.

I think the attempt to yoke the Shavian and metaphysical side with the domestic side alienated both people who like debates of ideas and those who like passionate emotional plays. This surprises me, I must admit since I like both kinds of drama and would want to see them married more often.

One thing I freely admit. The play would show to more advantage at the National. It is not an eight times a week piece, and the critics are no longer disposed to take Shaftesbury Avenue seriously as a frame for any play of serious intention.

Anyway, thank you for your kind message. May I wish you both very well for The Merchant?

Yours,

Peter

Our correspondence continued:

                                                20 February 1970

Dear Peter,

A few years ago in California I asked Christopher Isherwood why he chose to live and work there instead of in England.

He replied that criticism there, apart from one or two people, was faintly ridiculous and therefore possible to live with. In England he said it was bitingly intelligent, harsh and finally annihilating. He implied that creative artists would find it more and more difficult to breathe – never mind work – as time went on. He was right of course.

I wish more of us had joined Lindsay Anderson's stand against the type of criticism which seems contemptuous of its obligations to both artists and public.

We are all too immersed in our own problems to make a unified stand and demand the serious consideration the sort of work we attempt to do deserves.

With love,
Joan

He replied:

24 February 1970

Dear Joan,

Thank you for your marvellous letter. It seemed to express everything I've thought on the subject.

To me the whole critical thing is now deeply repulsive – the situation of a 'first night' like a gladiatorial combat: the judges sitting there with thumbs poised: the whole procedure of instant reaction, and the attitude of 'You do it – we'll tell you what's wrong.' It has all got nothing to do with the real theatre: I mean the reception of work directly by an audience, or feeling or love.

(Trouble is, what kind of reflective stand can one ever make? Are all performances dependent on reviews and I wonder what would happen if all the press were to be bypassed: would, hopefully, some strong law of discrimination operate? Or would the lowest common denominator always carry the day?)

I know what Isherwood means about California and criticism. I feel like flying there at once, and not coming back. To be so persistently clubbed over the head for intention *– that's God-awful . . .*

Thank you.
Peter

Back at the Toronto hotel, Peter told me about Burton's first performance in *Equus* when he took over the Psychiatrist's role on Broadway. He needed to prove to the film's producers that he was still up to it, because he knew that they had first wanted Brando or Jack Nicholson. Before his official opening night, he decided to test himself out at an unpublicized matinée. Peter remembered the disappointed groans of the audience when told that Anthony Perkins, the current star, would not be appearing at the matinée. And then their stupefaction at hearing: 'The role of Martin Dysart will therefore be played at this afternoon's performance by Richard Burton.' He had not been on stage for over ten years and it proved a nerve-racking experience for everybody. There was no drink problem because he was on the wagon, but he was not yet totally in control of his lines. He gave a fumbling and faulty performance, though the audience loved it. In the dressing room afterwards, as Peter struggled to find encouraging words, Richard cut him short: 'It was disgraceful,' he said bleakly, 'and it will never happen again.'

Another week went by in Toronto and we started shooting bits of the film without Burton. When he finally arrived it was in film-star fashion, wearing a mink-lined raincoat and surrounded by Suzy and the Entourage. We were back in the rehearsal room, mostly dressed in jeans and sweaters, and sitting at a table with our scripts, as he walked in. There was nowhere for the Entourage and Suzy to set up shop apart from an unprepossessing little kitchen off the main room. They gathered awkwardly in there, looking a bit nonplussed at the lack of amenities, not to mention the lack of fuss made of their arrival. Richard recognized the set-up immediately; it was like being back at the Old Vic: actors in working clothes, waiting quietly to get on with the work. He felt he had misjudged his entrance and he was shaking with nerves as he came to the table. The actors greeted him happily, I gave him a kiss and said how glad we were to see him, and Peter Firth, who was overawed, began shaking in sympathy as Richard sat down next to him. Sidney was very tough on him all through the week's rehearsing; he said he wanted to break down the barrier that he felt Richard had erected. 'He's in a straitjacket,' he kept saying at dinner.

Two days after we started shooting, Richard finally plucked up the courage to sit about in the studio without his Entourage, though Sidney had something to do with that too. He started crossing out our names on our chairs and substituting rival, or unfavourite, actors. Thus 'Richard Burton' became 'Edmund Purdom', 'Colin Blakely' became 'Oliver Reed', 'Peter Firth' was 'Roddy McDowall' and I became 'Barbara Windsor'. Needless to say, our American producer, unfamiliar with Britain's cockney blonde bombshell, thought I had been promoted to the royal family. We retaliated by crossing out Sidney's name and putting 'Ken Russell', whom we knew to be his most unfavourite director. From then on anybody sat on any chair, the ice was broken, we became a company of actors and Richard came out of his straitjacket, chatting happily about days at the Old Vic. When we talked about theatre and Shakespeare, his whole being became animated with remembered passion and the poetry would stream from his lips as though at the touch of a button. He was nursing an ambition to play King Lear and there was talk of him doing it at the Old Vic. He asked us all if we would play in it with him if he came to London, but by the end of the film he had lost his nerve. The English critics, he predicted, would sneer at the famous film star trying to recapture his faded glory. Like Isherwood, he felt safer in America where they were more grateful for attempts at serious work.

I acquired some valuable technical knowledge whilst filming *Equus*. For instance, if you have an emotional scene to do, it is advisable not to waste real tears on the first master-shot. Very little of it will be used, as the subsequent close-ups on each actor are going to be more interesting. And if yours is the third or fourth close-up to be shot, you will have already played the scene several times for your co-stars' close-ups. And so it's best to save your tears until you get to your own. Sydney was very helpful though he admitted to great difficulties where he needed to use the three of us on screen together. Richard was at his best around the eighth take, he said – Colin around the fifth take, but 'with Joan it's Curtain Up on Take One'.

Richard and I never spoke of the dreams of Oxford, or of Elizabeth, or of the National Theatre. He seemed very happy with Suzy. They had rented an old house where they spent

KING LEAR FOR GRANADA TELEVISION

iana Rigg and
orothy Tutin as the
icked daughters
oneril and Regan
osing for a special
otograph for Larry.

Larry as Lear on
the blasted heath.

Washington following a special show-
g of *King Lear* at the White House.

The crown of Shakespeare's herbs and flowers.

Julie-Kate, Tarquin and his daughter Isis, Richard and his wife Shelley, Tamsin and me – 'we put out his chair and some of his things'.

Grandson Troy with Hamlet the cat – 'the expression of new life everywhere'.

Richard and Donald MacKechnie.

With Douglas Fairbanks.

Below: Maggie Smith, my brother David, Lady
Richardson, Mary Evans, John Mills, Laurence
Evans and Mary Mills. Inset: Franco Zeffirelli.

MY SEVENTIETH
BIRTHDAY PARTY

Vanessa Redgrave and Ned Sherrin.

Frank Finlay.

Edna O'Brien and Helen Mirren.

Alec McCowen.

Tamsin and Julie-Kate with the cake saying '70'.

Twiggy, Leigh Lawson and Patrick Garland.

Julie-Kate and David Heyman.

Cleo Laine and Johnny Dankworth.

Chris Larkin, Richard and Tamsin.

Simon and Tamsin, Julie-Kate, me, Richard and Shelley, Troy and Alessandra.

John Stride and Edward Petherbridge – Rosencrantz and Guildenstern thirty-five years on.

Anthony Page, Norma Heyman, Maggie Smith.

Geraldine McEwan and John Mortimer.

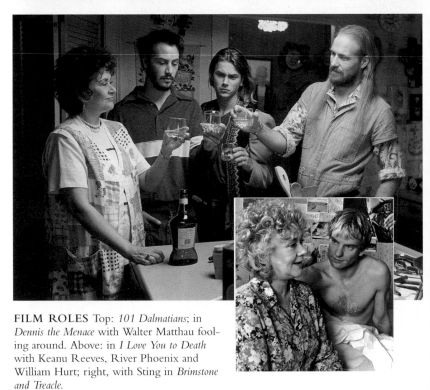

FILM ROLES Top: *101 Dalmatians*; in *Dennis the Menace* with Walter Matthau fooling around. Above: in *I Love You to Death* with Keanu Reeves, River Phoenix and William Hurt; right, with Sting in *Brimstone and Treacle*.

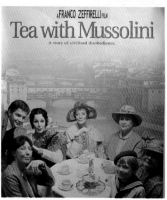

Anti-clockwise from above: Lily Tomlin (foreground), Cher, Maggie Smith, me and Judi Dench; with Armin Mueller Stahl in *Avalon*; comedy dance in *Dance With Me*; with Jim Broadbent and Mia Farrow in *Widow's Peak*; and Polly Walker, Josie Lawrence, me and Miranda Richardson in *Enchanted April*.

In the garden at the
Malthouse, and, below,
the next generation: Troy,
Alessandra and Wilfred.

their weekends at home, by the fire, rereading the works of Jane Austen, he told me.

We were to meet again on another film a few years later after Suzy too had gone. We had a glass of wine, and after mutual confessions of certain traumatic events in both our lives, he suggested, half-jokingly, that we might set up house together. There was no one in his life at the moment, he said, though I had heard reports of several. He went on to describe the delights of Céligny, his home in Switzerland, and how the children could have a wonderful time, whenever they wanted to visit. We laughed about what people would say, and I said, also half-jokingly, that for me it would be like jumping out of the frying pan into the fire. Anyway, I told him, I had a commitment for life, however difficult it might be. We had another glass of wine and went back to work.

Twenty-Four
....

Life Gets Difficult

Moving into the 1980s, we were no longer on an even keel. Larry had been back in hospital for a kidney operation and the recuperative period seemed to take longer this time. It would be pointless to deny that life now became very precarious due to his failing health; and great adjustments had to be made by us all. He was impatiently oversensitive about physical weakness; but how to stop him doing too much without making him feel inadequate was a constant source of worry. There was also the problem of *amour propre* and his barely concealed distress when I was the one who was working and earning a necessary addition to our income. Sometimes it would provoke angry storms, and other times a mournful mood: 'You'd all be better off if I were under the ground.'

The children were wonderfully supportive and always tried to laugh him out of his doleful humours. We were discussing reincarnation for some reason one evening, and after a grim remark from her father, Tamsin told him: 'You'd better not talk like that – you might have to come back as a grasshopper.'

'I'd very much like to come back as a grasshopper,' said Larry, 'it has a mercifully short life.'

There was a lot of 'hopping' in and out of his bedroom next morning, until he lightened up and yelled, 'All right, that's enough!' The doldrums never lasted long; he would snap out of it when we went off for short holidays together, and work prospects showed up again. And when friends came to stay he would be in good form, holding court and telling wonderful stories until late into the night.

In 1983 there was an extraordinary upsurge of energy and excitement when the idea of playing King Lear for Granada Television was put forward. Though doctors shook their heads and felt that it was beyond his strength, he was not to be deterred. Nor did I want them to hold him back from something he had set his heart on doing, 'even if I die in the attempt'. It was the most moving performance he had ever given, and the children and I felt quite shattered after watching him. Around him were actors who treated him with loving care and attention, marvelling at his will-power and sense of humour, despite his obvious fragility. And Dorothy Tutin and Diana Rigg, who played the wicked sisters, Goneril and Regan, gave him a special photograph of themselves smoking furiously as a joke to counteract the (awful) smell of peat in the studio. The achievement of *King Lear* gave him the spark needed to fire up his spirit and his energy. And we made a trip to Washington, where President Reagan arranged a showing of the film at the White House, and gave us a lovely informal dinner afterwards.

Then came the time when I was offered the part of Martha in Edward Albee's *Who's Afraid of Virginia Woolf?* for the National Theatre under Peter Hall's regime. Associate Director Michael Rudman asked if I would like John Dexter to direct it as we had worked together so well before. I talked to Larry about it and was dismayed by his reaction. He was annoyed that Dexter had been suggested and said he didn't want me to go back to the National unless he himself directed whatever I did there. In the event Dexter was not available. But apart from my reluctance to return again to the National as a 'husband and wife' package, I knew that Larry was still quite frail and not well enough to take on such work. I tried to reason with him but reasonability had flown out of the window. He grew angrier by the minute, saying it would provide grounds for divorce if I went ahead without him. I knew these storms could blow away as quickly as they arose, so I told him how much I wanted to do it, and hoped he would calm down in a day or two. And I began preliminary talks with Nancy Meckler who had been appointed director and whose work I much admired.

When my rehearsals began, Larry was also happily in preparation for a TV film of John Mortimer's *A Voyage Round My Father*. In the part of the blind patriarch, he would be mostly in a wheelchair so the work would not be too taxing. He seemed to have forgotten his anger about my decision to work at the National, and was in happy mood that morning as I cooked our breakfast and then waved him off to his rehearsal before leaving for my own. There was an unopened letter on the table, which I read, hurriedly, before getting into the car. It came from our solicitor who said how much he regretted to hear of our difficulties and our decision to part, and offered to help if they were not irreconcilable. I was in a state of shock and unable to concentrate properly at rehearsal. Albee's play is a marathon to learn for the leading protagonists, George and Martha, and Paul Eddington and I had the added burden of adopting the necessary American accents.

By night-time I had grown angry. And when Larry came in, beaming, through the front door of our house in St Leonard's Terrace, I told him coldly that I had received his solicitor's letter and would answer it the next day. 'What letter?' he asked. 'What on earth are you talking about?' He looked distraught when I explained and finally said, 'Would you believe me if I told you I'd forgotten ever having done it?' He rushed off in the morning to ask the solicitor what he had put in the letter as he had no recollection of it and I received another apologetic letter telling me to forget all about it. The strain of the play as well as the private turmoil began to tell on me and Larry's remorsefulness became as difficult to cope with as his anger had been. He went back to his old refrain of how much better off I would be without him.

I opened the play on tour in Bath, and Edward Albee came to the first night there and we all went for dinner afterwards. I was called away from the table to answer the phone. It was

Larry, still in remorseful mood, asking: 'If you were going to kill yourself, which method would you use? Head in the gas oven, or the river with stones in your pocket?' Then he remembered to ask how the play had gone. We talked more and he cheered up a bit and I rejoined my dinner companions. Albee was sitting next to me and I asked him if he had any notes on my performance. 'Everything you do is *right*,' he said. 'I have only one question – because I've seen you on stage before – where is your *joie de vivre*?'

Finally, and not surprisingly, my voice began to disappear too; I only managed three previews in London before it gave way completely, and I had to come out of the play. Doctors prescribed a long rest; I went to the South of France to stay at Tony Richardson's villa, and Margaret Tyzack took over the part of Martha. Later that year, Larry attended the Evening Standard Award dinner with Tamsin on his arm instead of me. And he watched Margaret Tyzack accept the Best Actress Award for her performance in the role I had vacated. Edna O'Brien was at his table that night, as the full realization of what had happened began to overwhelm him. She came back to the house in Chelsea with them and, after Tamsin had gone to bed, they talked it out. And Larry wrote this letter, and left it for me in an envelope bearing the following message:

Private. Miss Joan Plowright CBE. (No harm will befall from opening this.)

My darling, wonderful Girl,

There is nothing to say, except that I am sorry, sorry beyond words and deeply beyond any kind of measure.

It's no good me fashing around for excuses, or trying to recite a long history which might throw a better light upon my hideously unreasonable behaviour.

It is obviously going to take a long time for me to feel that you will ever have entirely forgiven me.

A wound as deep as that I have inflicted upon you my darling love cannot heal just like that. Health, strength and trust has to have reasonable time to mend a heart that has been so mercilessly hacked about. I must simply pray and devote all that I possibly can to leave it from being further troubled and apply what gentle aids may be acceptable . . .

I do try all I can, though this is not much, to keep a tighter hold on the ventricle, but I have not yet been exactly successful.

I want you to know that I love you as deeply as I am repentant.

L

After I read that letter I remembered the one I had sent to him twenty-odd years earlier, which had stated so bravely, 'I love you, my darling. I don't care what you have done or not done, what you will do or not do – nothing can change the essential you – which is an animal I love and feel I understand. And I shall love him forever.' At the time of my enforced departure from the play I certainly did care about what he had done or not done, and yet I also understood the pain and the depth of the frustration which had prompted those actions. And the love was still there somewhere beneath my crossness and the 'how could you' exclamations, though it was a little hard to locate at the time.

When I escaped to Tony Richardson's house near St Tropez, I took Richard and Julie-Kate with me. Larry was still at work on his TV film, and Tamsin was going with a study-group to Florence. Richard was on vacation from UCLA in California where Tony had become like a surrogate father to him, and had issued an open invitation to us all to stay at Le Nid du Duc whenever we wanted. His two daughters, Natasha and Joely, were there when we arrived, along with Kathleen Tynan and other friends.

Sitting outside over coffee with Tony and Kathleen, I recounted the tale of the lawyer's letter and my exit from *Who's Afraid of Virginia Woolf?* Tony, of course, found it all very stimulating and whooped with laughter, saying, 'It should have taught you how to do the play. I mean, it was George's Last Game, wasn't it?' Kathleen was more sympathetic and told him how that sort of thing could affect a woman's psyche; but Tony was having none of it and professed surprise that I had 'crumbled so easily'.

Tony's house in Hollywood was the scene for Sunday brunch and family gatherings, and hard-fought tennis matches, and Richard spent many a Sunday there with his friends. I remember an Easter party once, which our whole family attended. There were several small children and an Easter egg treasure hunt had been promised. The adults were drafted to take one child each and help with the clues if necessary, but the child was to be encouraged to do most of the work. The competition seemed to present such a serious challenge to the male ego that impresario Michael White felt compelled to snatch the Tynans' son, Matthew, who had the highest IQ, from under his mother's nose, thus ensuring that he came back first with the coveted prize.

Larry, too, was one of those supremely competitive men, and I remembered the time when Trader Faulkner, his friend from Stratford days, wrote me a complimentary letter about a performance of mine that he had seen. Faulkner was an aficionado of Federico García Lorca's plays, and Glenda Jackson and I had appeared in one together, at the Lyric, Hammersmith. It was *The House of Bernarda Alba*, a tremendous play, but a very difficult one for English actresses to tackle. It has an all-women cast, of which the principal characters are the widowed Bernarda, her four unmarried daughters, and La Poncia, her housekeeper, who is confidante to the girls and, in her own way, runs Bernarda as well as the house. Glenda was Bernarda and I played La Poncia, and we were fortunate to have the great Spanish actress, Nuria Espert, to direct. Rehearsals were arduous and difficult. The play made emotional demands on the actresses, which were far beyond any in English drama. And our youngest actress was unable to give Nuria the size of the passion she asked for. Though Nuria was willing to go on trying, Glenda thought the actress must be replaced. 'We can't afford to have a weak link,' she said. 'We don't have much time – this is the first all-female venture in London and the men are just waiting for us to fail and fall flat on our faces.' I wasn't as pessimistic about the male population but I did agree about the lack of time. Amanda Root took over the part and gave Nuria everything she asked for, and the production became another of those hits Orson talked about. It was transferred to the West End by producer, Josephine Hart (who later wrote the novel *Damage*), and was made into a TV film the following year.

Trader wrote his letter shortly after we had opened.

London   *13 September 1986*
Dear Joan,

Rafael Martinez Nadal, a close friend of Federico García Lorca and the man who went to see him off on the train from Madrid to Granada on 13 July 1936 (the last man to see Lorca alive in Madrid – among his friends), and an old friend of mine has just rung me. He said, 'I've seen eight Poncias in Spain – France – England etc., but never one to match Joan Plowright.' He's leaving for Madrid in the morning – wanted to write you – but he must be!!! now in his eighties. Looks an elderly sixty. He said, 'Hers is a very great performance.' I said I'll sit down now and tell her . . . Nadal knows. He knew Lorca during those years in the late 1920s and the 1930s and he is critical. This to tuck away in your mind. It was such a marvellous spontaneous typically Andaluz telephone call from the man who knows more about Lorca and his work than anyone alive. That sort of information must be passed on to the recipient. Olé! . . .

Much love, Trader

I gave the letter to Larry, who had been very enthusiastic and complimentary after our first night. This time his competitive instincts were aroused immediately. 'I must get back on the stage,' he said, as he dropped the letter onto the table. And I realized that in future it would be better to share such things with my children or my mother, and not with my husband, to whom it would always seem like one-upmanship. 'You took him on,' said my mother, when I told her. 'He can't help it, that's the way he is. You must find a way to cope with it.' Though she had always admired him, she had thought him a philanderer when our love affair first began, and feared that marriage was not on the agenda. Afterwards, of course, she could let her admiration flow freely, and was heard to say at the dinner table, 'There are two men in this world who should never die – Winston Churchill and Laurence Olivier.'

And one night in Lisbon in 1999, after we had been working together, Vanessa Redgrave and Jerry Hall and I had a girls' supper together where we talked about our men. We had all been engaged to present the Portuguese Golden Globus Awards for Film, Fashion and Theatre respectively. It was a glittering occasion but we were glad to get back to our hotel after the noise and confusion which always accompanies such events. It was around the time that Jerry had finally opted out of her marriage to Mick Jagger, having endured his frequent and much publicized infidelities for some years; but she still spoke kindly of him and said she loved him. When Larry came into the conversation she remarked in her soft Texan drawl, 'He must have been a handful.' There was no hint of condemnation in her words; they were accompanied with a sympathetic smile suggesting the forbearance of a long line of female ancestry who had accepted the vagaries of their menfolk and loved them just the same.

Larry made a great effort to keep a 'tight hold on the ventricle' and I made a similar effort not to seem too pre-occupied with work and not to be too bossy about what he should do or not do; and we had wise counselling from doctors and friends. Maggie and Beverley were now married and living not far from us in Sussex, and often came over at the weekends. Maggie and I were to act together for the first time in 1985 in *The Way of the World*, directed by Bill Gaskill. Millamant was the part she had been born to play, but she had not yet been seen in it in London. I had been asked to play Lady Wishfort once before but felt I was not yet the right age for the part. It was around the time that Peter Brook had asked me to play

Jocasta in his production of *Oedipus* at the National. And though I was flattered by his belief that I could do it, I was taken aback (and a little peeved) at the thought of playing John Gielgud's mother. 'It's nothing to do with age,' Peter had said, 'it will be an abstract production.' Abstract or not, I couldn't face it at the time and though I would have loved to work with Brook, I said no to Jocasta. In later years I would say ruefully to Maggie, 'I'm playing Tony Hopkins' mother-in-law in a film [*Surviving Picasso*] – and we used to act opposite each other as lovers.'

'I can beat that,' said Maggie. 'I'm playing Nigel Hawthorne's mother in *Richard III* and he's at least five years older than me.'

But now I was the right age for Lady Wishfort, and was happy to play it with what I knew would be a definitive Mistress Millamant. We opened at Chichester, playing through the summer and living in the country, both feeling thankful that we weren't yet having to travel to the West End, though that was where we were headed in the autumn.

Larry enjoyed a short film engagement with his old pal, Michael Caine, in *The Jigsaw Man*. And as we now had a lovely resident nurse, whom he adored, it was she who could prevent him from doing too much without incurring his wrath or hurting his pride. He took a much saner view of my desire to work, knowing that I would need a career to sustain me in the future, and generously encouraged me to accept short periods of film work in America.

Twenty-Five
....

Moving into the Cinema

I was well past my half-century when the cinema suddenly began to open its doors to me. And that late-burgeoning career became a source of great fascination. Directors with an affection and high regard for actors are rare, and it was my good fortune to work with Lawrence Kasdan.

I Love You to Death was a zany kind of black comedy, based improbably enough on a real-life story. It concerns a desperate and jealous young wife who tries unsuccessfully to have her womanizing husband assassinated; her main helper in this enterprise is her mother. Lawrence Kasdan had assembled a widely assorted cast, including Kevin Kline and William Hurt, both of whom had played in his film, *The Big Chill.* Kline played the pizza-parlour-owning husband and the multi-talented Tracy Ullman was his wife. I was her Yugoslavian mother, and Keanu Reeves joined William Hurt as the two pot-smoking hired assassins who prove so inept and hopeless at their task. And the young River Phoenix completed the main cast as a helper in the pizza parlour who is drawn into the family's drama. We rehearsed for about three weeks – unheard of, it seemed, for films – but necessary because of the need to discover a style of comedy playing which would mitigate the underlying blackness of the story. In the real-life story, the wife was sent to prison for attempted murder – and on her release the couple remarried and went on the *Oprah Winfrey Show* together.

We were mostly strangers to each other on the first day; but by the end of Kasdan's opening address, we were banded together as a supportive ensemble, ready to set off on a fascinating voyage of discovery. He acknowledged the knife-edge quality of the script and the way-out nature of the characters we were to play. He also said that we needed to have trust and confidence in each other so that we would be courageous enough to go 'over the top' if necessary. 'You are all from different backgrounds,' he said, 'and some of you will get there quicker than others, and by different means, but we are not here to judge each other – just to help.' He explained to us his method of working, which would include much improvisation in the first two weeks, and ended by saying, 'The exploration of the actors is a large part of the fascination for me.' I knew I would love working with him after those words, and it proved to be one of the most enjoyable times I've ever had on a film.

Kevin Kline and William Hurt had been students at the Juilliard School where the training was based on Michel Saint-Denis' methods at the Old Vic Theatre School. So we weren't from such different backgrounds after all. Keanu Reeves, who was not yet a megastar, came from the theatre too, and would return to play *Hamlet* at Guthrie's Minneapolis Theater some time later. And I remembered Bill Gaskill, a few years back, asking me to go and see his production of *She Stoops to Conquer*, saying, 'Come and see yourself when young.' It was Tracy Ullman he meant, who was playing the lead, and who since then has starred in her own brilliant TV show in America. And when Tracy and I went shopping together, everybody automatically assumed that we were mother and daughter.

We would lose our youngest co-star, River Phoenix, in tragic circumstances a few years later. But when we were filming together, it was River who took me to the health-food stores in search of vitamins and organically grown fruit and vegetables. He came to my trailer one day to ask if I thought he should join a theatre company for a year or two before he did any more films. 'I've watched you and Tracy and Kevin,' he said, 'and seen how quickly you can do a scene entirely differently, if Kasdan says it isn't working. I can't do that – I've only one way of doing it, which is just instinctive.' Of course his instinct had served him beautifully before in films like *Stand by Me*, but this particular script needed different technical skills, which he suspected had been acquired by us in the theatre.

I Love You to Death was much more successful in Europe than in America and its video life has gone on and on. I'm still being told by taxi-drivers, 'It's one of my wife's favourite films.'

As I write this in Grayshott Health Farm on 26 March 2000, the TV is giving information about two very special events. It is the night of the Russian elections and Putin is expected to be confirmed as President by midnight. It is also the night of the Oscars, and the other 'Orson', as Sam Mendes is referred to by his friends, is expected to be confirmed as Best Director for *American Beauty*, also by midnight. Expectations were fulfilled in both cases, and *American Beauty* also won Kevin Spacey the Best Actor Award.

My mind went back to Oscar night in 1993, when I had been nominated for *Enchanted April*. And the preparations for that weird and wonderful evening began at 12 noon with hairdresser and make-up artist, and didn't finish until 2 a.m. the next morning. I met two other British nominees, Emma Thompson and Vanessa Redgrave, in the Ladies, before we took our places; and though we raised our eyebrows in mock horror at the extravagance of it all, we had to admit that it was very exciting to be there.

The American reviews for *Enchanted April* had been much more ecstatic than the English ones. It was what they termed a 'feel-good movie' and it was helped enormously by its setting in Portofino on the Italian Riviera. The small Castello Brown where the film took place was the very same Castello which the author, Elizabeth Von Arnim, had rented some sixty years ago, when she had taken three other ladies on a special getting-away-from-it-all holiday. We knew exactly where to find the round sitting room, the writing room, and the dining room which opened onto its own garden terrace after reading her novel. In a wonderful position on a rocky promontory, the Castello had been sadly neglected over recent years. But the art department had gone out six weeks previously and done a wonderful restoration job, and replanted the garden. There were about 250 rocky steps to climb to get there each morning but it was such a magical place to work in that we didn't mind. And after we had made our way up from the picturesque harbour with its jostling yachts, we could marvel at the views of Portofino and the Gulf of Rapallo during breaks for the rest of the day.

Such a location of course is what makes film work score so advantageously over work in the theatre. It is infinitely preferable to spend summer weeks in Southern Italy.

But to return to Oscar night in 1993 when Vanessa and I were competing in the same category. We didn't win, but Emma kept the flag flying with her award for *Howards End*. It was presented by her co-star, Tony Hopkins, who loves it so much over there that he has now become an American citizen. In one way the Oscars are like the Cannes Film Festival: in that it is nice to have done it once, though the festival in southern France lasts a lot longer.

Juliet Stevenson, Joely Richardson and I attended Cannes with film-maker Peter Greenaway's *Drowning by Numbers*. It puzzled the audience, though they gave it respectful applause; but Peter had expected more – he was a favourite at Cannes and his work had been much admired there. When he first sent me the script there was a note in it which read: 'Nude scene on page 33 optional.' Thank goodness for that, I thought – I had never stripped off for a part in my life, and was hardly going to start aged fifty-nine. He said that it was intended to be like a Rembrandt painting of a nude lady, which he sent me a copy of, but as I didn't look anything like that, I said nobody was likely to appreciate the reference. He kindly allowed me to opt out of it and didn't (I hope) hold it against me.

It was the film producer and my good friend, Norma

Heyman, who asked me to play Mrs Munro in *The Clothes in the Wardrobe*. The film would be an amalgamation of a trilogy of novels by Alice Thomas Ellis, with four beautifully observed female characters – on a par with Elizabeth von Arnim's ladies in *The Enchanted April*. It is always difficult to cut and shape three interlinking stories into one script; and actors tend to want every facet of their own character included in the final version. Mrs Munro's life story was necessarily truncated in order to pay more attention to the story of Lily. But as Lily was to be played by France's Jeanne Moreau and her sister by Julie Walters, I was more than happy to accept. I had been a fan of Moreau since early *Jules et Jim* days, when my friends and I escaped from the theatre and spent our Sundays watching foreign films. And the Italian *Bicycle Thieves* and Jean-Luc Godard's *A Bout de Souffle* had made such an impression on us and left us feeling impatient with the unadventurous English films at that time.

Jeanne is now in her seventies, and we have remained friends since acting together in 1993. I am lost in admiration for her energy and creative drive, which have seen her transform herself into a director of note, both in theatre and opera. In 1995 she was again elected President of the Jury at the Cannes Film Festival. And our own Arts Minister at the time obviously thought it was not a suitable job for a woman, as he referred to the President of the Jury in print as 'Mr Jean Moreau'. Two years ago she became the first woman to become a member of the French Académie des Beaux-Arts.

She was marvellously cast as Lily in our film, and we had a drunk scene together, which we enjoyed enormously. From our very first meeting we felt on the same wavelength; we had each known, and worked with, both Tony Richardson and Orson Welles and we shared confidences as though we had been friends all our lives.

She sent flowers the next day with a card: 'I spent an extra-ordinary time with you the other evening. Thank you for sharing your memories. I am looking forward to our next meeting.' In New York we were involved in a TV satellite broadcast to promote our film, now known as *The Summer House*. We were so complimentary about each other that at one point she said, 'If we go on like this they'll think we're going to get married,' and the TV director warned us to be more careful about our asides, as they might be overheard and cause some misunderstanding.

The Enchanted April made its bow in America whilst I was filming with one of my most favourite actors, Walter Matthau. We were playing Mr and Mrs Wilson, the next-door neighbours in *Dennis* (the Menace). And that was the film, together with *101 Dalmatians*, from which my grandchildren would gain some reflected glory among their schoolfriends. On holiday once in a hotel in Spain, I was sunbathing in the nude on our large balcony, which had steps up to it from the hotel garden. My seven-year-old grandson had gathered a group of boys who all wanted to meet Mrs Wilson. He called out as he got to the top of the steps and I snatched up my bathrobe just as eight small boys spilt out onto the balcony. Afterwards he told me reassuringly, 'I saw your bottom but the others didn't.'

Walter and his wife Carol and I became close friends. And in her book, *Among the Porcupines*, the words she wrote – 'I loved the grief in him' – sounded a deep note of truth. There was a grief about him, which he would cover by presenting himself as a joker who refused to take anything seriously. Except perhaps for Mozart, whose music he knew inside out and loved. Always fooling about on the set, he dropped his trousers to the floor when we sang to him on his birthday. I gave him a gold toothpick as a present as he was forever handing wooden ones to me when we ate together in the studio restaurant. And he sent me a typically flippant note before the Oscar night ceremony when I was a nominee.

Joan Darling,
   Don't pick your teeth on camera. It's not nice!

Use the floss before you go to the ceremony.
Love and kisses,
Walter
P.S. I really hope you win, just to see more of you.

And it was during the filming with Walter in Chicago that negotiations were going on for me to appear in a Woody Allen film. Mia Farrow had parted from André Previn sometime previously, and taken all her children to New York, where she and Woody had enjoyed a relationship for the last six years. We had often talked about working together again after the collapse of Robin Phillips' Greenwich Theatre Company, but had lost touch in recent years with the Atlantic between us. But she wrote to me one day from New York to renew our friendship and give me her latest news.

Dear Joan
... Here I am in NYC ... I have two more children – a little boy and now a baby girl. They are wonderful of course and having a baby around again is pure joy. I am making the most of it and bringing her to work and everywhere. She is the proverbial apple of Woody's eye. 'Woody' is Woody Allen, my beau of six and a half years.
*   What is happening in your life? I've thought of you so often and Julie-Kate, Tamsin, Richard and Larry. I do hope you're all thriving ... What is it like now that the children are grown? It's terrifying how many years have gone by ... I am happier in my new life but have fond memories (and lonely ones) of Surrey. I look forward to hearing from you, I've missed you.*
*   Love to Larry and to you,*
*   Mia*

She had invited me to dine with her and Woody at Elaine's one evening when I made a fleeting trip to New York. And there was talk of me playing a small part with Mia in his next film, to be shot the following year. Then out of the blue sometime later came the news that Woody had fallen for one of the Vietnamese orphans to whom he had been acting as stepfather and had gone off with her. Mia was in great distress and legal action was being threatened by both parties. I was asked if I would testify in court on Mia's behalf, if necessary. Then my agent rang to say, 'What on earth is going on? Woody Allen's office have rung to say that they now don't think the part is worthy of your talents, and would rather wait until they can offer you a better one.' As it turned out, I wasn't summoned to court, though I had consented to be of help if I was needed. Mia and I eventually had the pleasure of working together again in *Widows' Peak* in 1993, with Natasha Richardson and Jim Broadbent as our co-stars. Mia brought her children to Ireland where the film was being shot, and fell in love with her mother's native land, saying she would like to live there when she retired.

Nova Scotia is not as pretty as Ireland but its countryside is more spectacular and it was here I would find myself in 1994 with film-maker Roland Joffé (*The Killing Fields*), who had started off as a director in the theatre. He had engaged Demi Moore for the leading part of Hester in Hawthorne's *The Scarlet Letter*, and Gary Oldman to play her priestly lover. I was Harriet Hibbins, a free-thinking rebellious woman who acted as midwife to Hester at the birth of her illegitimate child when no one else would go near her. Both our characters are sentenced finally to be hanged on the gallows (those were oppressive, barbaric times). And Demi and I had to endure a day of shooting with dreadful gags in our mouths – which was apparently the usual hanging procedure. The film's photographer grinned as he took Demi's picture that day and said, 'Shall we send one of these to Bruce?' She was still with her husband, Bruce Willis, in those days, and he came to stay for weekends. I watched him dealing gently with their three small daughters one morning at breakfast in the hotel, and remembered how Larry had offered to take over and sleep next door to our children one night on Nanny's day off. When I joined them next morning at 7 a.m., there was cereal and apple sauce all over the carpet and down the front of his silk dressing gown.

'I'd rather play Othello eight times a week than ever do this again,' he said.

It is often said that the quality of life depends upon the quality of the company you keep. And as my companions on Zeffirelli's *Tea With Mussolini* were of the highest calibre, the making of that film was a memorable experience. It was 108° in the shade in Florence, and Judi Dench, Maggie Smith and I were melting away in the period costumes and the wigs we had to wear as ladies from the 1930s era. But to wake up in a hotel just a few steps away from Santa Maria Novella, knowing that you will shortly be filming in the glorious Piazza della Signoria, is surely to be considered a privilege whatever discomfort the sun may cause. And to move location next day to the cathedral, and on days off, to be able to spend time in the Uffizi or Santa Croce, gazing at the frescoes and the tombs of Michelangelo and Galileo, makes it the kind of work most actors would give their eye teeth for.

Franco was in his element and very happy to be back in his home town. And happier still when he was presented with the Florino d'Oro, the highest award given by the city to Florentine artists. He was out celebrating when Judi, Lily Tomlin and I were at our costume fittings, though he had of course already approved the original designs, and would have screamed immediately we appeared on set if he hadn't liked them.

It seemed strange that in the forty-odd years that we had been in the profession, Judi and I had never worked together before. But she had been a Stratford girl, with Peter Hall, when Maggie and I were at the National. And in those days it had been a case of never the twain shall meet. Although she and Maggie had both acted in *A Room with a View*, it was the first time the three of us had worked together; and we all look back on the time with a huge nostalgic affection.

In Rome we had stayed at the Eden Hotel after moving ourselves from a less salubrious one, which I won't name, but which Judi and I both thought was a 'house of ill repute'. She and I had driven together from Florence to Rome, without

Maggie, who had some time off and had gone home. When we arrived at the questionable hotel, we met Lily Tomlin at the reception desk. She had already ordered her luggage to be brought down again from her room. She had her computer in front of her and was emailing friends in Los Angeles, asking for recommendations of other hotels. (It was a Saturday so the production office was closed.) But finally we were all happily ensconced at the Eden where we looked forward to a glass or two of Prosecco up on the roof, in the evening, and perhaps a game or two of Scrabble after dinner.

Cher joined us when we moved to San Gimignano, the historic small town with all those towers reaching up towards the sky. And the crowd of townsfolk and tourists, who had been watching the filming, swelled to much larger proportions with Cher's arrival on the set. She admitted that she had found the prospect of acting with us more than a little intimidating. But her fears were soon dispelled after a day or two, and she had her fellow American, Lily Tomlin, to confide in if she needed to.

Franco's renown (and his recent award) made it possible for doors to be opened which would have remained firmly closed to other film-makers. And we were allowed to film inside San Gimignano's cathedral, and within two feet of the precious Ghirlandaio frescoes and Memmi's *Madonna*, which fills the screen as the film comes to an end.

It is a leap from the cathedral and the Madonna to Grub Street Productions in Los Angeles. But variety is the spice of life and sunshine is good for the bones, and the series, *Encore Encore*, sounded as though it would be fun. The latest product of the team who had created *Cheers* and *Frasier*, it starred the very talented Nathan Lane as a failed opera singer; I was his Italian mother and Glenne Headley was my daughter and his sister. It had looked very promising to begin with, but somehow the creative team never got to grips with the style they were looking for. The script which we read and rehearsed on a Wednesday bore little or no resemblance to the one we were faced with on the Friday. And supporting cast members disappeared with alarming regularity as the plot changed and characters were dispensed with over the weekends. It was a 'learning experience' which I thoroughly enjoyed, despite its hazards. And the challenge of performing to a live audience each Tuesday evening with lines still in the process of changing, certainly kept everyone on their toes. After thirteen episodes and quite a good sized viewing audience, we called it a day. And today, in May 2001, Nathan is the toast of Broadway in the hit musical, *The Producers*, which has swept the board at the Tony Awards Ceremony.

Twenty-Six

Finale

On St Patrick's Day 1986, we celebrated our twenty-fifth wedding anniversary with a family lunch party at the Malthouse, and then drove to London where Edna O'Brien marked the occasion by giving us a wonderful dinner party. Harold Pinter, with whom I had just acted in his play, *The Birthday Party*, was one of the guests, together with his wife, Antonia Fraser. Alan Bates, Jeremy Irons and Sinead Cusack, Eli Wallach and Anne Jackson from New York, Ian McKellen, Sean Mathias, and the then-married Philip Roth and Claire Bloom were the other friends and colleagues gathered by Edna that night.

We feasted on oriental chicken with water chestnuts, purée of parsnips, potatoes dauphinoise, Russian meatballs, followed by apple charlotte (Larry's favourite) with dollops of crème fraiche. The champagne flowed and Larry made a speech on love and friends, and work and drink; and we sat around until late into the night, catching up on each other's lives.

I had given Larry a trio of statues for the garden that morning and he had given me a pair of diamond earrings, with this message:

In lovingest gratitude for so much, so much, and dearest hopes for our twenty-sixth – And unforgettable memories of our three years of rehearsal! It's been a long run all right, but you have a very special gift for those.

Always your

L

The next anniversary to be celebrated was Larry's eightieth birthday in 1987. A special entertainment had been devised by John Mortimer to take place in the Olivier Theatre. And leading actors at the National Theatre, past and present, paid tribute in a light-hearted pageant of theatrical history, placing Larry among the theatre's immortals, Henry Irving, David Garrick, Edmund Kean and Richard Burbage. Frank Finlay and Geraldine McEwan sang a bowdlerized version of 'Dem Bones, Dem Bones, Dem Dry Bones', which listed a catalogue of his well-known injuries received during film or theatre productions. Dame Peggy appeared as Lilian Baylis who gave him his first Shakespearean roles. And Sir Peter Hall allowed himself a little gentle self-mockery when he appeared as Shakespeare. At the end of the show a huge mock birthday cake was trundled onto the stage and Albert Finney called for silence. Then in time-honoured fashion, out of the cake popped our youngest daughter, Julie-Kate, to say, 'Happy Birthday Dad,' and start the singing. The standing ovation went on and on as we prepared to leave; and I thought back to that day twenty years ago in 1967 when we made what he thought was his last journey from Brighton to London and said goodbye to those few workmen at the Old Vic.

When Larry died in 1989 it came as a shock to everyone, even though we knew he had been living on borrowed time for the last few years. He had survived so much and won so many battles with illness that he seemed somehow to have become immortal. He had been at work recording scenes from Shakespeare at the Malthouse. Richard and Shelley and their baby were living there with him whilst I was away finishing off a film in Hollywood. We had invited various friends to take part in the scenes with him, including Maggie Smith, who had sounded a bit dubious: 'Oh, I don't know ... he'll just go on at me about my vowels.' He was halfway through the work when he had a sudden relapse, and I was rushed back home to be with him. Only three weeks previously he had said on the phone that if he felt strong enough he would like to come out to California for a holiday. He told me to ask our friend and American agent, Ben Benjamin, and his wife Carly, to look for a house that we might rent for a month. But it was not to be.

A family friend, Don MacKechnie, now living in Los Angeles, who had been Staff Director at the National Theatre and who had worked closely with Larry for some years, came over for the funeral. He wrote about it to Ben Benjamin, who was unable to be present, and sent me a copy of the letter, which I have treasured. It captures all the various emotions of that day: the sense of loss but also of acceptance, and for me the knowledge that I had been so privileged to share his life, whatever the burdens it carried. And I often thought of those lines written by William Hazlitt: 'A man of genius is not a machine ... There is no path so steep as that of fame: no labour so hard as the pursuit of excellence.' There would be a memorial service later in Westminster Abbey where his ashes are interred in Poets' Corner. But Don's letter concerns the day of the private funeral.

... when I arrived at the Malthouse I was encouraged to see the local constabulary out in full force at the end of the lane, and Joan and the family being looked after by a couple of good people that David Plowright had brought down from Granada to handle the press. It had been announced that the funeral was private with only family and close friends attending, but the presence of the press was inevitable. I was given a list of names and detailed to make sure that the sixty or so people in the tiny church would find their places. The service was to start at 3.30 and I decided to get to the church, unlike Mr Doolittle, well ahead of time. It was just as well I did as I had only been there a few minutes when Douglas Fairbanks, Lady Richardson, and Rosemary Harris all arrived for a 2.30 service. We decided they might like to go for a little drive and after looking at some of the floral tributes, they did just that. Douglas Fairbanks had flown overnight from New York and was, understandably, a little fragile.

St James's Parish Church, which was built in the twelfth century, and which our late dear friend sometimes attended when at the Malthouse, was an absolute picture. One of those very English churches with a slightly overgrown graveyard and, tucked away out of time and out of place, behind the village, and in the quietest, narrowest, overhung country lane you could imagine. Pure Thomas Hardy.

Among the stones leading to the church doors were spread numerous floral tributes. A single red rose from an admirer in the village; beautiful white carnations from Sir John who was filming in Italy; another resplendent white arrangement from Dame Peggy, and from Lady Richardson the most beautiful lavender-coloured daisies, forming a cushion – quite remarkable, Laurence's favourite colour and just a little card, 'From Lady Richardson and Ralph', bringing Sir Ralph back to us for a moment in time to usher his great friend along the last few yards to his exit. Bouquets from friends, colleagues, theatres all over the country and a magnificent arrangement from Elizabeth Taylor; 'Adieu, Elizabeth' was all the card said.

At three-ish people began to arrive, among them Sir John and Lady Mills, Sir Alec Guinness, Maggie Smith and Beverley Cross, Lady Walton, Sir William's widow, Franco Zeffirelli, Anthony Hopkins, Ronald Pickup, Robert Lang and Ann Bell, together with neighbours from farms next door to the Malthouse and, of course, an anxious little choir, huddled at the back of the church. A most distinguished, and catholic, last audience and the house was packed – standing room only as was appropriate. Sir Douglas and his party managed to get back in the nick of time as we sighted the first outrider of the police escort. The shutters on the cameras began to chorus quietly, and the hearse and the immediate family arrived. Joan and Richard, with Julie-Kate and Tamsin; Richard's wife Shelley, with grandson, Troilus; Tarquin, Larry's eldest son, and his daughter, Isis.

All preceded by LO, making a great last entrance on this planet, with a most spectacularly devised crown of herbs and Shakespeare's flowers atop his coffin. Everything was so befitting for him.

The sun shone out and made for us a glass that we could see his shadow for the last time, as it passed.

The single bell tolling prior to his entrance and ceasing into a deafening silence as he was brought into the sanctuary of the church.

The reverence from us all.

The respect from the famous.

The adoration of the people from the village who quietly, patiently, stood outside.

The wonderful behaviour of the press, who in their day, God knows, had harried Laurence from pillar to post, but here there was none of that paparazzi behaviour. And most of the press were in suits and all were in ties, that I saw.

And so he came into our midst for the last time in this life and so we sang and so we prayed and so we wept and so we rejoiced.

Wept for ourselves, I think.

Rejoiced for his great life and his new liberation.

Richard and Tarquin read from the Bible, and Gawn Grainger, who had been close to Laurence as an actor, writer and as a friend, gave a wonderfully down to earth and pertinent address to the family.

Anthony Hopkins simply stood and read the final lines of King Lear . . .

I have a journey, sir, shortly to go;
My master calls me, I must not say no.
The weight of this sad time we must obey;
Speak what we feel, not what we ought to say,
The oldest hath borne most: we that are young,
Shall never see so much, nor live so long.

Tony was impeccable, just standing there, hands to his sides, head slightly bowed and pouring all his love and talent into those few sentences, and helping Laurence on his way.

There was, suitably, a party afterwards, in his garden at the Malthouse, with flowers in full bloom and his presence everywhere. Much grace, much laughter and some tears.

I know that not a day will pass when I don't do something that will have *been brought about by his guidance, his generosity, his spirit of adventure, his practicality and his demonstration of a good hard life, well lived.*

We had put his chair out and a few of his treasures. We toasted him in champagne. And then, in the middle of the party, we looked up and two RAF fighters, which had overflown the house in practice quite by accident, had left two vapour trails which merged into a cross in the sky above the house. It was uncanny. Joan looked up at it when it was pointed out to her, and said, 'I believe in such signs.'

Such stories spinning in the garden from such a cross-section of generations and professions. Doctors, carpenters, farmers, lawyers, agents, writers and, of course, actors and directors. The young male nurse, Mark, who, towards the end was trying to give Laurence a little liquid refreshment in the middle of the night, said, 'So I cut an orange in half and put one half into a gauze and squeezed it into Sir Laurence's mouth. I thought he was asleep, but I knew it would help. As I was squeezing it onto his lips, he opened one eye and looked at me and said, "It's not fucking Hamlet, you know, it's not meant to go in my ear." '

But above all, the lasting image was Laurence's resplendent garden. The borders in full flourish, the hedgerows neat and tidy, the apple trees burgeoning with new fruit, all continuity and the expression of new life everywhere . . .

And the expression of new life continued as two more grandchildren, Alessandra and Wilfred, were born; and a new pony arrived; and the trees he had planted at the Malthouse grew taller and gave more shade, in preparation for the global warming promised in the future.

And the family and close friends gather round his memorial stone in Poets' Corner at Christmas-time each year. We place roses round the stone, light candles, sing a carol, tell stories and read a poem or two.

And we continue to work and live life to the full, as he always did.

In the second week of August 2000 I was at Naples Airport, on my way home from another Italian holiday at Torre di Città in Ravello. I didn't see Gore Vidal this time; he was about to depart for New York to attend the opening night of a revival of his play *The Best Man*. It had been timed to coincide with the election campaigns of his distant relative Al Gore and George Bush, neither of whom in his opinion, he said on the phone, could lay claim to that title. And after a shambolic election day, followed by demands for the Florida recount and charges of a Republican conspiracy and an appeal to the Supreme Court, it would take several weeks before one of them did. And George W. Bush became the President of the United States.

At the airport I read an interview in the *Financial Times* with Simon Russell Beale, who was about to play *Hamlet* at the Royal National Theatre, and who said there had only been three *Hamlets* there before him, and named actors who had played the role since 1972 during Peter Hall's reign. The interviewer reminded him gently that Britain's National Theatre had been founded in 1963 with Laurence Olivier's golden reign and that its opening production had been *Hamlet* with Peter O'Toole.

As I was about to make a film with O'Toole in Toronto, the double wipe-out of Larry and Peter naturally caught my attention. Though they had suffered some disagreements on how the part should be played, they had remained on speaking terms, but never worked together again despite their mutual admiration. It was always difficult for any actor to be directed by Larry in a part that he had previously played himself, and O'Toole has an entirely different approach to acting and his own individual style.

Earlier in the year, O'Toole had won the Olivier Award for Outstanding Achievement, which I had presented to him and, in the usual fashion, kissed him and stood back whilst he made his acceptance speech. Recalling his work with Larry, he said, turning and smiling at me, 'We got on very well' – (pause) – then swivelling back to the audience – 'at first.' It was impeccably timed like everything he does, and got him his first big laugh. After the award ceremony we drank three or four glasses of champagne despite the fact that he was under doctor's orders to abstain, and as we reminisced about our first years in the theatre, I remembered the letter he wrote to me in Los Angeles after Larry's memorial service.

Hampstead   *28 November 1989*

Dearest Joan,

It was truly loving and kind of you to have included me in the procession for Larry. It was an awesome and mighty day and one that will stay with me for ever.

A forlorn little ruffian in the post-war period heard the silver trumpet that was the voice of Larry and saw his dangerous presence and was summoned and dared to do the work which I now do and love so much.

Ever,

Peter

Perhaps this is the place to add two more letters from among the hundreds that arrived, not only from the profession but also from people in all walks of life, who had been touched by his genius in some way or another. The first was from Dame Susan Garth, OSJ, a neighbour of ours at Roebuck House.

Roebuck House, London SW1   *29 October 1989*

Dear Joan,

Do you remember me? We shared a wall at Roebuck House. I slept on my side of the wall . . . perhaps you and Larry slept on the other side.

We met briefly. I had recently returned from the horrors of Biafra where I had managed to save the lives of children. You had asked me to your party . . . otherwise as Larry said I would have had to 'enjoy' the occasion from the other side of the wall. I did enjoy the party and was touched to witness the tenderness of Larry as he so frequently kissed the nape of your neck.

He had asked my advice on whether you should adopt a Biafran orphan. I thought not. Perhaps I was wrong.

I am sending you this little note as I was so moved to see you and your darling children at today's memorial. You looked so beautiful. I listened to the tributes in tears.

The God-given talents of your beloved Larry will continue to enrich the lives of many millions yet unborn.

I send you my love and prayers.

Susan Garth

The second letter, undated, was from Sir John Gielgud.

Dear Joan,

I find it almost impossible to write you anything adequate about Larry's death. The whole profession will be mourning with you and you will be overwhelmed with messages of sympathy from all over the world. It is difficult for me to believe that he is gone, but what a rich legacy he leaves behind; not only of his brilliant talents and extraordinary range of achievements — but the memory of his own vital courageous personality, his determination and power as performer, manager and director, the originality of his approach to every new and challenging venture, his physical bravery not only on the stage, but in the valiant way in which he faced his few failures and defeats, above all his refusal to give up when he had become so ill. As you know we were never intimate friends over these long years. He only spoke to me on one memorable day — I think it was just the time he had fallen in love with you. We talked at the Algonquin for about an hour and he told me of some of his tortured times with Vivien and a few other personal problems — a confidence which touched me very much. I was, I confess, always a bit afraid of him. He had a certain remoteness and spiritual authority which I imagine Irving also had. Perhaps it was a fitting part of his own acting genius and his gift for leadership.

His meeting with you and the blessing you brought him in giving him the children he always longed for must to some extent at least have given him a great reward despite all the miseries and complications of the South Bank. How he continued to go on giving such fine acting performance over those appallingly difficult years was an amazing triumph of concentration and devotion.

I am sad not to have seen him these last years but I hesitated to intrude on the family life he had so richly deserved and I felt it might distress him to find me still lucky and well enough to go on working while he himself was so sadly disabled.

Please don't dream of writing – my affectionate thanks for all you gave him and always my fondest wishes and admiration.

John

It is 21 June, the longest day of the year, 2001 and last night thousands of people gathered at Stonehenge to celebrate the Summer Solstice and watch the sun rise in the morning. At the weekend my family and friends will be with me at the Malthouse, which is thankfully inhabitable again, after the damage caused by severe floods last autumn. There is adventure ahead next month when I go to Paris – still the most evocative and beautiful city I know – to start another film with Zeffirelli. Before that, on 21 July, I shall be back in the county where I was born to receive an honorary degree conferred by Hull University. The ceremony will take place in Lincoln Cathedral, which I often visited as a girl. And childhood memories will come crowding in again of family conflicts, school plays and drama festivals. ... And of the time when I rode my pony, with no knowledge of where life would take me, through the cobblestone streets of Hibaldstow in North Lincolnshire.

Index